GUNS OF OUTLAWS

"Have you any idea of what a man must endure who leads such a life?
No, you cannot. No one can unless he lives it for himself."
—Frank James

". . . we go a'ridin' into town, a-whompin' and a-whompin'
every livin' thing that moves within an inch of its life.
Except the women folks, of course."
—Slim Pickens, *Blazing Saddles*

GUNS OF OUTLAWS

WEAPONS OF THE AMERICAN BAD MAN

GERRY AND JANET SOUTER

CRESTLINE

Brimming with creative inspiration, how-to projects, and useful information to enrich your everyday life, Quarto Knows is a favorite destination for those pursuing their interests and passions. Visit our site and dig deeper with our books into your area of interest: Quarto Creates, Quarto Cooks, Quarto Homes, Quarto Lives, Quarto Drives, Quarto Explores, Quarto Gifts, or Quarto Kids.

Inspiring | Educating | Creating | Entertaining

This edition published in 2017 by Crestline, an imprint of The Quarto Group, 142 West 36th Street, 4th Floor, New York, NY 10018, USA T (212) 779-4972 F (212) 779-6058 **www.QuartoKnows.com**

ISBN-13: 978-0-7858-3547-9

Acquisitions Editor: Elizabeth Demers
Project Manager: Madeleine Vasaly
Design Manager: James Kegley
Layout: Helena Shimizu

On the front cover (left to right): Jesse James. *Library of Congress*; Pile of Guns. *Author photo*; Billy the Kid. *Library of Congress*; Clyde Barrow and Bonnie Parker. *Library of Congress*; Tommy gun. *Dja65/Shutterstock*

Printed in China

10 9 8 7 6 5 4 3 2

MIX
Paper from
responsible sources
FSC® C104723

ACKNOWLEDGMENTS

The authors wish to thank the following for their assistance in writing this book:

Lynn Carson, of the Dalton Defenders Museum, Coffeyville, Kansas

Dale Chlouber of the Washington Irving Trail Museum

Dave Cooper, photographer, and Robert Rea, president, of the Franklin County Historic Preservation Society, Benton, Illinois

Jim Covell of the New Mexico Gun Collectors Association

Shelly Crittendon and Amanda Crowley of the Texas Rangers Hall of Fame and Museum, Waco, Texas

Peter Cutelli, of the St. Louis Weapon Collectors

Zac Distel and Kelly Williams of the Frazier History Museum in Louisville, Kentucky

Thomas Haggerty of the Bridgeman Art Library

Jessica Hayes and Jessica Hougen of the US Marshals Museum in Fort Smith, Arkansas

Laura Hoff, Laraine Daly Jones, Caitlin Lampman, and Rebekah Tabah of the Arizona Historical Society

Samuel Hoffman and Tom Pellegrene of the *Journal Gazette* in Fort Wayne, Indiana

Marguerite House of the Buffalo Bill Center of the West in Cody, Wyoming

Susan Jaffe and John Paul of Guernsey's Auctions, New York

Lisa Keys and Nikaela Zimmerman of the Kansas Historical Society, Topeka, Kansas

Loren McLane of the Fort Smith National Historic Site in Fort Smith, Arkansas

Dale Peterson of the Minnesota Weapons Collectors Association

Silka Quintero of the Granger Collection

Michael Runge of the City of Deadwood Archives, Deadwood City, South Dakota, and also Rose Speirs and Carolyn Weber of the Adams Museum in Deadwood

Jason Schubert of the Davis Arms and Historical Museum, Claremore, Oklahoma

Hayes Scriven of the Northfield (Minnesota) History Collaborative

Elizabeth Van Bergen of Christie's Auction House

Roy Young, editor of the *Wild West History Association Journal*

A special thank you to the following:

Kathie Bell of the Boot Hill Museum in Dodge City, Kansas, for the hours spent searching through the museum's archives and the museum staff for taking the time to help us photograph the weapons in Boot Hill's extensive collection. Also, the staff of Dodge City's Long Branch Saloon for their help, advice, and Old West hospitality

Marguerite House of the Buffalo Bill Center in Cody, Wyoming, for her time and efforts in researching the museum's database

Hans and Eva Kurth of the Cody Dug Up Guns Museum, Cody, Wyoming, for taking the time to help us photograph their unique collection

Patrick Quinn of Rock Island Auctions for his expertise, time, and encouragement providing digital images attributed to outlaws and lawmen

CONTENTS

INTRODUCTION

THE DEADLY GUNS of the bandit trade tell the story of American outlaw culture. Those same guns blazed hot in the hands of the underpaid lawmen who doggedly pursued the American bad man's greed-fueled determination never to pay for what he could steal.

Six guns, rifles, shotguns, and pistols evolved into exotic weapons of murderous destruction, leaving a trail of artifacts that reaches far back into the violent history of the United States. Firearms' evolution is not the tail that wagged the dog, but is instead the residue that marks the rise and fall of the outlaw trade from the eighteenth century to the 1940s, when the last of the legendary outlaws, Al Capone, Chicago's boss of bosses, left Alcatraz Prison and later died in his bed, a disease-ravaged, babbling shell of a man whose name had become a chilling synonym for lawlessness around the world.

Outlaws and the lawmen who pursued them came in all shapes and sizes, colors, and genders as did their implements of aggression and protection. In these pages we'll examine and discuss the actual guns they carried as well as lookalikes and trends in technology, all gathered from museums, historical societies, and private collections. The difference between *owned by* and *used by* is pursued as far as provenance permits. This is not a catalog. It is as much archeology as it is history. Like the swords of ancient kings, these artifacts bear the scuffs, rust, and scabbard-wear of use, or of the curious vanities of their owners—engravings, inlays, plating, and hand-carved notches commemorate survival, or the defeat of a rival who was two seconds too slow.

We'll also explore life on the "owlhoot trail"—an imaginary twisting outlaw path—and visit where outlaws lived, where they worked, and where they died. The mythology of their lives and skills is a dense thicket of hearsay, facts, fantasies, truths, delusions, and steaming heaps of once- or twice-digested lore that makes for great stories, but can be bottomless traps for the historian. For instance, there are many versions of the deaths of Billy the Kid, Butch Cassidy,

Wyatt Earp's Colt Single Action Army belly gun with three-inch barrel and no ejection rod. Built to get the drop and that first quick shot. *Guernsey's Auctions, New York*

and Pretty Boy Floyd—all sworn to in writing. The gunfight at the O.K. Corral is a virtual blizzard of half truths and misdirections, and at least one unique gun is widely described in great historical detail, but never actually existed.

Life for many in the Old West, the New West, and the eras of Prohibition and the Great Depression was a struggle. Most of the outlaws who packed their pistols and left home were victims of real or imagined injustice. Some inherited old feuds. Others fled from broken homes that were crushed by a hardscrabble existence. A few embraced the owlhoot life to pry the rich man's boot off their neck and taste the rewards of a life lived hot and fast. Many famous outlaws were semiliterate losers with entire careers based on one chance encounter.

Justice was meted out by men not far removed from the lawbreakers they pursued and captured (when convenient) or killed (when desired). Dedication in a lawman was rare, but highly prized when discovered. The pay was low and many needed second jobs to buy bullets or feed their families. It was not unusual for outlaws to put on a badge, nor for admired lawmen to stray across the line and thus considerably raise their standard of living.

Watchdog volunteers were at hand in many communities to level the playing field when dishonest men—and women—became annoying nuisances. Quick judgments rendered by flinty-eyed vigilantes often ended with premature application of a short noose dangled from a tall tree. On the other hand, too many local deputies armed with squirrel rifles and duck guns found themselves facing automatic drumfire in the hands of hardened killers.

From the double bang of the flintlock to the chatter of bucking submachine guns, we'll ride the owlhoot trail from antique to modern times and try to live as close to the bone of reality as we can while squinting into the fog of legend. Return with us now to yesteryear when the outlaws lived bold and died hard; when courage and guts prevailed behind a scarred and dented badge, the rise and fall of the American outlaw.

A Hyman Lebman special full automatic Baby Machine Gun built from a Model 1911 semiautomatic pistol. It fires an eighteen-round magazine of .45-caliber bullets in about five seconds. *Federal Bureau of Investigation*

CHAPTER 1

THE
OUTLAWS
ARRIVE

Choose Your Weapon

I N THE NINETEENTH century, striking out to find a new start, a new life, or a new chance to grow beyond the bounds of society, which for many people rarely extended more than a hundred miles from a person's place of birth, was no less daunting than traveling to Mars. And what was the third most important thing that went into that wagon bed after the family Bible and mother's tea set? In most cases, it was a double-barreled shotgun. The shotgun was the gun that tamed the West. Nothing fancy, just a fist full of double-ought buckshot to put a jackrabbit in the stew pot, or a get-along tickle of rock salt to discourage unlawful attentions toward the family's best milk cow by four-legged critters—or two-legged thieves. It protected the flow of treasure and commerce that built towns and empires. In

This six-gauge double-barreled breech-loading shotgun was designed for meat hunters to shoot into flocks of geese, partridge, and other game. Scatterguns were perfect for shooters with minimum practice. *Rock Island Auction Company*

The flintlock was the natural evolution of the original Chinese fire stick, in which flame applied to compressed gunpowder caused an explosion, or rapid gas expansion, that then propelled a missile. Producing the flame was the trick. The later matchlock (or arquebus) required a cord tip saturated with saltpeter that was thrust, smoldering, into the gunpowder chamber through a touch hole. The next mechanical solution was the wheellock, which used spring-driven clockworks to spin a rough wheel against a flint to produce sparks. Finally, the gun mechanics produced an ignition spark by striking a flint against a small steel striker plate in the Dutch snaphaunce. Refining that concept created the flintlock.

Preparing the flintlock for discharge requires a measured quantity of coarse (corned) gunpowder poured down the musket's or pistol's barrel followed by a ball of slightly smaller diameter than the barrel's bore. The ball is wrapped in a greased linsey or cotton patch to hold it in the barrel and rammed down on top of the gunpowder charge with a ramrod that is then replaced in its ferrules beneath the barrel. A small pan at the foot of the striker plate, or frizzen, is filled with finer ground ignition gunpowder that is protected from wind or wet by a sliding panel. Thumbing the hammer (doghead) to full cock opens the pan. The tricker (trigger) is tripped with the forefinger.

The flint sweeps down, striking the frizzen and sends sparks into the priming pan, which ignites a plume of flame that squirts down into the gun powder through a touch hole. This flame ignites the powder in the barrel and the gun fires its ball, or whatever load is rammed on top of the powder. Preloaded cartridges carrying the correct powder load, ball, and patch were carried in a wood and leather box on the belt. Each cartridge was torn open, poured into the muzzle, and rammed down. The primer powder, carried in a horn or flask in a pouch or on a thong around the neck, was poured into the open pan, which was closed until ready for firing.

To fire rapidly, the rifleman tap-loads his weapon, foregoing the patch and dumping the ball down the barrel, settling it against the gunpowder by firmly tapping the gun butt against the ground and using the coarse gunpowder for both priming pan and propellant charge. This rough handling ruins accuracy and fouls the mechanism in a short time with unburned powder residue. In an emergency, however, an expert rifleman can fire four shots a minute, filling a battlefield with a hail of gunfire.[2]

The wheellock pistol (called a "dag") was a handful with all of its wood and brass furniture besides the wound-spring clockworks mechanism that spun steel teeth against a flint to produce sparks. The ball-ended grip made a dandy club. *Rock Island Auction Company*

the hands of the law, the shotgun meant business. Held hip-high by an outlaw, it was business.

Almost nobody today uses the term "outlaw" in reference to lawbreakers. Outlaws originated in Britain as far back as when people formed settlements for crop raising and protection. Anyone who stole, or murdered his neighbor, or committed treasonous acts was considered outside the law, and anyone in the village, or town who aided this person—or even failed to report his whereabouts— was lumped into the arrest warrant when a *posse comitatus* (Latin phrase: "Law of the country," or any males over the age of fifteen that a sheriff may conscript for their vigilance) was formed to hunt him (or her) down. That was the beginning of vigilante justice, which came over to the American colonies on the boat with the earliest English immigrants and the rest of their laws and customs.[1]

The early outlaw arsenal ranged upward from the cudgel and garrote to the double-edged knife and ultimately to the flintlock pistol. During the revolution, it was a while before the Continental army began to police the vicious gangs that held open season on friends of the king, or Tories (the Tories had their own gangs as well). With colonial justice itself barely fleeing the British rope from village to town, convening courts of judgment posed a problem. As with most insurgencies, telling the zealous patriots apart from the cut-purse killers was difficult.

The flash and flame of the flintlock pistol made it the prestige weapon of choice during the Revolutionary War, even if its short barrel reduced accuracy to a handful of paces—or about forty feet. This inaccuracy in sets of dueling pistols virtually guaranteed—depending upon the distance marched off—the survival of one or both parties. Flintlock pistols were also expensive as most were made from imported parts, and they required an elaborate collection of accessories to load and clean them, which also made them slow to operate.

A bullion wagon from Deadwood, South Dakota, carrying $250,000 in gold from the Homestead mine is guarded with a formidable battery of Winchester repeating shotguns. *Library of Congress*

Highwayman makes an escape, discharging his pistols at pursuers. Successful thieves stole enough gold to afford firearms, while footpads stayed with knives and cudgels. *Wikimedia Commons*

A 1700 French flintlock pistol with elaborate wood and brass furniture gilding the functioning firearm—a gentleman's gun. *Rock Island Auction Company*

When Gen. George Washington first laid eyes on his army in 1775, crowding into Boston to shame the Redcoats who had retreated to their ships in Boston Harbor, he almost called it quits and galloped back to Mount Vernon. Though eager and anxious to fight, the majority of the men in the scattered militias who reported for duty couldn't hit the ground with their hats when it came to musket marksmanship. Most were not the flinty-eyed deerstalkers of American lore, the riflemen of the deep woods who could cut the mark at four hundred yards. This milling mob was a cross-section of the coastal and inland villages: clerks, tinkers, coopers, mercantile men, and business men. Farmers shouldered their antique fowling pieces. Some showed up wielding eight-foot pikes and Native American tomahawks.

As Washington had to face the most feared army in all Europe, filled with rank on rank of Seven Years' War veterans, with nothing but this brave, well-meaning rabble who might bolt at the first thunderous scourge of the drums or the gleam of bayonets, he needed an edge. He chose buck and ball. This paper cartridge ammunition load contained a charge of powder, a .65-caliber ball, and three .31-caliber buckshot. The soldier bit off the powder end of the cartridge,

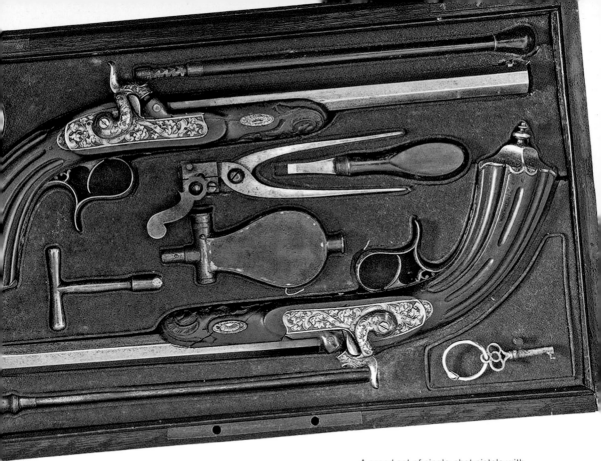

A cased set of single-shot pistols with 1820–1830 percussion locks. A complete accessory set was needed to keep them in firing order. *Rock Island Auction Company*

poured some in the musket's priming pan, and dumped the rest of the cartridge down the barrel. He counted on the paper wrapping wad to wedge the slightly smaller ball down against the powder and to reduce the exploding gas blow-by that cost the shot some of its power. In a smoothbore musket, the soldier could hope to hit a standing man at one hundred yards. For penetration, the buckshot proved effective at fifty yards, but at one hundred yards only raised a nasty welt.

Using the shoulder-to-shoulder, volley-fire-on-command combat of the eighteenth century, buck and ball increased the volume of lead poured downrange into enemy ranks. The British, however, were not amused. They considered this shotgun-type load to be an illegal war crime. In many cases, prisoners, or wounded caught with buck-and-ball loads in their cartridge box were summarily put to the bayonet.

Because the muzzle loading took so much time, the average shooter was held to two—possibly three—shots a minute, and then the ball went God-knows-where.[3] A room, alley, or forest glade was suffused with a double blast of gun smoke from the flash pan and muzzle, allowing the shooter to affect

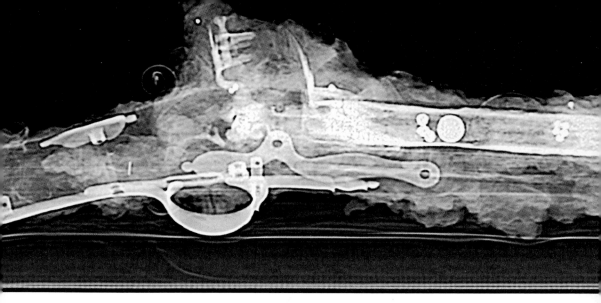

An X-ray of a flintlock rifle loaded with buck-and-ball ammunition showing the positions of the powder charge, ball, and buckshot before firing. *Wikimedia Commons*

an escape before his intended victim could locate him in the haze and reply in kind.

While the flintlock may have been more dramatic, the most feared weapon, according to court records dealing with concealed weapons in the early nineteenth century, was the double-edge Bowie knife, or its fighting companion, the Arkansas toothpick. These twelve-inch fighting blades were worn in scabbards beneath the jacket and required considerable intestinal fortitude to wield, as the hot blood and vital fluids of one's opponent sloshed about. However, its maintenance required only a session with a grinding stone once in a while and a dab of grease on the blade for quick retrieval and for easy withdrawal from a sucking wound.[4]

The tomahawk, or long-handled hand ax, was also popular in the wilderness. A prized Native American weapon, it was also useful as a camp tool. Some had a hollow handle and a pipe bowl opposite the ax blade for enjoying tobacco—or other herbs.

The single road agent, or highwayman, required at least two to three pistols arrayed in pockets or stuffed in the waistband. Large, so-called horse pistols were within easy reach, carried in holsters draped across the saddle's pommel. Galloping about invited disaster if the vibrations loosened the missile in the barrel and a fast draw left the gunpowder and ball behind in the toe of the holster. The flintlock was oily, greasy, and flakey, ruined by damp and subject to ignition if dropped. Every part on it was made to fit, so field repairs were a problem without the tools of a gunsmith. And yet, flintlocks remained in use in the deep wilderness far into the nineteenth century, prized

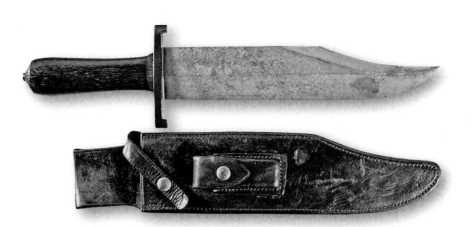

A Bowie knife designed for fighting with a double-edge blade and brass hilt to parry an opponent's slash. The heavy knives were carried in a leather scabbard for quick presentation. Designed by James Bowie, frontiersman and Texas patriot, who died at the Alamo. *Rock Island Auction Company*

by Native Americans and valuable to the mountain men who lived and hunted far from white civilization.

Gunpowder can be made in the field from saltpeter (potassium nitrate), charcoal, and sulfur. To collect saltpeter, drink a bottle of rich grape wine, pee in a manure-filled drum with a bottom drain and filter, add water, and dry the mixture that drips out in open trays. Charcoal can be made from willow wood cooked in a can over a fire. Sulfur deposits occur near steaming underground springs.[5] Raw lead has a low melting point (a campfire stimulated with a homemade, foot-powered bellows) and can be poured into a single or double handheld ball mold. Add a dash of antimony of tin to the lead and you have a ballistic stable bullet.

Only the invention of the percussion cap saved the outlaw trade from these messy flintlocks. A Scottish clergyman,

The tomahawk was a prized backup weapon in the era of single-shot rifles and pistols. The long handle gave leverage to a slash. It was a handy camp tool, and the hollow handle with a pipe bowl at the end allowed for smoking tobacco or other herbs. *Rock Island Auction Company*

Rev. Alexander Forsyth, enjoyed hunting, but was frustrated by the flint-lock's delay between the flash in the pan and the ignition of the powder in the barrel, which tipped off his marsh bird targets. To reduce that delay, after many experiments, he proposed a pellet of fulminate of mercury stuffed in a copper cap that, when struck by the triggered hammer, shot a squirt of flame down the gun's touch hole into the powder chamber. The cap also served to keep the touchhole covered and weather-proof. A gun could be carried, ready to fire at any time—and the press-fit cap allowed practical multishot weapons that could be carried on the person.

From the time of his invention in 1807 through the first third of the nine-teenth century, gun makers incorporated the reliable, percussion cap system into a variety of packages from heavy, bayoneted infantry rifles to tiny single shot pistols that fit neatly into a waistcoat pocket. However, the big news was the relatively small multishot handgun. Two- and four-barrel derringers became popular even as towns and villages in the East drew up ordinances against concealed weapons. Down South, among the planters and cavalier populations, the constant threat of a slave revolt and a perceived Scots-Irish tendency to short tempers over matters of honor demanded a personal arsenal.

The lack of accuracy beyond the length of a dining room or the width of a card table was overcome with sheer volume of firepower. A variety of pepperbox revolvers came on the market in the 1820s and 1830s, which provided from four to six or even eight shots from a single weapon. A road agent armed with a pair of six-shot pepperbox pistols could put up a terrific battle against a coach

Three percussion caps found on a battlefield. The antique clay pipe stub is a size reference. Their crimped ends and soft copper or brass construction assured a trustworthy ignition when the hammer dropped. *eBay*

guard's single-shot musketoon, or even the blast from a bell-muzzled blunderbuss. The pepperbox offered any number of barrels that rotated around a single axis, each with a percussion cap nipple. The effect was that of a half-dozen single-shot pistols arrayed in one weapon.

Allen and Thurber made a particularly efficient model where the trigger squeeze rotated the barrels and cocked the hammer. When a barrel aligned the rotating cap under the hammer, a lever released and the hammer dropped. The downside to the multibarrel solution was sympathetic detonation—one flaming shot triggered the powder in the adjoining barrel, which triggered the next barrels around the axis, accidently clearing away a table of card players besides the lad caught with an extra ace in his waistcoat pocket.

Of course, if it was your intention to clear out the whole cheating bunch of rascals, the perfect pistol for you was the duckfoot. One powder charge simultaneously ignited any number of barrels spread out like the fingers of a hand—or toes of a duck—and any sullen mob threat was instantly turned into garbage.

As the population rumbled westward, outlaws dogged the trails, setting up islands of sin and murder amid the vast lawless prairies and mountains. The government inadvertently helped these desperadoes, as it encouraged settlement to grow voters and to advance political agendas. The railroads needed profits from land sales, cattle, crops, minerals, and buffalo hides. Outlaws plucked these low-hanging fruits of progress while taking advantage of burgeoning firearms and blade technology to further their aims.

Some gents did not even wait for the guns of the revolution to cool down before they took up the outlaw trade. Tories who had been booted off their land

A pepperbox pistol was the earliest successful form of the revolver, giving the shooter as many shots as practical in one handy gun. This model is a double action—barrels are rotated, hammer is raised and dropped—all with one squeeze of the trigger. *Rock Island Auction Company*

For intentional chaos across the poker table, or on the quarter deck of a ship in riot, nothing calms a crowd like a duckfoot. These splayed barrels all ignite at once, producing a scene of horror and bloodshed with one tap of the trigger. *Rock Island Auction Company*

A bell-muzzle blunderbuss with an added bayonet. Usually used for defending a stagecoach or bullion run, the huge barrel was loaded with buckshot, nails, or whatever was available, and the extra-wide muzzle assured a wide dispersion of great pain and destruction. *Rock Island Auction Company*

by the new state governments, and others who had enjoyed easy pickings off the cooling corpses of battlefield dead of both sides, made an easy transition to outlawry. Every state was isolated by the new Articles of Confederation. The United States was still a patchwork quilt that included lands claimed by Spain, England, France, and Mexico with communications traveling at the speed of a trotting horse. Taking advantage of this chaos, many outlaws never crossed the Mississippi into the wilderness. The original thirteen colonies and adjoining territories had enough outlaw hunting grounds to go around.

CHAPTER 2

OUTLAWS
OF THE
NATCHEZ
TRACE

I N THE EARLY nineteenth century, nearly every state had a rustic backwoods that sheltered outlaw bands. Originally a game trail blazed by bison in search of salt licks in the Nashville wilderness of Tennessee, the Natchez Trace became a trading highway for the Chickasaws and Choctaws. Before the Louisiana Purchase in 1803, the trace was our earliest national road; called the Columbia Highway, it was a trade route leading into the West. As traffic volume grew, the military helped maintain the trace and the private inns and trading posts—called stands—along its length. Before steamboats began plying the Mississippi, western planters, slave traders, and farmers followed the trace north and east to sell their goods, and returned south and west with their earnings. National treasure flowed up and down the trace, but a wagon full of hides was less attractive to an outlaw than a purse heavy with gold.

THE HORRIBLE HARPES

The Wilderness Road snaked through dark and overgrown woods where, in the 1790s, travelers moved at their own peril when the horrible Harpes were about. These two brothers—savage, brutal Micajah ("Big") and ferret-like Wiley ("Little") Harpe—claimed this patch of Kentucky as their own hunting ground. Their father had been a Tory—a "friend of the King"—during the Revolutionary War and, in 1798, fled west for his life with his brood. The boys, having grown up surrounded by wartime hatred, decided working the soil for a pittance was less rewarding than burying their betters in the rich Kentucky loam. They became murderers who also stole travelers' valuables.

Because they had no ready cash to start up their criminal enterprise, their initial weapon of choice was the tomahawk. During their early wandering years they spent time with the Cherokees, learning Native American woodcraft and the use of the tomahawk hand ax, decorated with carving and brass tacks, and sharp as a razor. They worked the road every day, appearing to be wayfarers, parsons, or woodsmen, looking for work, all the time sizing up their victims. There would be a distraction, a break for a roadside snack, passing the jug, a few laughs, and then one hard stroke with the tomahawk and it was done. They favored killing near a river where they slit the victim's stomach open and filled his body with stones to sink it.

Taverns became great hunting grounds and kept the Harpes in money. They killed one man in the night just because he snored. One day, they offered up hard cash for a pair of loaded rifles from two men they had met and befriended. With the transaction complete, the Harpe boys shot the men, kept the rifles, and took back their money. Now, armed with modern flintlock rifles, they put aside all the pretense and playacting needed to get close enough to stab their victims, and just shot their unfortunate targets from ambush.

Eventually, even in the vast Kentucky and Tennessee wilderness, the Harpes'

Hired coaches were particularly rich targets for outlaws' depredations. Witnesses left behind were a liability. Justice was final and sudden to captured thieves by local vigilantes. Severed heads were stuck on poles as warnings. *Wikimedia Commons*

Cave-In-Rock is a natural cavern on the Illinois River that served the same function as other caves along the Ohio and Mississippi rivers. Besides providing shelter from the elements, they became havens for outlaws of every stripe and the last tragic stop for many travelers on the Natchez Trace. *Illinois State Parks*

high body count aroused notice. They attempted to hide out in the outlaw sanctuary, the Cave-In-Rock on the Ohio River. The resident outlaws, con men, and cutthroats who called the cave home were brutal river pirates, luring heavily laden flatboats, pirogues, and canoes to their doom with promises of lodging and drink. Even these thieves and murderers could not stand the presence of this pair of savages and threw them out.

The Harpes were captured and jailed, but escaped. A family living in a remote cabin gave them shelter. When the husband returned to his cabin the next day, he found it in flames, his wife savagely abused with her throat cut and his only child's throat cut with the same knife. In a killing rage, the husband gathered a posse of neighbors and pursued the Harpes for days until they ran them to ground. A pursuer fired his flintlock at the fleeing Big Harpe and missed, but the ramrod stuck in its ferules beneath the barrel. Another posse member tossed over his primed and loaded rifle and the next shot went home, bringing down Big Harpe.[6]

The posse members argued that Big Harpe should stand trial, but crazed Harpe carried on about his murders and how he was put on earth to be the

Inns along the trace offered rest, relaxation, and robbery to wayfarers. Guides, grog, and gumbo were offered as services to travelers at a price before the steamboats began navigating the Ohio, Illinois, and Mississippi Rivers. *Wikimedia Commons*

scourge of mankind. The posse held a final vote and determined that they would shoot him, but the grieving spouse would have none of it. He drew a large skinning knife and slowly sliced off Big Harpe's large head, the brute finally breathing his last. The staring head was wedged in a tree crotch at a bend near the crossing at Robertson's Lick and for years the spot was known as Harpe's Head.[7]

JOSEPH THOMPSON HARE

> "We took three hundred doubloons from one man, seventy-four pieces of different sizes and a large quantity of gold in bars. With the others, I found seven hundred doubloons and five silver dollars and four hundred French guineas and sixty-seven pieces the value of which I could not tell until I weighed them. I got $12,000 or $13,000 altogether from the company, all in gold."

Not a bad haul for the eighteenth century when a gold doubloon was almost a week's wage for nonfarm labor. Joseph Hare was the opposite of the horrible

Harpes. Instead of living rough like a beast in the cane breaks, Hare liked fine clothes, was well-armed on a good horse, and organized an efficient gang of cutthroats. He came from good Methodist stock, but decided early that stealing offered an adrenaline rush greater than working and thus became a pickpocket and cutpurse.

He kept ahead of colonial law by skipping back and forth across the border between Spanish and American Louisiana. His first road agent attempt failed when he forgot to brandish his pistol before demanding of a fellow traveler, "Stand and deliver!" The other chap got off the first shot, holing Hare's hat. In the smoky confusion, Hare managed to gallop away with only injured pride.

About ten months of successful bandit enterprise followed. At one point local vigilantes pounced on a band of swamp murderers, caught their leader, and, as was the custom, lopped off his head, claiming they had captured the notorious Joseph Hare. Later, closer identification of the slack-jawed head stuck on its riverbank pole (the official warning to other outlaws), showed they had rid themselves of Wiley Harpe who had only temporarily escaped the grizzly fate of his older brother, Big Harpe.

Hare's gang, meanwhile, was eating well, throwing expensive parties, and using their new passports to enjoy Spanish hospitality. This overindulgence soon made Hare fret about his abandonment of the Methodist religion and he slipped into moods of deep contemplation. While engrossed in the purchase of a silk-lined suit of clothes befitting a gentleman, he forgot to keep watch. A local militia scooped him up and dumped him in a jail cell where he spent the next five years writing tracts and confessions of his many sins—too many sins, as it turned out.

His self-confessed criminal career soared from vagrancy and civil mopery to capital murder. In four months, the court decided returning Joseph Hare to society was a bad idea. On September 10, 1818, one thousand potential victims looked on with relief as Hare was swept off his feet in a well-fitted gentleman's suit to jerk and strangle at the end of the hangman's rope.[7]

CHAPTER 3

MANIFEST DESTINY

Never Steal Anything Small

NTO THE NINETEENTH century, the primary obstacles to westward expansion—besides rugged geography—were roving bands of angry Native Americans who had been "civilized" off their hereditary lands. There were also great numbers of Mexican banditti pointedly questioning the United States' right to lands their Spanish and Indian ancestors had lived on for hundreds of years. The US government saw only the flip side of the coin. The Native Americans' seemingly primitive, nomadic lifestyle—and touchy disposition when cheated via government treaties—was impairing President James K. Polk's signature vision of Manifest Destiny for the young United States.

The Mexicans had lost Texas in 1836 to American squatters who had been invited to settle the territory and act as a buffer against the Comanches, whom the Americans resented for stealing their cattle. Now the Mexican government made threats, rattled swords, and shook fists over the *Norteamericanos'* desire to strip further Mexican land from the ancient Spanish legacy. President Polk— who had vowed to serve only one term in office—seized on Mexican demonstrations of force along the Rio Grande border as a threat to invasion and, in his hurry to add to the United States' territory during his brief stay in office, he trod the Constitution under foot and sent troops to punish Mexico. He then informed Congress the country was at war.[8]

The Mexican War finished at the Battle of Chapultepec where American forces stormed the fortress held by the retreating Mexican Army with many casualties and heavy fire power—the first war to employ modern Colt percussion revolvers. *Wikimedia Commons*

While the actual fighting lasted only a year and a half, between 1846 and 1848, at the end of hostilities, the United States acquired more than five hundred thousand square miles of new land, including California and New Mexico. For the outlaws, eking out a living preying on dirt-poor pilgrims and surviving among the hordes of settlement-hostile Native Americans and avenging Mexican *vaqueros* was touch and go. Now, however, with the West Coast buttoned up with arriving US troops, forts, and civilian courts the home-grown, genuine American outlaws needed to up their game.

TIBURCIO VÁSQUEZ—*VAQUERO* WITH A GRUDGE

The US victory over Mexico had also given the American outlaw class a sense of superiority over their Mexican counterparts, figuring any encounter with banditti would be at very most a dogfall—an even match. Unfamiliar with the horsemanship, shooting, and roping skills of the Mexican *vaqueros*, the Yankees often came out on the losing side. In 1852, Tiburcio Vásquez, whose great-grandfather had arrived in California in 1776, was a teenager enjoying a local fandango with music, food, and *señoritas* when a fight erupted and a white constable was killed. Though innocent, Vásquez fled with his older cousin, Anastacio Garcia. Their friend, Jose Higuera— another party guest who was also not guilty—was lynched the next day. Unable to return, Vásquez remained

The Mexican *vaquero* set the mold for the American cowboy. Master horsemen skilled with the lariat and whip, *vaqueros* populated much of California and the Southwest until the Mexican War of 1846–1848, after which migration of settlers voided ancient Spanish land grants, forcing *vaqueros* back across the border. *Wikimedia Commons*

Tiburcio Vásquez was caught up in the transition from Mexican to American California. Falsely accused of killing a white man, he and friends became horse thieves and bandits. They justified their crimes as defending their rights against the trespassing gringos. *Wikimedia Commons*

with Garcia and a group of other Mexican castaways to learn the outlaw craft. He became an expert horse thief and formed his own gang.

Like the later Civil War guerillas in Missouri and Kansas who continued to terrorize and pillage their home territories in the name of sectional patriotism long after the war was over, Vásquez justified his depredations as punishment against those who stripped away the rights of Mexican businessmen and land-owners. Although locked up in San Quentin Prison many times over the 1860s, his civic duty led him and his gang on a crime rampage, sacking towns, robbing stores, and plundering stage coaches. Eventually, on August 26, 1873, while robbing the Snyder Store in the town of Tres Pinos, he reportedly gunned down three innocent bystanders, for which he would pay the ultimate price.

Though his methods were old-fashioned thievery, at least one of his weapons was a firearm of the future, the Henry Rifle. Tiburcio Vásquez owned one of the fourteen thousand Henry rifles built between 1860 and 1866. Its concept came from the Volcanic repeater pistol that fired from a sliding bolt fed by an under-barrel tube using a lever action. Unfortunately, the Volcanic fired a one-piece conical lead bullet with its powder propellant packed in the base like a tiny rocket ship. The bullet was limited by the small amount of powder that could be stuffed into the hollowed-out bullet base. The design, created by B. Tyler Henry in 1852, replaced the one-piece bullet with a .44-caliber rimfire cartridge that used a disposable copper and later, a brass case for the powder and primer.

The early Henry had a bronze receiver that was later tooled from iron. It fired as fast as the lever action could be swung down for extracting the spent case and recocking the hammer up to load a fresh bullet spring-fed from the tubular magazine. This action preceded the later idolized Winchester rifle.

The Henry's downside was that heat radiated from the barrel, and loading from the muzzle end was slow and took the rifle out of action. It was also subject to jamming from mud blocking the exposed magazine's spring follower slot. But this early fixed ammunition rifle was coveted by Union soldiers who used it to spoil many a Confederate charge. The .44-caliber rimfire cartridge was underpowered, but lasted until the Winchester .44-40 center-fire became the gold standard of cartridges for either rifle or pistol.

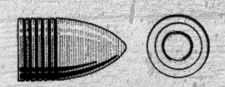

The Volcanic bullet was a self-contained mini-rocket ship design with the primer and powder charge stuffed into the hollow base of the lead missile. This concept limited its power and range. *Wikimedia Commons*

This Henry repeating rifle belonged to Tiburcio Vasquez. The Henry was the precursor of the Winchester lever-action rifle firing the .44-caliber rimfire cartridge fed from a tubular magazine beneath the barrel. It had many faults, but the Henry's firepower made it a popular saddle gun. *Buffalo Bill Center of the West Museum, Cody, Wyoming*

"A spirit of hatred and revenge took possession of me. I had numerous fights in defense of what I believed to be my rights and those of my countrymen. I believed we were unjustly deprived of the social rights that belonged to us," Vásquez dictated just before he was hanged in Santa Clara, California, on March 19, 1875.[9]

The Civil War of 1860–1865 quickly became a working laboratory for firearm concepts. While the armies on both sides were mired in Napoleonic mass firing tactics that cut men down like fields of wheat, inventors were feverish in their search for anything that would give the soldiers an edge in combat and thus provide lucrative contracts that could carry over to the civilian markets.

Samuel Colt arrived on the scene at age twenty-one after a life spent in search of the next new thing. A born entrepreneur, Colt first tried his hand at explosives and got bounced out of school. His father shipped him off to become a merchant seaman. While at sea, he noticed that the ship's steering wheel's mechanics included a clutch that always stopped the free-spinning wheel and held it. He cobbled up a model of a pepperbox pistol and incorporated an automatic barrel stop after a pawl, activated by the trigger, moved the barrels around the center shaft axis. He banged together a working model, which promptly exploded. Alas, he gave up the idea and became a showman, seizing upon a popular parlor entertainment. Audience members were given a snort of nitrous oxide (laughing gas) that caused gales of hilarity. His success as a touring doctor of science earned him a decent wage, and enough money to revisit his rotating revolver idea. He fashioned a model where only a cylinder rotated loaded and primed chambers behind a single barrel. This time, he gave the idea to a proper gunsmith to make a prototype.

Sam whisked his revolving gun off to Europe to secure patents and then returned to the United States in 1836, having patented the Paterson folding-trigger percussion revolver. Its success was based on its

Samuel Colt was an entrepreneur who tried to make a reputation as a scientist-inventor, using everything from explosives to laughing gas until he took a boat trip and stumbled onto the principle of the revolving cylinder firearm.
Library of Congress

assembly-line manufacture that used interchangeable parts. Unfortunately, Sam Colt was a terrible businessman, squandering profits on hype, high living, and extravagant gifts to influential people. However, the gun design was better than its builder's business skills and survived long enough to get into the hands of the Texas Rangers.

The Rangers were a Texas state police acting as roving troubleshooters, often involved with Mexican bandits and with Apache and Comanche raiding parties. While the Native Americans' weapons included a sprinkling of flintlock and percussion trade muskets, their use of the horse (for transport and food), the bow and arrow, and the lance or coup stick made them the "finest light cavalry in the world" according to the US Army. A Comanche warrior could fire a half-dozen accurate arrows in the time it took a Ranger to reload his single-shot pistol. In practiced hands, the Paterson Colt became a game changer.

Ranger Capt. Samuel Walker employed the Colts when his fifteen-man unit repelled a party of seventy Comanches with sheer firepower. As the Mexican War brewed, he traveled to New York on January 4, 1847, and ordered one

Samuel Walker decided the Paterson Colt could be improved after using it as a Texas Ranger sidearm. He recommended changes that set the standard for most successful percussion revolvers to come and his design saved the Colt company. *Wikimedia Commons*

This Belt Model Paterson Colt was a game-changer for the mounted horseman, offering five shots of medium caliber balls without reloading. The spur trigger was revealed when the hammer was cocked. *Rock Island Auction Company*

thousand revolving pistols, contingent upon a few changes. He wanted a man-stopper caliber, a fixed trigger inside a brass guard, six shots instead of five, and a faster reload system. The result was the Colt Walker, a .44-caliber, six-shot man-killer weighing almost four pounds. It was made to be carried in saddle holsters with sixty grains of black powder behind every ball. The Walker Colt was the most powerful handgun ever built, before the advent of the .357 Magnum in the 1930s. At one battle during the war, five hundred Mexican troops were routed by seventy American soldiers wielding the Walkers.

Shaving weight and bulk from the Walker and dropping the powder load from sixty grains to fifty, the Colt Dragoon followed in 1850 and soon after, the Baby Dragoon and the 1849 Pocket Model proved the revolver concept could be scaled down. By 1851, the Colt Navy Model, larger than the Pocket Model, but smaller than the Dragoon, became the standard for efficient, reliable revolvers. Along with the sleeker Army Model, Colt's percussion hand guns served with terrible glory throughout the entire Civil War.

The 1847 Walker Colt was a brute. Designed to be carried in saddle holsters, the six-shot revolver packed sixty grains of black powder behind a .44-caliber ball. It had a kick at both ends. This gun was mass produced at the Whitneyville factory. *Rock Island Auction Company*

Turning the Walker into a sidearm required downsizing, and resulted in this 1849 Colt First Model Dragoon with a seven-and-a-half-inch barrel, slightly smaller powder charge behind the .44- caliber ball, and considerably less weight. *Rock Island Auction Company*

Further slimming trimmed the Dragoon down to the 1851 Colt Navy, which became the outlaw's standard percussion revolver through and after the Civil War period. Confederate border raiders and Union cavalry often carried up to four loaded Navy Colts when they charged into towns and encampments. *Caldwell Auctions*

The successful outlaws who could afford—or managed to steal—the expensive revolvers were ecstatic. The percussion cap and the rotating cylinder allowed them to ditch their bulky, oily, fussy, flintlock single-shot pistols, arrayed about their persons with all the clunky iron, wood, and brass furniture that they required—all for one shot and then a hasty retreat. Colt held the monopoly on revolvers until 1857 when the floodgates opened and a torrent of variations on the revolver theme poured out from factories along the East Coast and throughout the Midwest, manufactured to accompany rolling wagons and trainloads of tenderfeet, farmers, dirt miners, merchants, buffalo skinners, saloon builders, and lawyers.

Only the Civil War slowed the migration west, but that conflict inflated the number of firearms. Eventually, a virtual tsunami of pistols, rifles, and shotguns of every conceivable description swept westward. And dotted among migrants dreaming of a new beginning, a second chance, a shot at the nine-teenth-century American Dream, were the hard-eyed gunslingers who would take what they wanted with unleashed torrents of hot lead.

The Colt 1860 Army Model combined the efficiency of the 1851 Navy with racy curving lines replacing the Navy's bumps and hard edges where grit could collect. The classic Colt silhouette remained. This gun has the attached walnut shoulder stock. *Rock Island Auction Company*

CHAPTER 4

THE
OUTLAW
INCUBATOR

GROUNDWORK FOR THE Civil War had simmered since 1776 when Thomas Jefferson inked the words "All men are created equal" into the Declaration of Independence. While the concept of slavery divided Americans economically and morally, too many saw an opportunity in this division. Inequality and distrust bred fear and hatred. As the gulf between North and South grew, legislation and competing visions of American exceptionalism further splintered state and federal governments.

Bankers and manufacturers, with the aid of politicians on both sides, set schemes in motion to capitalize on events before all control was lost in the maelstrom of actual combat. Arms makers stockpiled raw materials. Contracts for muskets, cannon, and ammunition were sought. In the industrial North, girding for war was a matter of repurposing already productive factories and a skilled work force. In the South, the agrarian planter society had a more difficult time. As soon as war was declared, Southern coastal ports would be blockaded, railroads halted at state borders, and the flow of both raw materials and finished goods stopped.

But the greatest blow would be financial. Using the European model, the banks in the United States were family-owned affairs like those of the fifteenth-century Florentine princes and the great house of Rothschild in England, a custom dating back to the moneylenders in the time of Caesar. However, in the

South, the sums of money passing through their banks could not compare with the fortunes available for loans in the North. The solution was to make loans for crops, land purchases, manufacturing, et cetera, using inflated or sham collateral. Money raised by the banks was funneled into arms purchases and wartime expenses of the Confederacy.

As the war progressed and the Confederacy saw its money being devalued, banks began to close on reams of worthless paper. As cities fell to the Union Army and Union financiers (carpetbaggers) moved into their acquired banks for audits, the loan schemes were discovered. To clear the books, many Southerners were shoved off their land; shops and businesses were shuttered, and the economic grass roots of the South were ripped from the ground.

Not only licked in combat, but stripped of land that had been owned by familial generations, former Confederates were disenfranchised and removed from the voting rolls. Their anger swept across class lines and many unreconstructed Southerners kept their guns loaded and ready. Union-owned banks, appointed African American politicians, collaborating plantation owners, and carpetbaggers became targets of skilled raiders turned outlaws, who made new use of skills learned in five years of war. Missouri banks alone paid out hundreds of millions of dollars in unsecured loans to the state's Southern sympathizers in return for sham collateral. Sheriff sales cleared owners from a half-million acres of farmland. The land sales also intensified the ire of bushwhackers, who lived in the indebted counties and overwhelmingly came from families who lost their property in the widespread litigation.[10]

Hunted by federal authorities long after the official war ended, the more vicious guerilla bands, previously cloaked in butternut and gray as soldiers, now had nowhere to run. Majors, captains, and lieutenants became leaders of gangs of hard-bitten former Confederates, but who now were loyal to the bandit kings

Carpetbaggers (named after their traditional luggage) were the scourge of Reconstruction in the South. Representatives of Northern financiers and political patronage leeches descended on the vulnerable banks, land owners, and political appointments to take advantage of the crippled Southern economy. *Wikimedia Commons*

who could provide the most plunder. Many young men had grown up too fast with a hot revolver in each hand and only the owlhoot trail ahead of them.

RESIDUE OF WAR—THE RAIDERS

"I have been hunted for twenty-one years, have literally lived in the saddle, have never known a day of perfect peace. It was one long, anxious, inexorable, eternal vigil."

—Frank James, Quantrill Raider and outlaw[11]

The agreement ending the Civil War—signed in the parlor of a home in Appomattox Courthouse while two exhausted armies camped in nearby fields— was an unsatisfactory conclusion to other battlefields left in limbo. One of these bloody slaughter grounds had spread across Kansas and Missouri where free-state jayhawkers fought Confederate bushwhackers without quarter. Whole towns had been put to the torch in the conflagration of total war. Male civilians were shot down in front of their families. Captured raiders became slowly turning corpses strung up by the neck. It was a hit-and-run war, a cavalry war of civilian guerilla bands armed with a dog's breakfast of hunting, sporting, and aged firearms any farmer might own, but mostly with shotguns and coveted new revolvers.

Lawrence, Kansas, was attacked by Confederate Bushwackers on August 20, 1863. These guerilla raiders from Missouri led by William Quantrill and "Bloody Bill" Anderson combined hatred of anti-slavery sentiments with slaughter of Union troops—and stealing anything not nailed down. Virtually all male inhabitants were killed and the town burned. *Wikimedia Commons*

The strategy was always the same. Put out the call for volunteers, mount up the biggest band on good horseflesh, and move out toward an unsuspecting town or troop encampment. Each man loaded all the revolvers he possessed. The Colt and Confederate copies and any other large caliber weapons fired three-piece ammunition: percussion cap, gunpowder, and ball. The six-shot cylinders required time and attention to reload. Each guerilla tried to carry more than a pair of revolvers within easy reach.

A brass-frame Spiller & Burr CSA copy of a Remington percussion revolver reflects the shortage of steel for weapons as forges were captured by the Union or forced to move from city to city. *Rock Island Auction Company*

An 1863 Leech and Rigdon Confederate copy of a Colt 1851 Navy revolver. *Old South Military Antiques*

A Confederate copy of Colt 1851 Navy made by Beaumont & Adams of London and shipped to the Confederate states by running the Union blockade of CSA ports. *Rock Island Auction Company*

The Springfield or Enfield rifled muskets used by the Union and the Confederacy were clumsy weapons to handle astride the hurricane deck of a galloping horse. Moreover, they only offered one shot before the shooter had to wield the ramrod, bite off the paper end of a cartridge, pour the gunpowder into the muzzle, and then press the greased lead ball down to be rammed into the barrel to the breech where a percussion cap fitted over the nipple would be detonated by the triggered hammer—only to repeat the process all over again for the next shot. This was okay for massed infantry, but impossible for mounted cavalry on galloping horses.

For a long gun, the raiders favored the double-barreled shotgun. Virtually every farmer owned one that put meat in the pot, discouraged predators from the hen coop, or sent two-legged varmints on their way with a load of rock salt. Loaded with buckshot, the shotgun was lethal up to about seventy-five yards and required little skill to operate. In the 1860s, these shotguns were also muzzle loaders, but they were less fussy when cramming in the loose powder, loose shot (or roofing nails, or nuts and bolts), and a wad of cotton linsey required to hold everything in place. Sometimes half a tobacco chaw spit down the tube would do. Staring into the twin three-quarter-inch barrels of the standard ten-gauge weapon could clear a path through any mob of defenders without firing a shot.

A daguerreotype portrait of a Confederate soldier posing with his double-barrel shotgun and a Colt or Colt-copy revolver. Civilian shotguns were employed by the rebels early in the war because most civilian recruits owned one, and they provided two shots instead of just one from a musket. Gradually, rifled muskets replaced the short-range shotguns. *Wikimedia Commons*

Hunters used these ten-gauge cannons to blast flocks of sitting birds. Exit the passenger pigeon. However, their kick was almost as lethal as their blast.

The end of the war cut short the raiders' depredations, but not their taste for thrills. Riding with William Quantrill[12] or Bloody Bill Anderson into these breathtaking butcher jobs, stirrup to stirrup with comrades eager for vengeance and blood, was a rush. Living to tell the tale imparted an ego-swelling invulnerability. Both Quantrill and Anderson died in the saddle carrying arsenals of weapons. Quantrill carried several *Lefaucheux*—pinfire revolvers made in Belgium—that fired the first successful fast-loading fixed ammunition. Like most outlaws, he embraced new technologies that gave him the edge. Yet, after the Union victory, those Bushwhacker Confederates who survived became war criminals.

The Scots-Irish made up the majority of the lower- to middle-class cavalier citizens of the slave-owning states. Time had not softened the chip on the shoulder they carried against authority, be it the British crown in the old country or the US government in the new. The peacetime

William Quantrill was a leader of Confederate border raiders who attacked anti-slavery settlements in Kansas and Union military camps. He was eventually hunted down by Union troops and killed in an ambush on May 10 at a Kentucky farm. He died in a military hospital on June 6, 1865. *Wikimedia Commons*

The Lefaucheux pinfire revolver was a Belgian invention that seated the primer inside the cartridge case with the powder behind the bullet. The pin was struck from the top and punched down into the primer to ignite the charge. It was very vulnerable to hard use and detonation outside the firearm. The rimfire and centerfire primers were better. *Wikimedia Commons*

plundering only fueled their animosity. Wealthy politicians in the North who looked to Reconstruction to exact revenge on the unruly South, the plutocrats who pushed the railroad west, and the land speculators who took advantage of individuals and institutions received the brunt of this new anger against authority. They gave out-of-work guerillas a whole new array of targets—banks, railroads, payrolls, express shipments—anywhere ready cash was stored or transported.

THE RENO GANG

Some outlaw gangs created during the Civil War attracted a popular following, viewed romantically as men driven to postwar lawlessness by the catastrophes of wartime loss. Relatives, property, dignity, and hard-earned financial security were swept away in the brutalities of battle. Whether real or imagined, the injuries suffered drove these men to the owlhoot trail. And then there were the born snakes, rotten to the core from their mother's milk and the back of their father's hand, those whom everyone feared and hated. That was the Reno Gang.

In 1835, the Reno family moved into Jackson County, Kentucky, onto 1,200 acres near Seymour and began to breed children. Frank arrived first and then came John in 1838, Simeon ("Sim") arrived in 1843, Clinton in 1847, William in 1848, and Laura in 1851. The boys (except for "Honest Clint") were stinkers from the starting gun, conning fellow school students and travelers out of money and valuables with crooked card games. As they grew older, their tastes switched to arson and soon mysterious fires began flaring up on their neighbors' properties, which could then be bought and added to the Reno homestead.

Frank Reno was the eldest Reno brother. He was also the gang's ringleader and the nastiest member of that cutthroat tribe. The Reno Gang used the Civil War more as a cover for their robbery and murder sprees rather than a cause they believed in. *New York Times Learning Network*

The Civil War broke this cycle of petty crime and increased their income when the Reno kids became bounty jumpers. A gentleman with enough money could buy a surrogate to serve the gentleman's obligation in the army draft. Bounty jumpers took the money and reported for duty, but when the opportunity arrived, they deserted with the cash to find another sucker. And then the Reno boys became brokers, hiring out willing jumpers for a cut of the bounty. Soon, these full-time jumpers got to be well-known among recruiters and, to avoid jail time, they joined up with the Reno brothers for bigger scores. In particular, they congregated around a Seymour hotel called the Rader House where hapless pilgrims checked in for the night and never checked out, or they were pounded to a pulp and their belongings divvied up among the outlaws.

By the standards of the time, the Reno brothers became relatively wealthy through all their scams, murders, and muggings. Their influence affected elections as the war ended in 1865 and they achieved virtual invulnerability to the law as politicians owed their jobs to the Renos' brutal influence with voters. Their successful scourge required a bigger payroll and bigger scores to keep sufficient cash and willing gunmen on hand.

On October 6, 1866, at 6:30 in the evening, an Ohio & Mississippi train left Seymour with three Reno Gang members aboard: John and Sim Reno, along with Frank Sparks. When the train was beyond the town, the three forced their way inside the express car. John poked a Navy Colt into messenger Elam Miller's face and he surrendered his keys. The masked outlaws scooped up ten thousand dollars in gold coin and thirty-three dollars in bank notes from one small safe. When they tried to pry open a larger safe, they had no luck. They pulled the stop-signal rope on the locomotive and when it slowed, they heaved the safe out of the express car. A little further along, they all stepped off the slowing train.

The Reno Gang obtained, according to Jackson County Court records, "one safe the value of Thirty Dollars, Three Canvas Bags of the value of One Dollar Each, Ten Thousand Dollars in Gold Coin and Thirty Three Dollars in Bank Notes." Frank and William Reno were nearby holding the horses. They all made another attempt to batter the safe open, but failed, leaving roughly thirty-five thousand dollars at trackside when they rode off. This first train holdup in history was witnessed by George Kinney, a passenger.

Thanks to quick work by the Alan Pinkerton Agency, which was contracted for the protection of the railroad express company, and the eye witness statement, the Renos were rounded up at the Rader House hotel in Seymour. Awaiting trial, the boys made bail. One evening, the Pinkerton eyewitness, George Kinney, answered a knock at his door. A fusillade of bullets silenced his testimony and the boys went free.

With Kentucky too hot, the Renos shifted their robbing and murder to Missouri. There, they continued their crime spree with various members coming aboard and drifting away while Frank, John, Sim, and William carried on as the core of the operation. Yet, the Pinkertons were closing in. One bunch of gang members hit an Ohio & Mississippi train express car on July 10, 1868. The raid turned out to be a trap and a blazing gun battle brewed up in the car, wounding most of the robbers, who were all scooped up later by the Pinkertons. Three of the wounded bandits were caught and hustled aboard an O&M train headed for the county jail. On July 20, near Seymour, the train was stopped on the dark tracks by a large mob of silent men, all wearing scarlet masks. The Jackson County Vigilance Committee had been formed to eradicate the Reno brothers and the three bandits were strung up from a nearby beech tree.

Fleeing the vigilantes and the Pinkertons, Frank made it all the way up to Windsor, Canada, before being extradited back to the United States and united with his brothers, Sim and William, also in Pinkerton custody. The detectives were determined to get these three to court and transported them to New Albany in southern Indiana by steamboat and into a large stone prison to await trial. The relentless Jackson County Vigilance Committee had other plans.

In the deep night of December 2, 1868, a train showing no lights softly coasted into New Albany's Pearl Street station and hissed to a stop. A group of one hundred men, all wearing scarlet masks, stepped down and began to form ranks. Their leaders wore their suit coats inside out and had numbers chalked on the inside backs of the jackets, which separated them into military-like squads and platoons. The man with "No. 1" on his back stepped to the front and addressed the ranks.

Alan Pinkerton developed the concept for a nationwide detective agency at a time when law enforcement was stopped at city, county, and state border jurisdictions when pursuing lawbreakers. The Pinkerton's motto, "We never sleep," was close to the truth when agents were employed in the field. Though often overzealous, they were an effective threat. *Wikimedia Commons*

"*Num salus populi suprema lex*," he intoned—"The wish of the people is the supreme law"—and the silent sepulchral band stepped off in solemn formation. Armed with

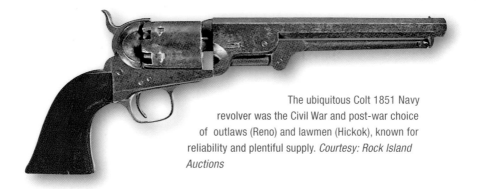

The ubiquitous Colt 1851 Navy revolver was the Civil War and post-war choice of outlaws (Reno) and lawmen (Hickok), known for reliability and plentiful supply. *Courtesy: Rock Island Auctions*

revolvers and clubs, down the dark streets they marched with measured tread, to the prison door where "No.1" knocked. The jailer opened up and was overwhelmed, as were the sheriff and two county commissioners who were standing watch. A quick search produced the keys and the vigilantes swarmed up the stairs. A second jailer was intimidated into opening the next iron door and only the cells remained.

Frank Reno was dragged from his cell by the silent men in the scarlet masks and received his hemp necktie. The other end of the short rope was made fast to an iron railing and he was shoved out over the stairwell, falling until brought up with a snap. The youngest Reno, William, was next, hurtling over the railing with a terrified scream.

Finally, the vigilantes laid hands upon Sim Reno who struggled and fought like a madman, eyes wide with terror, flailing, biting, babbling, and kicking until, in the southwest corner of the lockup, he was strung up with his feet grazing the ground and finally strangled to death a half hour later. Charley Anderson, another Reno owlhoot, was a bonus lynching. Heaved over the railing, his rope broke and he had to be fitted with a fresh collar and pitched over a second time, until they got it right.

Two hours after they arrived, the Jackson County Vigilance Committee marched silently back into the still night and reboarded their train.

THE NORTHFIELD RAID: THE YOUNGERS, JESSE AND FRANK JAMES

On September 7, 1876, eight men rode out of the Minnesota woods down a dusty road toward the town of Northfield. Frank and Jesse James, riding alongside Cole, Bob, and James Younger, were all graduates of the Confederate Quantrill's Raiders. They were skilled in ripping into a sleepy town just to see the feathers fly and crashing out the other side leaving death, flames, and misery in their wake. Riding with the James and Youngers were Clell Miller, Bill Chadwell, and Charlie Pitts, hard and resolute men at the top of their games. There was a familiarity to this morning ride in an early fall chill as the canopy of trees rustled above their heads, a recall of the days when Navy and Army Colts flashed and bucked

in pursuit of the lost cause. But this time the raiders were on their way to rob Northfield's First National Bank.

They had taken the train from their home ground in Missouri, purchased fine horses and McClellan saddles, loaded their cartridge belts with .44-caliber bullets and cleaned their Smith & Wesson American Model No. 3 revolvers. Cole's was nickel plated as befitted a true professional.

Above: Bob, Cole, and James Younger (in the middle) with their sister, Rita, in a family portrait wearing their Sunday best. First as raiders and then as robbers, the gentle demeanor got packed away on the owlhoot trail to Northfield, Minnesota. *Library of Congress*

Top left: In 1863, Frank and Jesse James turn game faces to the camera as they begin their apprenticeship in the Confederate raiders. Their appearances would change many times over the years with beards and mustaches, but here, they are just two tough kids. *Library of Congress*

The gang needed the money to maintain their high-living lifestyle, but Jesse James also had vengeance in mind. One of the bank's largest investors was Adelbert Ames, former Mississippi governor—a carpetbagger installed during postwar Reconstruction, hated by Southern whites, and married to the daughter of the reviled governor of Louisiana, Benjamin "The Beast" Butler. In 1875, to avoid impeachment—and a brutal tar and feathering— Ames had fled to Northfield and become a flour miller. He was also one of the bank's largest investors. This bad-blood raid would be just like the good old days.

Four of the gang rode from the south, up Division Street into Northfield, past the bank. Two stopped there at the corner of the Scriven Building while the other two rode through Mill Square to the Exchange Saloon. The pair at the bank dismounted and went inside where Bob Younger got change for a twenty-dollar bill— while he and Charlie Pitts had a good look around. From there, they mounted up and crossed the square to meet three others of their party. They conversed, shook hands and split up. Over the next four hours, the men wandered in twos and threes about the town, chatting with passersby, talking politics over ham-and-egg breakfasts, and waiting for the crowded street to thin out. This casual casing of the bank was hardly the raiders' style, but they knew the Pinkerton Detective

Cole Younger's Smith & Wesson Model No. 3 Schofield .44 was nickel plated for maximum flash and intimidation. Many outlaws opted for plated and engraved sidearms. He shot his way out of Northfield with this gun. *Library of Congress*

Charlie Pitts's S&W Russian .44 has the trigger guard extension for a gloved hand. His S&W is slower to shoot, but quicker to load with its break-top dumping of empty shells. At the Hansa Slough, he died with it in his hand. *Guernsey Auctions*

Bill Chadwell's Starr .44 is the best of their line when they changed over to cartridges from their Civil War percussion models. It laid where he dropped it next to his body in front of the bank. *Guernsey Auctions*

Frank James's Smith & Wesson .44, like Cole's, is nickel plated. He may have used this gun to blow out the brains of the Northfield bank clerk. All the outlaws carried .44-caliber ammunition that was available everywhere. *Artattler*

Agency was on their tail for previous crimes and the gang wanted this to be an easy score with no fuss from a cowed bunch of dirt farmers.

However, Northfield was a close community. Everybody knew everyone else and eight strangers arriving and meandering about in the middle of the day caused something of a stir. Each of these men wore an off-white linen duster—a loose, two-piece garment consisting of a sleeveless caftan beneath a draping cape. While it was a practical accessory, giving the arms great freedom and covering the loaded cartridge belts and a pair of large Smith & Wesson revolvers, the duster also looked like a sort of uniform. The men were also well-mounted. It was unusual to have so many saddle horses in town at once. Most townsfolk traveled in buggies and spring wagons. And finally, these riders had the look of men "on the prod," a swagger and watchfulness that was not simple curiosity.

At 2:00 p.m., Clell Miller and Cole Younger rode across the iron bridge over the Cannon River, walking their horses toward Division Street. Frank James, Bob Younger, and Charlie Pitts saw them coming and entered the bank. Bill Chadwell

The Scriven Building in downtown Northfield, Minnesota. The bank is at the far left, and most of the shooting and dying took place here as the James and Youngers rode back and forth shooting at armed citizens who were, in turn, shooting them to pieces. *Northfield Historical Society*

and Jesse James waited across the square guarding the other road out of town. Inside the bank's cramped lobby, employees Alonzo Bunker, Frank Wilcox, and bookkeeper Joseph Lee Heywood stared at three nickel-plated Smith & Wesson revolvers aimed by the three grim-faced and resolute robbers.[13]

The shortest of the bandits, Frank James, shouted, "Throw up your hands, for we intend to rob this bank—and if you holler we will blow your God damned brains out."

Outside in the square, a number of citizens had noticed the meandering strangers come together in front of the First National Bank. J. S. Allen leaned out and looked around the corner of the Lee & Hitchcock Store next to the bank and saw the three duster-clad men go inside. He hurried down to the bank as Clell Miller pulled the door shut. Seeing Allen, Miller grabbed him by the collar and hissed, "You son of a bitch, don't you holler!" Across the street, Henry Wheeler had been sitting in a chair on the wood sidewalk and saw Miller snatch at Allen. He had been aware of the parade of duster-men strolling about town, and now their purpose suddenly became clear. Wheeler leaped to his feet, shouting, "Robbery! They're robbing the bank!" And he took off at a dead run into the Wheeler and Blackman Drug Store. Miller fired a shot that sizzled over Wheeler's head.

That gunshot brought Cole Younger, Jim Younger, Jesse James, and Bill Chadwell into action. As Miller stood by the horses in front of the bank, the others began galloping and dodging about, their banging revolvers clouding the street with gunsmoke. The Northfield residents set about with a grim resolve as weapons and ammunition were passed out from every store that had a stock. Mostly, these were long guns. This was hunting country.

The Lee & Hitchcock Store next door to the bank and the Manning Hardware Store around the corner on Mill Square became ready arsenals. Elias Stacy snatched a shotgun from the J. S. Allen Hardware, pressed in two brass shells, clapped the barrels shut, and aimed at the nearest outlaw. Clell Miller was swinging his leg over his saddle when Stacy triggered a load of birdshot that hit the gunman in the head, knocking him from his horse. Disoriented, Miller remounted with blood running down his face.

Anselm Manning left his hardware counter and watched the bandits galloping up and down the street, shooting at anyone who stuck their head out, and saw residents waving pistols, shooting out windows, and spraying lead everywhere. He remembered a Remington Rolling Block rifle propped in the store window. This rifle fired .45-70-caliber buffalo killers and he knew how to use it. Stuffing his pockets with ammunition, he raced out the door, cocking the hammer and opening the breech block as he ran. He slid a cartridge into the chamber, closed the breech, and paused to look around the corner of the Scriven Building down Division Street toward the bank entrance. Seeing saddle horses and two robbers hiding behind them, without hesitation, he laid his sights on the nearest horse and killed it. When he went to reload, he found the empty shell wedged tightly in the breech. Manning turned and ran back toward his shop to extract the shell.

In the bank, all was chaos. Frank James and Charlie Pitts were beating up on James Heywood who claimed he could not open the safe because of a time

The Remington Rolling Block rifle was a single shot, usually heavy-caliber, rifle built for military and sporting use. The simple action of cocking the hammer, then cocking open the breech, made for fast reloading. Along with the Sharps .50-caliber, the Remington was a popular gun with buffalo hunters. *Rock Island Auction Company*

lock, which the robbers knew to be a lie, because they were familiar with the Yale Chronometer Time Lock. No bank would have it engaged during banking hours. They cut his throat and beat his head with a pistol butt. Alonzo Bunker spotted a .32-caliber Smith & Wesson revolver on a shelf beneath the counter and moved toward it. Bob Younger snatched the pistol away and dropped it in his pocket.

Frank James cursed and fired his revolver just above Heywood's head. The blast was deafening. Powder smoke filled the air. Bunker threw his hands in the air and made a mad dash for the back door screaming, "Murder! Murder!" He crashed through the door, trampled over Theodore Miller, the undertaker who was coming to the bank, and kept running until Pitts took steady aim and put a ball in Bunker's shoulder, but adrenaline and pumping feet kept Bunker going until he was out of sight.

Henry Wheeler had been searching for the nearest gun when he remembered an old Civil War breechloader he knew was at the Dampier House Hotel two doors away. The carbine was a Smith .50-caliber that fired crude fixed ammunition, a greased lead ball held in a gunpowder-filled gutta percha (made from South Pacific tree latex) cylinder with a hole in the other end. It was ignited with a percussion cap on a nipple once the breech was closed much like closing the barrels of a shotgun. Wheeler took four cartridges from the hotel desk clerk and ran upstairs to look down on Division Street. Below him, James Younger was a perfect target, mounted on a squirrely horse in front of the bank. Wheeler aimed the old carbine; breathing hard, with silver stress spots dancing in his eyes, he cocked the hammer and pulled the trigger, but only a puff of dust went up behind Younger.

Wheeler broke the barrel downward, removed the blackened cylinder, put a fresh cap on the nipple, shoved in another cartridge, and closed the barrel back up in place with a clunk. Next, he aimed at Miller who was bent over in his saddle. Wheeler aimed lower this time, cocked, and fired. Clell Miller lurched

Designed in the 1850s, the Smith used a rubber-cased .50-caliber cartridge and a separate percussion cap. The ammunition was fragile to transport, but functioned well when it was adopted by the Union in 1860 before the Civil War began. *Wikimedia Commons*

in the saddle as the slug the diameter of a quarter slammed into his shoulder, chopped through bone and tissue, and severed his subclavian artery. He rolled from his saddle, mumbling his last words while his severed artery emptied out into his body and he died.

Down the street, pausing in his desperate game of cowing the citizens of Northfield, who would have none of it, Bill Chadwell broke the action open on his Smith & Wesson revolver to eject the empty shells and cram fresh .44-caliber cartridges into the cylinders. Anselm Manning, desperate to get off another shot at the gunmen as bullets whistled around his head, saw the six-foot four-inch Chadwell astride his horse looking for targets. Bringing his Remington Rolling Block rifle to his shoulder, Manning aimed, cocked the hammer, and squeezed the trigger. Chadwell reeled back and pitched off his horse with a hole in his chest. He lay on his stomach propped up on his elbows, obviously in great pain, shivered, and then rolled over, dead in the street.

One of the outlaws dismounted, stripped off Chadwell's cartridge belt and revolvers, and leaped back into the saddle. At the same time, Cole Younger was imploring the outlaws inside the bank to give it up and get out.

"For God's sake come out! They're shooting us all to pieces!"

As the horsemen continued to fire in all directions from the center of Division Street, a group of patrons streamed up from the basement entrance of a nearby saloon to see what all the fuss was about. Cole Younger desperately reined his horse forward and back, circling to find targets in the haze of gunsmoke when he saw these men come rushing into view. He cocked his Smith & Wesson, aimed at the last man up the stairs and fired. Nicolaus Gustavson, an old Swede deep in his cups and who knew little English, toppled over backward with a fatal head wound.

Charlie Pitts and Bob Younger came piling out of the bank, leaving behind a grain sack containing a little over eight dollars and change for their troubles. Their guns joined the others. Behind them, an angry and frustrated Frank James paused in the bank to vent his fury. The beaten and bloody book-keeper, James Heywood, slumped in a chair. Frank fired one shot at the injured man, missed, then crossed the lobby to point blank range and fired again into Heywood's head, blowing brains out the other side.

Across the street, while some unarmed citizens began throwing rocks at the beleaguered robbers, Manning had reloaded his Remington rifle and was playing duck and dodge with Bob Younger, each trying to get a clear shot at the other.

Meanwhile, Henry Wheeler, upstairs in the Dampier House, had reloaded his Smith carbine and saw Younger shooting in Manning's direction. With his third cartridge, Wheeler cocked the heavy hammer, sighted on Younger, and fired. The shot shattered Younger's elbow and spun him. The savvy outlaw tore the revolver from his useless right hand and kept up the fight with the left.

Frank James and Charlie Pitts mounted their horses, spurring for the iron bridge and the road out of town. Bob Younger, with his horse dead and blood drooling down his white duster, trotted after them. He cried out, "My God, boys! You're not going to leave! I am shot!" Hearing his brother's cry, Cole Younger reined his horse and turned his back on the bridge to safety. With his brother stumbling toward him, desperately wounded, Cole spurred his wild-eyed mount back into the furnace of flaming guns and sizzling bullets. He galloped to Bob's side, shucked a foot from the near stirrup, and held down his hand. Bob jumped into the empty stirrup, seized Cole's arm with his left hand, and swung up behind his saddle. Cole bent low over his horse's neck and raced for the iron bridge with Bob holding on, literally for dear life. The pair clattered across the bridge's wood planks and hightailed out of town.

The raid was finished seven minutes after the first alarm. Two townsmen were dead: Heywood, a hero at his post in the bank, and the Swede, Gustavson, who would die later from his head wound. A pall of gunsmoke hung over Division Street for a time while the injured were tended to, but it didn't take long for the telegraph wires to begin humming with the news to towns along the raiders' flight from Northfield. For weeks, an estimated thousand men combed the great Minnesota woods to the prairie's edge, narrowly missing the wounded outlaws who had turned loose their exhausted horses. Finally, at a bend in the Watonwan River near the town of Madelia, Minnesota, the wretched robbers

Cole Younger gave up this last revolver to the posse as they closed in. His Moore .32-caliber, seven-shot rimfire pistol has a slide-out-to-the-right-side cylinder for loading and punching out empty shells with a rod that fitted beneath the barrel. It violated Rollin White's patent for bored-through cylinders and Moore lost the lawsuit. Moore was ahead of his time. *Northfield Historical Society*

were run to ground by Sheriff James Glispin's posse. Charlie Pitts tried to make a fight of it and took a ball in the chest, killing him instantly. Bob was hit again, as were Cole and James Younger. Jesse and Frank had split from the group and successfully made their way back to Missouri.

The end of the raid played itself out when the bloody and bandaged Youngers were paraded in a wagon down Madelia's main street as trophies—much more fortunate than their cohorts, Clell Miller and Bill Chadwell, whose bloody bodies had decorated planks on display in Northfield for the citizens to contemplate. In Madelia, the survivors were cheered for their grit and waved back at the crowd.

Jesse and Frank James continued on the owlhoot trail, but they were never the same again. Jesse assembled another gang, but without the Youngers, or anything resembling the boys who had ridden with Bloody Bill or Quantrill back in the day. He took on young trail trash looking to add a stint with the famous James Gang to their resumes. Frank became a reluctant partner and even Jesse tired of living rough in the woods, the Pinkertons' pursuit, and the fear of betrayal. Members of the gang drifted away as their cut from train and stage coach robberies became less and less as railroad express safes began carrying less cash. Spotty loot gleaned from passengers made up the shortfall.

By 1882, Frank was living on a farm under the alias "Woodson," and Jesse was "Mr. Howard" in a house looking down on St. Joseph, Missouri, with his cousin, Zee (whom he had married), and their two children. He was a respected—albeit very private—member of his community, though no one seemed to notice the Colt Single Action Army revolver, nor the Smith & Wesson American Model he carried in shoulder holsters beneath his suit jacket. He had also grown a beard and was planning to rob the Platt City, Missouri, bank for one big final score before setting himself up as a regular citizen.

With the gang virtually disbanded, Jesse befriended two recent members, young men in their twenties, who were eager as puppies to side him in any enterprise. Bob and Charley Ford also had made a deal with Missouri Governor Thomas T. Crittenden for forty thousand dollars to deliver Jesse alive into custody, or for ten thousand dollars for his corpse. Not being big risk takers, they opted for the latter. The brothers lived as guests with Jesse and his family. After dinner, on April 3, 1882, they retired with Jesse to the parlor. His holstered pistols lay on a table as he fiddled with straightening a picture on the wall. Bob Ford drew his Smith & Wesson .44-caliber revolver and cocked it. Jesse James knew that sound and started to turn around. Bob Ford became a legend with a squeeze of the trigger "and laid poor Jesse in his grave."

A collection of Jesse James's guns from counter-clockwise: the nickel-plated .44-caliber Smith & Wesson revolver was a very popular rival to the Colt; his ubiquitous 1851 Colt Navy percussion; a Remington 1863 New Army percussion; and, at the top, Jesse's 1873 Colt Peacemaker with ivory grips. *Frazier Museum, Louisville, Kentucky*

Bob Ford became famous as the man who killed Jesse James. Ford was a latecomer to the James gang, a wannabe who hoped Jesse's fame would rub off on him. He achieved that fame as one of the most despised men of the West. He lived on in song as "the dirty little coward who shot poor Mister Howard" until a shotgun ended his days. *Wikimedia Commons*

Bob and Charley snatched up Jesse's revolvers and ran from the house followed by the screams of Jesse's wife, Zee, as she stood over the spreading pool of blood beneath her husband. Crittenden ended up on the wrong end of public opinion for essentially hiring the Fords to kill Jesse. He paid out part of the promised reward, but kept a low profile. Charley Ford contracted tuberculosis and became a morphine addict, eventually committing suicide. For ten years, Bob Ford, the trigger man, sold photographs of himself and never stepped back from his reputation as a cowardly back shooter. He opened a tent saloon in Creede, Colorado, in 1892.

Jesse James laid out in his Sunday best shirt and pants in the undertaker's parlor where kin and gawkers could look on his serene face instead of down the barrels of his revolvers. *Wikimedia Commons*

The 1873 model Remington revolver had all the Colt's good points and added a few rugged structural touches. It was popular and only suffered because it came into the market after the Colt's long presence. *Dale Peterson Collection*

A local down-at-the-heels miner and drunken tosspot, Michael O'Kelley, reasoned he could improve his station in life by killing Ford. He borrowed a shotgun; stuffed it with all manner of scrap, nails, screws, and such; tamped the load over a sizable dose of black powder; and strolled into the saloon. He said, "Hello, Bob," to the man behind the bar and, as Ford turned to face him, triggered both barrels. Ford's head detonated from the force of the blast and the "dirty little coward who shot poor Mister Howard" was laid in his own grave.

On October 5, 1882, Frank James turned himself in to Governor Crittenden in the governor's office, dramatically presenting the wide-eyed official with an 1875 Remington revolver. Holding it by the barrel, the outlaw offered it butt first. After a series of farcical trials and laudatory articles by the newspaper journalist John Newman Edwards depicting the James boys as victims of prejudice and lies, Frank James was declared a free man—even following the eyewitness testimony of Frank Wilcox, the Northfield, Minnesota, banker who, standing in the gunsmoke-choked bank lobby, had looked Frank James square in the eye and saw him kill James Heywood.

When Cole finally left Stillwater prison after serving twenty-five years, he hooked up with Frank James to form the Great Cole Younger and Frank James Historical Wild West touring show and wrote a self-serving book, *The Story of Cole Younger by Himself*, which he sold at the shows and told his version of the Northfield raid, a story that claimed Frank and Jesse were never there. According to Cole, the other two men who got away were a chap named Woods and another fellow named Howard.[14] Coincidently, Woodson was Jesse's middle name and Howard was his last alias.

COFFEYVILLE, KANSAS, AND THE DALTON BOYS

The Dalton brothers were nice and polite, according to their school teacher.[15] Bob, Grat, and Emmett were cousins of the Younger boys, who were friends of the James brothers. The Daltons had also lost their homestead after the Civil War. Despite the bitterness, their family and neighbors farmed in Kansas, then in Missouri and, finally carved up the ground in the Indian Territory and Oklahoma. Growing up, the Daltons absorbed the heroic stories of outlaw depredations, but kept to the straight and narrow path.

They had been born during the war and its aftermath when their cousins and other disbanded raiders had run roughshod over the burned-out countryside. Still, as they approached manhood, they chose to uphold the law as deputy US marshals, serving at the pleasure of Judge Isaac Parker's court in Fort Smith, Arkansas. The Wild West was mellowing as settlement, transportation, and the law followed the western migration toward the turn of the century.

Bob Dalton. *Rock Island Auction Company*

Grat Dalton. *Wikimedia Commons*

Packing firearms for a living, tracking down horse thieves, tax cheats, murderers, and rustlers can sour a man. With a Colt or Smith & Wesson revolver riding high on the hip and a Winchester in the saddle scabbard, the Daltons faced a cynical dangerous world. They quickly tired of shelling out twenty-five cents for soda bread and a tin of beans and having nothing left in their pockets but lint. A marshal's pay was erratic and low. Having been raised on the flashy tales of their kin, the boys knew there were lucrative alternatives.

It was not long before Bob started earning side money from crooked land deals. Grat had a drinking problem and did short jail time for public drunkenness. Soon, horse theft was added to Bob's and Emmett's arrest records. Finally, they gave up all pretenses of being wronged by the US marshal's service and just stole because they wanted the money. With friends and relatives protecting them along

Emmett Dalton. *Rock Island Auction Company*

Oklahoma's Cimarron River country, they branched out, hitting railroad express shipments of banknotes. Bob's fianceé, Eugenia Moore, posed as a potential express customer to inquire about banknote shipment schedules.[15]

Their train robberies produced a successful *modus operandi*. The Dalton Gang arrived at the train depot wearing masks and carrying Winchester rifles. As former lawmen, they preferred the long gun because of its firepower and long reach compared with the revolver. Lawmen relied on ambush and surprise to get the drop on their quarry. When they were hunting men day in and day out, they needed every advantage to survive.

The Daltons stuck to this training. With the railroad employees trussed up and the station searched for anything valuable, the telegraph wires were cut. When the train arrived, it was greeted by the gang who shut down the locomotive. The outlaws battered their way into the express car and looted it methodically. They did not molest or shake down the passengers, and after they transferred the money to their horses, the boys rode away firing a fusillade of rifle shots back at the train to keep heads down. With this successful formula, and the press subsequently extolling their virtues as outshining the James or Younger gangs of old, the brothers' egos were pumped up to attempt even more dazzling stunts.

A Winchester Model 73 belonging to a Dalton, collected in Coffeyville, Kansas, after the aborted raid on two banks. *Dalton Defenders Museum*

With their eyes on a big prize, the Daltons invited journeyman outlaws Bill Powers, Dick Broadwell, and Bill Doolin to accompany them. They planned a whirlwind tour of Coffeyville, Kansas's two banks: the First National and the C. M. Condon Company across the street. Eschewing masks for false mustaches and fake beards, the group arrived in Coffeyville on the morning of October 5, 1892. All were armed with Colt and Smith & Wesson revolvers plus their trusty Winchesters and an attitude of invincibility. They were going to do what no bandit had ever done: rob two banks in the same town on the same day. Bill Doolin was not present at the outing. He had claimed his horse had pulled up lame and he passed on the ambitious score. His absence left even bigger cuts of the pie for the remaining quintet.

Above: Bob Dalton carried this Colt Single Action Army model .32-20-caliber revolver built on a .45-caliber frame in his right boot when riding on a raid. If needed, he only had to bend down to reach it. *Dalton Defenders Museum*

Left: The Condon Bank is one of the two Coffeyville, Kansas, banks hit by the Dalton Gang. No outlaws had ever successfully robbed two banks in the same town on the same day. The Daltons proved it could not be done. *Dalton Defenders Museum*

BANK RAIDED BY DALTON GANG — 1892
COFFEYVILLE, KANSAS

Because the brothers had grown up around Coffeyville, almost everyone who saw the Daltons ride in wondered why Bob, Grat, and Emmett were wearing false whiskers. When the five dismounted in a narrow alley off Maple Street and then strolled—Bob and Emmet to the First National, and Grat with Powers and Broadwell to the Condon—all became clear. Everyone who was not already armed headed for the hardware store to begin feeding ammunition into their long guns and revolvers.

The wait was brief. Bob and Emmett moved briskly from the First National's lobby, shielded by bank employees. They hustled toward the alley and the horses with a feed sack holding roughly twenty thousand dollars. As soon as Grat, Broadwell, and Powers stepped from Condon behind their terrified hostages, holding their booty, the citizens of Coffeyville made their presence known.

A rippling blast of pistols, rifles, and shotguns hammered the outlaws. Hostages scrabbled for cover on hands and knees as lead slugs sizzled overhead, shattering glass, powdering brick, chipping stone, and thudding into running, stumbling targets. The Daltons, Powers, and Broadwell made it into the alley only to be confronted by more townsmen funneling in from the opposite end. An enfilading blast of gunfire peppered the outlaws and their horses.

Wounded animals screamed, tore loose their reins, and bolted, frothing and spurting blood from a dozen wounds. Bob Dalton killed two defenders with his Winchester and took a fatal round in the gut from livery stable owner John Kloehr. When Grat saw Bob drop dead, he aimed at the livery man, but Kloehr

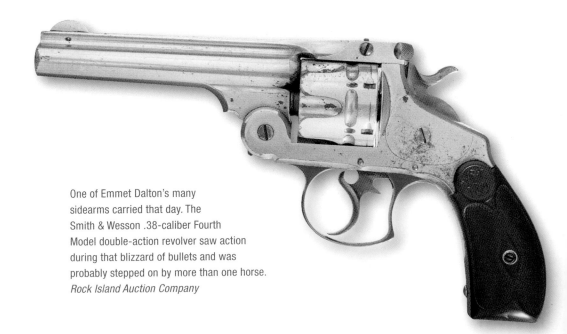

One of Emmet Dalton's many sidearms carried that day. The Smith & Wesson .38-caliber Fourth Model double-action revolver saw action during that blizzard of bullets and was probably stepped on by more than one horse. *Rock Island Auction Company*

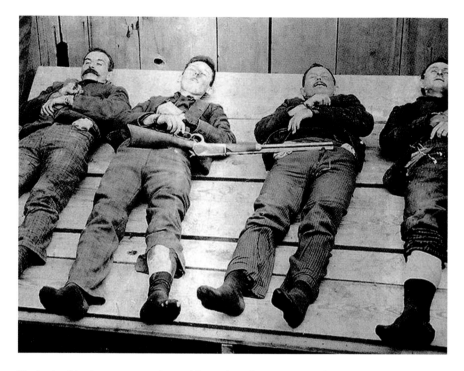

The bank raiders' corpses were dragged from where they were gunned down by the townspeople and laid out for the home folks to view their handiwork. Postcards of the boys went for thirty-five cents each. They are: Bill Powers, Bob Dalton, Grat Dalton, and Dick Broadwell. Emmett Dalton was riddled, but survived. *Dalton Defenders Museum*

killed Grat with his next shot, a ball through the throat.[15] Broadwell managed to get into a saddle only to stop a heavy-caliber round, which knocked him to the ground.

Emmett tumbled from his saddle and, clutching the money bag, tried to scrabble away from the hail of bullets chopping into him. He collapsed, shot to pieces with more than twenty-three bullet and buckshot wounds.[16] The raid had lasted only twelve minutes.

Emmett survived and was shipped off to prison. The last portrait of Bob and Grat Dalton, Dick Broadwell, and Bill Powers laid out on wood planks in per-forated clothes for the photographers made a fine advertisement for the folly of hubris—and sold for thirty-five cents each.[16] The raid was also a testament to the unwillingness of hardworking citizens to knuckle under to worthless gunmen. Four Coffeyville citizens died defending their town. The West was growing up. All the old stories, the old myths, grudges, and feuds were becoming crusty with age and irrelevance.

CHAPTER 5

A PAIR OF LEGENDS:
HICKOK AND DOOLIN

THESE TWO WESTERN legends could not have been more different. "Wild Bill" Hickok began his path to legendary status as a young man in a nascent and dangerous west. He was tall, athletic, and handsome with flowing long hair and piercing eyes.

He gravitated toward adventure and dressed to attract attention with his shoulder-length curls, Prince Albert frock coat, and custom-made boots. Hickok practiced long and hard with percussion model Navy Colt revolvers and heavy rifles as a hunter for the railroad. His job took him to end-of-track towns that grew into tough cow towns as the herds arrived to feed the eastern market. His flamboyance, fearlessness, and frequent shooting scrapes—usually from behind a badge—influenced the press as well as the lugubrious mythmaking writers of the penny dreadfuls, whose paperback books mixed an ounce of fact with a quart of sentimental fantasy.

Bill Doolin was a Johnnie-come-lately to the pantheon of Western legends, coming into this world in 1858 just as Wild Bill was starting his career. Doolin was a man of simpler needs and left home a young man to become a cowboy. The wild streak in him crossed paths with former cowboy, now outlaw, George "Bitter Creek" Newcomb and discovered there were illegal, but profitable, shortcuts to the long, tedious life on the cattle trail. He hooked up with the

Above: William Butler "Wild Bill" Hickok in his prime: handsome, confident, a steady gaze, and very fast hands with a pair of Navy Colts. *Wikimedia Commons*

Right: The Navy Colts tucked into his belt with the butts forward became his signature. He cocked the hammer as the revolver was leaving his belt, a risky proposition, but the move gave him a full second faster drop on his opponent. *Wikimedia Commons*

Dalton Gang before they became the Dead Dalton Gang at Coffeyville, Kansas. Seven days after the deaths of the Daltons, Bill Doolin and Newcomb held up the DM&A train as it pulled out of the Caney, Kansas, station and made off with $1,500. A few weeks later, they robbed a bank in Spearville, Kansas, of $1,697 and in 1893, took in $1,000 when they robbed a Santa Fe train near Cimarron, Kansas.

But by the late 1890s, Doolin had distanced himself by demonstrating a streak of integrity, as well as a natural cunning, that helped him lead his own gang, the Long Riders. Even the lawmen who hunted him showed him respect—but not enough to give him the first shot. Both Hickok and Doolin were masters at their respective trades and both died with their boots on in a cloud of gunsmoke.

WILLIAM BUTLER HICKOK SETS THE PISTOLERO MOLD

Legendary Wild Bill Hickok had been a US deputy marshal, county sheriff, and town marshal in tough cow towns like Hays City and Abilene, Kansas. But even with his prowess packing a pair of 1851 Navy Colts, he still needed help. When not patrolling the West's mean streets, Bill usually found himself a chair in a gambling house—with his back to a wall—forestalling the parade of reputation hunters who would shoot him in the back just for the notoriety. While he provided the morbidly curious with demonstrations of his shooting ability on targets from fifty to two hundred yards distant, the length of a saloon bar or the width of a card table were the more frequent challenges he faced in his social circle.

His preference for three-piece ammunition of the Civil War era had its own self-preservation logic. All too often in the early days of mass production, brass cartridge cases received short doses of gun powder in the assembly line. Cartridges stuffed in a leather loop gun belt were subject to damp seeping in around an improperly seated primer, or lead bullet. Moreover, cartridges were expensive—especially for the roller-coaster economics of a regular gambler—and not everyone carried the plethora of calibers that were sprouting up. Hand loading the proper charge of black powder with a carefully greased ball seated down into the cylinder chamber and closed with a copper percussion cap at the other end, pointed down a cleaned nipple, and then further sealed at the business end of the cylinder with a swipe of waterproofing grease made for a gun that would hit what it was aimed at.

The Colts served him well from behind a badge to laying down a straight flush to win a poker pot until the late evening of October 5, 1871, when he was city marshal of Abilene. A gambler, Phil Coe, with fifty armed and dangerous Texas cowboys at his back, fired a shot in town—strictly against the law. Hickok arrived on the scene and demanded Coe's revolver. Coe tried to give it to him one bullet at a time—and missed, punching a hole through Hickok's frock coat. Wild Bill fired twice, both shots ripping into Coe's boiler room. As Coe dropped, the surly cowboys stirred and there was a commotion behind him. Bill spun around and fired at a man with a drawn gun. He killed his own deputy, Mike Williams, who had run out to side with him against the mob. That took the steam out of Wild Bill for quite some time. He was fired from his job when

"ARE YOU SATISFIED?"

Once Hickok combined the jobs of peace officer and gambler, he was a constant target for the disgruntled. His gunfight with Phil Coe, where he also killed his own deputy by accident, shows how his reflexes worked. Nobody startled Wild Bill Hickok. *Wikimedia Commons*

Abilene went out of the cattle business and wandered off, ending his career as a peace officer.[17]

He hooked up with Buffalo Bill's Wild West Show, appearing as a stage actor with Bill and Texas Jack Omohundro, but his drinking grew worse and his eyes started to go bad. When he left their partnership, they gave him a matched pair of Smith & Wesson American Model No. 3 revolvers, which he carried with him for a couple of years up into Colorado mining camps. By the time he drifted down into Deadwood as a partner in Charlie Utter's shipping company, his holsters once again held Colts. This time, he carried a pair of Richardson Colts—Army Model revolvers converted to .44-caliber cartridge use that were popular in the transition period between the Civil War and the mid-1870s.

On August 2, 1876, Hickok violated his cardinal rule of always sitting with his back to a wall when gambling. Furthermore, he left the heavy artillery home and packed only a Smith & Wesson .32-caliber No. 2 rimfire pistol with a stubby spur trigger in his belt. Jack McCall, a local tosspot whom Hickok had

Charley Utter's Smith & Wesson
.44-caliber rode with him while
he bullwhacked ox wagons of shipping
supplies for his and Wild Bill's company.
Charley and Calamity Jane Canary ran the business
while Bill needed an income to support his gambling
and drinking. *City of Deadwood Archives*

Colt had a vast inventory of Army
and Navy Model percussion revolvers
on hand and even more banging away in the field.
What to do but find some way to convert all this iron
to use the new cartridges? Wild Bill chose this Richardson
conversion, kept the feel and balance of his Colt Navy, and
updated his game. *City of Deadwood Archives*

humiliated in a card game, worked up his whiskey courage and shot the frontier legend in the back of the head with a double-action revolver in Nuttall & Mann's No. 10 Deadwood saloon. Hickok's blood-spattered poker hand was two pair: aces and eights—forever after known as the dead man's hand. Charlie Utter had a tombstone carved and the legend continued to grow.

Much of Hickok's real and mythical reputation as a fighting man can be laid at the door of the border scriveners who elevated Wild Bill into a kind of demigod. Some were genuine admirers, some tongue-in-cheek, and others malicious. Hickok typified the era of the man-killer or shootist, better known today as the gunfighter—a term in use as early as 1874, but not popularized until post-1900. Back in 1881, however, a Missouri editor wrote that the gentleman who had "killed his man" was quite common, and if "his homicidal talents had been employed in the enforcement of law and order, he would be ranked as a 'great Western civilizer.'"

Charley Utter and a Native American, Steve, saw to it Bill was buried with a suitable marker—one that even names his killer—just outside of Deadwood. *Wikimedia Commons*

Predictably, some writers have eagerly seized upon the word "civilizer" to explain Hickok's role in the control and eradication of the bad men who infested many frontier towns and habitats, ignoring the fact that when acting in an official capacity, every time he drew and fired his pistols and a man was killed, he was answerable to the coroner and not necessarily applauded for ridding the community of such characters.

We will probably never know how Wild Bill really felt about gunfighting. Old-timers recalled his bravery under fire, or the deadly purpose he displayed when he drew and fired at another man who was as intent on killing him. Buffalo Bill Cody, in one of his last interviews, said that Hickok cocked his pistols as he drew—which gave him a split-second advantage—and was always "cool, kinda cheerful, almost, about it. And he never killed a man unless that man was trying to kill him. That's fair."

If we ignore Hickok's Civil War service, during which he is reported to have killed a number of bushwhackers and guerrillas, it was 1865 before he was again involved in a face-to-face shootout. This was between himself and his friend Davis K. Tutt, a Confederate-turned-Union man who, like Hickok, was an inveterate gambler. The pair played cards on the night of July 20 in Springfield, Missouri, and Hickok lost. Tutt claimed he was owed thirty-five dollars, and Hickok said it

Hickok might have grown tired of packing those twin Colts everywhere, especially to his round of gambling saloons. To ease his burden, he began carrying a small Smith & Wesson .32-caliber spur trigger revolver in his waistcoat. This gun was enough to reach across a card table. *Rock Island Auction Company*

was twenty-five dollars. Dave took Wild Bill's Waltham watch pending payment. The pair then spent most of the twenty-first arguing over the amount. Hickok stated that Dave had loaned him money many times in the past, but he did not believe that he owed his friend thirty-five dollars and they should compromise. But Tutt stormed off and reappeared on the public square at 6:00 p.m. sporting the watch. When Hickok told him to stop, Tutt drew his pistol, and Hickok did the same. Seventy-five yards apart, both men opened fire, the shots sounding as one. Tutt had turned sideways (in dueling fashion) and missed, but Hickok's ball entered Dave's right side and exited through his left, piercing his heart.

Arrested and put on trial for manslaughter, Hickok was found not guilty by a jury influenced more by the judge's remarks on one's rights of self-defense than by the opinion of the prosecuting counsel. Tragically, neither man had wanted the fight, which is a far cry from the anti-Hickok statements made in the 1920s by men who claimed to have witnessed the shootout, some of whom had not even been born when it took place.

It was to be another four years before Hickok again killed another white man (in those days, killing Indians did not count as homicide), during which

continued on page 70

In the period during and following the Civil War, firearms technology raced forward in design and terrible efficiency. Of the many improvements, the development of fixed ammunition led the way. From the separate missile, propellant, and igniter the components were brought together in a one-piece cartridge. During the war, breech-loading rifles, such as Sharps, Smith, Burnside, Spencer, and others, each used a unique two-piece cartridge: powder and ball fixed together and ignited by a separate percussion cap.

In the 1850s, the Volcanic pistol combined the powder and igniter in a hollowed-out lead missile that fired as fast as the action could be worked. The amount of powder that could be stowed in the concave base of the missile limited the rifle's or pistol's power. When Volcanic was bought out by B. Tyler Henry, the missile became a solid bullet pressed into a copper case with primer dribbled into the rimmed base that dried and exploded when struck by the gun's hammer. After the shot, cocking the action ejected the empty case and loaded a fresh primed and powdered cartridge. That was the answer. Now, a .44-caliber rimfire cartridge would fire in any gun chambered to accept it instead of every cartridge being proprietary to a specific make of gun. The limited rimfire cartridge was supplanted by the more powerful centerfire primer plugged into the concentric middle of the cartridge base.

New centerfire cartridge rifles and pistols were designed to accept the new ammunition, but what about the thousands of cap and ball revolvers already sold and in use, or inventories of unsold pistols? Rollin White had obtained a patent for a drilled-through cylinder that accepted fixed cartridge ammunition. It was licensed by Smith & Wesson, which in the mid- to late 1850s produced pretty little .22-caliber rimfire revolvers and licensed .32-caliber and .38-caliber models. They owned the market until the patent expired in 1857 and the other manufacturers agonized, jumping through hoops to get around the patent with terrible guns. Lawyers got rich defending that patent against infringement.

Smith & Wesson kept building those pretty little pistols and never took advantage of their monopoly to create larger, more practical weapons until after the patent expired. By that time, Colt had designed cartridge conversion kits for Army, Navy, and Pocket Model revolvers, replacing the under-barrel loading levers with spring rod ejection systems and drilled through cylinders with side-drop loading and unloading gates.

Other manufacturers took advantage of the patent situation. Some, like Thuer and Richardson, produced conversion kits for percussion Colts that loaded cartridges from the rear into replacement drilled-through cylinders. William Mason built a breech loader for Colt in 1871 firing the .44 rimfire and then added a top strap above the open-top rotating cylinder for a more rugged design. Eventually, the .45 Colt man-stopper

Left: Colt's earliest multishot cartridge revolver with a cloverleaf cylinder was called their house gun.
Wikimedia Commons

Right: An 1873 Peacemaker Colt recovered from the Little Big Horn battlefield following George Armstrong Custer's massacre by the Sioux and Cheyenne Native Americans. The letter behind it attests to its provenance as belonging to Company K of the Seventh Cavalry.
Wikimedia Commons

cartridge was developed for this Richards and Mason revolver ordered by the army. The Colt Single Action Army Peacemaker 1873 revolver was the ultimate beneficiary of the post–Civil War patent games. It became the first choice of outlaws, lawmen, and range-riding cowboys, famous for its durability, reasonable accuracy, and its adaptability to a variety of calibers—and is still produced today.

In the new market of metallic cartridge, rear-loading pocket revolvers, Colt not only introduced its three derringer models (as of 1870) or the Colt House Gun and the Open Top Pocket (the last two as of 1871) but, in 1873, also introduced a subsequent design called its New Line revolver models, based on William Mason's patents.

The 1870s and 1880s provided sales opportunity to the Colt company via the spread of European-American society ever farther westward across the continent, and the demand for firearms that it engendered in various ways. As white Americans displaced Indians, both sides were eager for firearms. On the white side, both the US Army and civilians were customers of Colt. The army carried Colt revolvers through the last of the Indian Wars. On the Indian side, Colt weapons were captured when possible, or bought from whoever was selling. Even among whites in towns where Indians had been vanquished, a thriving demand for guns existed, from the criminals to the police to self-defending civilians. Memoirs of Americans speak of what it was like growing up in Western towns where most people had guns and open carry was common (such as in Kansas and Missouri, which were considered "out West" at the time—now considered the Old West).

continued from page 67

time the press had been busy building up his reputation both as a man-killer and pistol dead shot. Following his election as acting sheriff of Ellis County in August 1869, Wild Bill shot and killed Bill Mulvey who, when drunk, had refused Hickok's order to disarm and continued shooting at anyone who moved. A month later, Wild Bill was called to a saloon where Sam Strawhun and friends were raising a ruckus and threatening to shoot anyone who stopped them. Whether Strawhun threatened to shoot Wild Bill or thrust a broken glass into his face is hotly debated, but Sam was buried the next day, unmourned, and Hickok received congratulations for ridding Hays City of such a debauched character. Wild Bill still lost the November election to his deputy, Peter "Rattlesnake Pete" Lanahan.

Almost a year later, in July 1870, when Hickok paid a visit to Hays City, either on personal business or in his authority as a US deputy marshal, he was set upon in a saloon by two troopers of the 7th Cavalry, Jeremiah Lonergan and John Kile. During the scuffle, Lonergan pinned Hickok down and Kile pushed his pistol into Wild Bill's ear, but it misfired, by which time Hickok had his hands on a six-shooter. Lonergan received a ball in the knee and Kile, who was shot twice, died the next day. Hickok, meanwhile, hid out on Boot Hill, determined to sell his life dearly if other troopers fancied their chances. None did.

Wild Bill now left it to his reputation to deter most would-be rivals, while the legend-builders eagerly spread the word. But it is doubtful even they realized how much Hickok's murder at the hands of the back-shooting coward Jack McCall in a Deadwood saloon in August 1876 would immortalize Wild Bill Hickok as a Western legend.

BILL DOOLIN AND THE LONG RIDERS

No one ever claimed outlaws had to be smart. Bill Doolin, who had ducked out on the Daltons with a lame-horse excuse and missed rolling in his own blood on a Coffeyville street, probably took a moment to reflect on his good fortune. Next, he might have turned his attention to picking a tough-sounding new name for his new gang. He and his recent recruits had come up with: the Wild Bunch, the Oklahombres, and, most ominous, the Long Riders—referring to the long dusters they wore to hide and protect their weapons. The dusters also gave them the relentless uniformity of disciplined troops—however undisciplined they actually were.

By the 1890s, nicknames were all the rage. Doolin's wretched crew at least had colorful handles. There was "Bitter Creek" Newcomb, "Tulsa Jack" Blake,

There are two photographs of Bill Doolin readily available: this beat-up tintype of a clear-eyed, well-groomed gentleman, and the other one most people have seen: Bill laid out on an undertaker's slab. A lot of living took place between these two photos— some good and most bad. The life of an outlaw took sudden turns.
Spartacus.schoolnet.co.uk

Tom Doolin's hideout single shot derringer made by Moore's Patent arms in .41 caliber. Most outlaws carried one for when a six-gun ran dry and a seventh shot was needed. *Wikimedia Commons*

"Dynamite Dick" Clifton, "Red Buck" Waightman, and "Little Dick" West. Packaged with a few other bad-tempered malcontents, they became a scourge. One shining light in Doolin's bunch was Bill Dalton, who had previously tried to go straight and seek a future in politics. When his brothers got chopped down at Coffeyville, he figured shooting people and stealing money was better than running for office. He joined Doolin robbing banks, trains, express shipments, payrolls, mercantile stores, and anywhere money could be found in quantity at the expense of a few bullets.

It was claimed that Doolin's Riders gave money to down-on-their-luck farmers, beef growers, and anyone who needed tiding over. The debt was repaid in loyalty and aid when the law came calling. Between jobs, the Riders licked their wounds, cleaned their guns, got some sleep in the OK Hotel, and drank up their swag in either Murray's or the Ransom Saloon in the sad little town of Ingalls, Oklahoma.

Toward the end of the century, the law had closed down most of the wide open Western towns. Meandering trail herds heading east now had access to so many railheads that long cattle drives requiring dozens of cowboys were gone. Cow towns had found other sources of income or closed their doors, leaving only dusty streets full of tumbleweed and memories. Ingalls was held

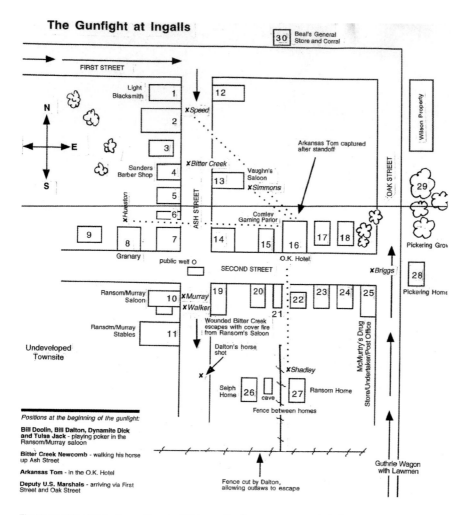

The Gunfight at Ingalls

The town of Ingalls in Payne County, Oklahoma Territory, was no great shakes when it was new. It had survived the crackdown on wide open towns by the 1890s. Ingalls became a roost for outlaw gangs seeking rest and relaxation between killings and is famous for the gunfight that pitted fed-up US marshals against Doolin's Long Riders. *Washington Irving Trail Museum*

together by spit and a promise, and the reluctance of the law to wipe it out once and for all.

In 1893, US Marshal Edward Dumas Nix heard many of the Long Riders were ensconced in Ingalls, presenting an opportunity to see justice done. He gathered twenty-seven deputy marshals, all heavily armed, and formed a covered wagon train posse heading for the little town. They camped by a river bank and were spotted by a small boy whom they tried and failed to capture. He dashed into town shouting, "the marshals are coming." Even with surprise compromised, the marshals' covered wagons rolled into Ingalls and stopped opposite the saloon and hotel.

Out the door of the Ransom Saloon came Bitter Creek Newcomb and climbed aboard his horse. One of the jumpy marshals leaned out of the wagon and winged him with a rifle shot. Newcomb fired two shots and cantered away. The next thing that came through the door was a roar of guns, clouds of smoke, and spitting flames. Marshals scattered, tumbling out of the wagons, returning the outlaw volley with one of their own, blasting the saloon façade to flinders and shattered glass.

Arkansas Tom cut loose with his .30-30 Winchester from the hotel second floor. Eventually, he found himself alone as his buddies hightailed across the prairie. Soon, he was out of bullets and out of time facing a posse of really angry marshals. *Wikimedia Commons*

From the hotel, "Arkansas Tom" Jones rose from his sick bed on the second floor, jacked a round into his Winchester and, with a clean shot, killed Deputy Marshall Thomas Hueston. In reply, Deputy Jim Masterson lobbed a stick of sputtering dynamite into Jones's bedroom. Meanwhile, with the saloon's flimsy architecture suffering badly from the rain of bullets, Bill Dalton, Red Buck Waightman, and Tulsa Jack Blake sprinted for the livery stable, mounted their saddled horses, and galloped into the street, revolvers blazing. Deputy Lafayette Shadley shot Dalton's horse, dumping the outlaw into the street. Dalton returned fire, killing Shadley. Bill Doolin at this time downed another deputy with a single shot. By now, the street and plaza were filled with rolling coils of white powder smoke, shouting men, screaming horses, and the scrabble of scurrying boots.

George Murray, owner of Murray's Saloon, had thrown in his lot with the outlaws and kept up a running gunfight from his partly open door. Those marshals still on their feet poured a withering fire at the threat, chewing up the door frame and the bartender. Outlaws who were still ambulatory found horses, fired wildly, and made a scramble for the prairie beyond the shot-up town.

Bitter Creek, though badly wounded early in the fight, broke free, as did Bill Dalton when he found another horse. Dynamite Dick stopped a ball in the neck, but hung onto his saddle horn in a dead gallop down the street. Arkansas Tom, driven to the hotel attic as the building disappeared around him, now stood on a chair in the attic window, pumping his Winchester as fast as he could keep it loaded. Suddenly, he realized he was the last of the owlhoots still standing and everyone in the street was shooting at him. When called upon to surrender,

Bill Tilghman, Henry "Heck" Thomas, and Chris Madsen were the Three Guardsmen. They terrorized outlaws seeking hideaways in the Oklahoma and Indian territories. These three deputy US marshals were the backbone of the loosely knit marshals' organization sworn to patrol this deadly piece of real estate. They finally buried or jailed all of Doolin's Long Riders. *US Marshals Service*

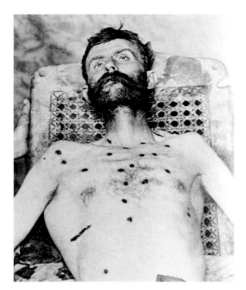

Bill Doolin just before he was planted. One night, Heck Thomas and a posse spotted him leading his horse down the road and decided not to take chances on another of Bill's escapes from custody. Heck shouted, "hands up!" Bill raised his rifle and stopped sixteen buckshot and two Winchester balls with his chest. *Wikimedia Commons*

he sat down quietly and waited for the surviving posse members to come and fetch him.

Three dead marshals lay about, as did one outlaw and the rogue bartender. Unable to pursue the wounded and struggling Long Riders because the lawmen had arrived in wagons, the marshals could only lick their wounds and consider what might have been. Once again, the old professional man hunters were called to put an end to Doolin and his gang.

Bill Tilghman, Heck Thomas, and Chris Madsen saddled up. Of the eleven original Long Riders, all died of lead poisoning over the ensuing years. Charlie Pierce and Bitter Creek Newcomb paid a call on Newcomb's teenage girlfriend, Rose Dunn, called "Rose of the Cimarron," who had nursed them following the Ingalls's battle. Her two brothers, who were bounty hunters, showed up hail and hearty. As the two Long Riders dismounted, the Dunn brothers poured half a box of bullets into Charlie and Bitter Creek for the reward money.

In 1896, Doolin was eventually captured and clapped into the jail at Guthrie, from where he just as quickly escaped. Marshal Heck Thomas and a small posse pursued him. Watching Doolin stroll down a dusty road, Heck recalled Federal Judge Frank Dale's suggestion that Bill had caused enough trouble for one man and should be brought in boots first. Following a couple of busy minutes at the rural roadside, the outlaw's remains were posed on a table for photographers. They counted sixteen buckshot wounds and two Winchester holes in the skinny, pale corpse. He preceded the last Long Rider, Little Dick West into the great beyond by two years when, in 1898, Little Dick was cut down by another member of the famous trio, Marshal Chris Madsen. The Three Guardsmen had closed the books on the Doolin Gang.

CHAPTER 6

CROSSING
THE LINE

The Johnson County War

POLICING THE NINETEENTH- and early twentieth-century West was, essentially, a thankless job. The duties ranged from keeping loafers from cluttering up the benches at the train depot to peeling drunks off the wood sidewalks to putting a ball or two into a drink-crazed cowboy trying to shoot down everyone in sight. Some towns didn't have the wherewithal in taxes to afford a lawman's salary. The same went for counties and even states. Except for the army, there was no federal policing agency and the military was ill-equipped for investigative work. Law officers spent long hours in the saddle in all weather tracking down cattle and horse thieves, conmen, itchy-fingered gunmen, and crazed malcontents. He also had to keep at least one eye on the constantly fragile political climate.

A deputy had to buy his own ammunition and often provide his own weapon, clothes, and saddle tack. A good horse had to be able to stand still while its rider emptied a Winchester or a pair of smoke- and flame-belching revolvers into a nest of outlaws. Town police jobs relied on fees and fines for income. For example, unlicensed dogs euthanized with a pistol butt paid fifty cents of the fine to the policeman. A horse removed from blocking the sidewalk paid another quarter.

The good people didn't get Wyatt Earp or Bat Masterson for dead dog fines. Towns often turned a blind eye to lawmen who owned an interest in a saloon's faro table, or half the earnings of a few prostitutes working cribs below the town deadline that separated the sleazy joints and dance halls from piety hill where the decent folks lived. The lurid side of life was a constant temptation to the men who carried a badge.

Men like Mysterious Dave Mather, Wyatt Earp, and even the Three Guardsmen, who put the Doolin Gang in the ground, padded an occasional expense report, owned a piece of a dance hall, or did not share all the collected fines with the city budget. A few men like the young Daltons crossed the line between lawless and lawmen so many times, they finally went over full time to the owlhoot trail.

The Johnson County War at the end of the nineteenth century pushed not just a single peace officer, but a whole community across the line. The murders, thefts, betrayals, and brutality were justified as protecting a way of life.

In the 1880s, Wyoming's wide open grass lands fed the cattle herds of many large ranches and cattle companies owned by eastern investors. At roundup time, the cattle were gathered in by their registered brands for shipment by rail to the great midwestern and eastern packing houses. Not only the grass, but the water rights were apportioned out by need, utilizing rivers and lakes scattered across the state. With the end of the Civil War, and the western expansion by

Mysterious Dave Mather was a jack of all trades on both sides of the law. He was a Dodge City saloon fixture during its days when you couldn't think straight for the racket made by bodies hitting the ground. *Wikimedia Commons*

Mysterious Dave's Colt Army Model 1860 percussion revolver with five notches on the grip for men killed—something to do with a pocket knife on a boring Tuesday afternoon. *Boot Hill Museum, Inc., Dodge City, Kansas*

the railroads, immigrants poured in from the east and west coasts scooping up tracts of previously open land the railroads had optioned along with their track right-of-ways.

These sight-unseen purchases were for farming and small ranches, but when the families arrived, the farmers often found land that would only grow sagebrush and rocks. Greenhorn ranchers discovered the wide open range and water use was vigorously regulated by the large ranches and cattle companies who saved the cost of feeding their cattle by simply letting them graze the free grassland. These wealthy landowners had established the Wyoming Stock Growers Association (WSGA) and intended to protect their rights. They also controlled the price of beef back east, producing maximum profit from minimum expenses as big cows begat little cows and required only a one way ticket to the Armour or Swift steak factories in Chicago and Kansas City.

Throughout the 1880s, the conflict grew until Frank Wolcott, who owned a large ranch, helped plan a once-and-for-all solution that involved hiring fifty regulators or range detectives to track down small ranch and farmer rustlers. These thieves were making off with unbranded calves to build herds and feed starving families. The detectives were paid five dollars a day plus fifty dollars for each rustler they killed. Among these regulators was Frank Canton.

Born Josiah Horner in 1849, he drifted from Virginia into Texas in 1871 and took up the outlaw life, rustling cattle, and robbing banks—which were all hanging offenses. In 1874, he shot two soldiers in a gunfight, killing one, and was eventually arrested after robbing a bank in Comanche, Texas. Horner escaped from the Texas Rangers and lit out for Ogallala, Nebraska, changed his name to Frank M. Canton, worked on a ranch, and gave up his outlaw life. He eventually became undersheriff of Pawnee County, Oklahoma.

Above: These "detectives" were hired by the train carload, outfitted, and paid a wage in addition to a bounty on every rustler they caught with a slaughtered steer or changing a brand. The cattle companies sponsoring the Wyoming Stock Growers Association regulators preferred dead to alive to save time and court complications. *Wikimedia Commons*

Left: Frank Canton was an enigma. Basically, he was a lawman with a distinguished record, but he signed on as a leader of the Wyoming Stock Growers Association, accepting their bounty. He eventually became disillusioned and quit to continue his career as a law officer. *Wikimedia Commons*

Word reached him of the big payday Wolcott's Wyoming regulators offered for men with his skills. He signed on with the WSGA and, as if unsure which path to follow, was also elected sheriff of Johnson County. Canton married and then returned to the WSGA while also wearing a deputy US marshal badge. Finally, on April 9, 1892, he got a bellyful of the Johnson County War.

Nate Champion was a small rancher opposed to the WSGA. He helped form the Northern Wyoming Stock Growers Association and became a thorn in Wolcott's side by organizing the small ranchers. Under the pretext of arresting rustlers, Canton led a body of WSGA regulators to Champion's KC Ranch, surrounded the main building, and laid siege to it. The gunmen killed one man, captured two others, and cut loose a blaze of gunfire into the ranch house with no intention of capturing Champion. In a journal Champion kept during the siege—where his return fire killed four of the regulators—he wrote a final entry:

> Well, they have just got through shelling the house like hail. I heard them splitting wood. I guess they are going to fire the house tonight. I think I will make a break when night comes, if alive. Shooting again. It's not night yet. The house is all fired. Goodbye, boys, if I never see you again.

Nate Champion's 1878 .45-caliber double-action Colt Frontier revolver after being toasted in the fire that burned down his KC ranch cabin. The detectives enfiladed the wood house and then tossed in burning torches. He ran out to make a fight of it. Note the bird's head grip for his small hands. *Guernsey Auctions, New York*

Champion made a dash out the ranch house back door, firing his Winchester Four gunmen guarding that exit shot him twenty-eight times, pinned a note reading "Cattle Thieves Beware" on his tattered shirt, and scratched out the names of attackers written in his journal.

Frank Canton had regrets about the Champion affair, but had little time to ponder his actions. The next day, Johnson County Sheriff "Red" Angus led a vengeance-bent immigrant posse to the TA Ranch and laid siege to the WSGA Regulators. A galloper was sent by the WSGA to the nearest telegraph station and within two days, the US Sixth Cavalry arrived to arrest the regulators, who gladly surrendered to escape extermination. Political maneuvering saw to it that no one was ever prosecuted for various murders and arsons.

Besides the Champion killing, Canton had gotten involved with investigating supposed rustler Ella Watson (a.k.a. "Cattle Kate"), who, it was claimed, built up her cattle spread with stolen beef. From 1888 to 1889, together with rancher and widower Jim Averell, she

Sheriff Red Angus was sickened by the range war violence and mustered a volunteer army to ride out and confront the detectives en masse at the TA ranch, laid siege, and was winning until the US Army arrived to escort the politically connected detectives to safety. *Wikimedia Commons*

This Colt Model 1878 double-action .45-caliber Frontier revolver belonged to Red Angus. It is the same as Nate Champion's Colt before the KC ranch barbeque. *Guernsey Auctions, New York*

had prospered, to the consternation of the WSGA. Finally, following a regulator's rustling claim against the couple, they were trussed up, hustled into a wagon, and were both lynched. Unfriendly witnesses to the crime were either shot, disappeared mysteriously, or were poisoned before the trial. All charges were dismissed.

Disgusted, Canton threw in his cards and headed for Fort Smith, Arkansas, where he became a respected deputy marshal, serving the "Hanging Judge" Isaac Parker's court, and often rode with the Three Guardsmen. One evening in Pawnee, Oklahoma, while Canton ate dinner, a former rustling prisoner of his, Bill Dunn—one of the Dunn brothers who murdered Charlie Pierce and Bitter Creek Newcomb of the Doolin Long Riders—sought him out with vengeance in mind. As Canton crossed the street from the restaurant, Dunn drew his revolver and fired at the marshal. The bullet sizzled past. Canton drew, aimed, and fired a ball into Dunn's head.

Frank Canton, now a respected lawman, turned himself in as Josiah Horner to face the music. With his marshal service considered, he received a full pardon, kept the Canton name, and lived a respectable life, dying in bed at age seventy-eight in 1927.

Ella Watson ("Cattle Kate") horned into the ongoing range war, building up her own spread while allegedly making some dollars on the side as a sultry soiled dove— a working girl. Her jolly appearance masks a shrewd mind and a lousy sense of timing. *Wikimedia Commons*

BILL COOK—INDIAN TERRITORY CROOK

You can't please everybody. One of Judge Isaac Parker's prisoners, Bill Cook, had started out serving under the judge as a scout for Fort Smith's US marshals, guiding the lawmen through Indian Territory. When Bill started a small cottage industry, selling whiskey to the Indians, he was arrested and sentenced to forty days in jail. This only inspired him to go into business for himself.

James Averell teamed up with Ella Watson to create a successful spread. Their good fortune attracted the WSGA, which sent over a deputation of hard cases who bundled the couple off to the nearest tree and hauled them up by the neck. *Wikimedia Commons*

Ella's small .32-caliber revolver with its folding trigger could be concealed behind garters beneath her voluminous skirts. *Rock Island Auction Company*

Following his release in June 1894, he assembled a group of twelve desperados, including his brother Jim; "Cherokee Bill" Goldsby; Elmer "Chicken" Lucas; Thurman "Skeeter" Baldwin; Jess Snyder; William Farris; Curtis Dayson; Jim French; George Sanders; Sam "Verdigris Kid" McWilliams; Lou Gordon; and Henry Munson. From Chicken to Skeeter to Verdigris, it was a shady crowd at best.

They were a full-service outlaw gang and stormed through Oklahoma Indian Territory, robbing anything they set their mind to: banks, trains, post offices, stores, and people.

As lawmen hunted them down, Bill Cook's bunch slowly shrank in numbers. Some were arrested; others were killed or wounded in shootouts. Several marshals were murdered or injured as well. When authorities confronted Bill, Jim Cook, and Cherokee Bill with a warrant for Jim's arrest, a gunfight ensued during which Cherokee Bill shot and killed lawman Sequoia Jackson and Jim Cook was wounded. The other two transported Jim to Fort Gibson and left him there—where he was promptly arrested.

Judge Isaac Parker's courtroom at Fort Smith, Arkansas, displaying its usual heavy case load. They were always short of deputy marshals to patrol the vast, rugged Fourteenth District. Bill Cook became a scout to avoid jail time and then got back to outlaw business as usual. *Library of Congress*

Cherokee Bill—formerly Clifford Goldsby—was half black and a quarter Cherokee with a huge chip on his shoulder. He rode with Bill and Jim Cook and managed to kill seven men before he was dragged into Parker's court. *via Weasey Publishing*

Throughout the summer of 1894 hardly a day went by when Cook's entourage wasn't engaged in some sort of banditry or gunfight. On July 14, they held up a stagecoach; two days later, they robbed a man named William Drew. Two days after that, they stopped the Frisco train, but came away with only a handful of cash—the express manager had hidden the bulk of the money behind boxes.

On July 31, they took five hundred dollars from the Lincoln County Bank in Chandler, Oklahoma. They killed one person and wounded others but lost gang member Elmer Lucas when he was shot and captured by marshals.

The outlaws hid out in Sapulpa, Oklahoma, until authorities tracked them down on August 2. Gunshots rang out and when the smoke cleared, one lawman was wounded, two gang members were killed, and one was captured.

More robberies and killings followed throughout the autumn of 1894. By the end of the year, the rest of Bill Cook's cohorts had been arrested or killed in gunfights. In the months that followed, the bang of Judge Parker's gavel signaled a long-term incarceration for Curtis Dayson, Thurman Baldwin, Jess

Snyder, and William Farris. The only exception was Cherokee Bill Goldsby, who climbed the gallows' thirteen stairs on March 17, 1896.

After yet another arrest in January 1895, Bill Cook spent his remaining days in the federal prison in Albany, New York. He coughed his life away on February 15, 1900, dying of consumption. His body was returned to Hulbert, Oklahoma, for burial.[18]

Though Bill Cook has become a little-known footnote among the many gangs that ravaged the territories and died an imprisoned consumptive in 1900, Cherokee Bill Goldsby added bloody luster to the story. When he stood on the gallows, he replied to a request for a few words with, "I have come here to die, not to make a speech." *Wikimedia Commons*

While Cherokee Bill got all the press, Bill Cook was chased all over by a flock of marshals. He emptied this Harrington & Richardson .38-caliber cheap stingy gun at his pursuers and then threw it at them. The owlhoot trail could be all uphill. *Fort Smith National Historic Site*

In articles, eyewitness accounts and remembered versions of actual events involving gun play in the Wild West, cowboys, lawmen, and outlaws are always "levering a cartridge into their Winchester," "snatching their Winchester from the saddle scabbard," or "peppering the hideout with their Winchesters." Every lever-action, high-capacity long gun became generically known as a Winchester. How many times has an owlhoot "snapped off three shots from his Whitneyville-Kennedy?" "Threatened the rowdy gunmen with his Marlin" sounds like his arms are wrapped around a large sword-nosed fish.

The Winchester lever-action rifle was an icon in its time. It evolved from the original Volcanic rifle and pistol system created by Benjamin Tyler Henry before the Civil War. In the era of single-shot, muzzle-loading rifles and early breech-loading carbines just reaching the military cavalry and skirmisher units, the Henry was a quantum leap forward. Its ammunition—.44-caliber rimfire fixed cartridges

When Theodore Roosevelt bought into a Dakota cattle ranch and went west for health, he immersed himself in cowboy life, although the Tiffany knife handle and engraved Winchester 76 were dude giveaways. He had a lifelong love of the Winchester rifle. *Wikimedia Commons*

in copper and, eventually, brass cases—was stored in a tube beneath the barrel under spring pressure. Each cocking of the lever beneath the stock's handgrip withdrew the bolt, levered a cartridge up to the breech, cocked the hammer, and seated the cartridge by returning the lever that closed the bolt. The trigger tripped the hammer and a second cocking ejected the spent brass case as a new cartridge slid up into the breech.

The Henry also had a few flaws. The tubular magazine had to be loaded from the muzzle end. The magazine had an open slot—for counting remaining shots—that ran its length, allowing mud and dust into the tube. No wooden fore end shielded the shooter's hand from the hot barrel during heavy use, and the .44-caliber rimfire was no man stopper with a 216-grain bullet over 15 grains of black powder. But for sheer firepower, the Henry rifle was treasured during the war, on the postwar prairie, and anywhere sheer firepower was required.

The first Winchester rifle—the Winchester Model 1866—was originally chambered for the rimfire .44 Henry. Nicknamed the "Yellow Boy" because of its receiver of a bronze alloy called gunmetal, it was famous for its rugged construction and lever-action mechanism that allowed the rifleman to fire a number of shots before having to reload: hence the term repeating rifle. Nelson King's new, improved patent remedied flaws in the Henry rifle by incorporating a loading gate on the side of the frame and integrating a sealed magazine that was covered by a wood forestock.

From 1866 to 1894, the Winchester was prized by its owners. However, basic design problems continued to invite competition. The open top of the Winchester frame required to eject the empty cartridge case sometimes allowed the shell to drop back down into the receiver, jamming the action. The bullet fired by the rifle had to have a rounded nose to prevent detonation of the bullet ahead of it while

A Winchester 73 with the side panels removed, showing the toggle linkage that moved the ammunition for the tube magazine up into the action, cocked the hammer, and slid the cartridge into the breech. A simple system but open to improvement. *Wikimedia Commons*

spending time seated in the tubular magazine. That rounded nose also offered limited ballistic capabilities for long shots on windy days.

Looking for a share of the market, Andrew Burgess, a former Civil War photographer, paid a visit to the New Haven, Connecticut, Whitneyville factory, which dated back to Eli Whitney, the eighteenth-century innovator who helped create the assembly line and appliances made of interchangeable parts. Burgess had an idea for a lever-action rifle firing the heavy-caliber .45-70 government cartridge. The 1878 Burgess-Whitney packed a wallop after a long reach and found a market with many early buffalo and meat hunters. The beefed-up cannon was better suited to travel in a wagon bed rather than a saddle scabbard or hiking a hunting trail.

To add versatility to the Burgess design, Sam Kennedy and Frank Tiesing lightened the 1878 model to fire the new .44 Winchester centerfire cartridge for the 1880 model. They produced 23,500 rifles between 1880 and 1886 and then turned out models hammering out the .45-60 cartridge. Next, they converted their Sharps or Spencer-type S-shaped cocking lever to a full-hand loop lever for .45-75, .40-60, .38-40, and the heavy .50-95 paired with the lightweight and popular .32-20-calibers.

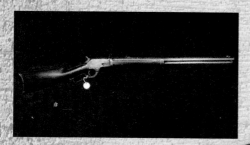

The Burgess eventually became the Colt-Burgess until Winchester suggested they would not begin building revolvers if Colt dropped a lever-action rifle line. Colt made it so. *Merz Antique Firearms*

The Whitney-Kennedy was a straight knock-off of the Winchester concept with a few cosmetic changes. The Spencer-type snake cocking lever was clumsy and hurt its sales. It finally went to the Winchester-type lever, but never recovered market share. *Rock Island Auction Company*

John M. Marlin hung out his own firearms production shingle in 1870 after becoming a tool and die maker and working for Colt during the Civil War. He designed a virtual Winchester clone in 1881, but Marlin's contribution to the competition—one that lasted—was the flat-top receiver. Now, the empty bullet casing ejected out to the side. Beginning in 1889 through 1905, this feature allowed new optical sights to be installed on the optical center of the breech and barrel for greater solidity and accuracy. Also, the .44 Winchester Center Fire—a.k.a. .44 WCF and .44-40-caliber—became a popular combination rifle and pistol round requiring only one caliber of ammunition to be carried for both rifle and revolver.

To complete the improvements of the lever-action rifle, beginning in 1892, the new Savage rifle appeared. It was hammerless, which further aided the use of optical sights, but its main feature was the rotary magazine. This allowed cartridges to be fed into a rotary cylinder inside the receiver instead of nose to tail in an under-barrel tube. Spitzer-type pointed bullets could now be used in the repeater. This pointed Mauser bullet featured greater accuracy, higher velocity, and a still greater variety of cartridge calibers. The Marlin and the Savage 99 rifles brought the system started by Henry, established by the iconic Winchester, and improved by the Whitneyville-Kennedy (Burgess) into the twentieth century.

Marlin produced the most innovative improvement by having empty shells ejected from the side of the action, leaving the top solid. Marlin rifles allow scope sights to mount along the breech's center line, an important sales point that still exists. *Rock Island Auction Company*

Savage changed everything with this hammerless model 1899 firing a .300-Savage caliber cartridge with a pointed (Spitzer) bullet fed from a rotary magazine. A hot bullet in a scope-sighted rifle was a long-range winner—and still is today. *Rock Island Auction Company*

CHAPTER 7

BLACK AMERICAN COWBOYS

BASS REEVES—BLACK MAN BEHIND A SILVER BADGE

HE WAS BORN a slave in Arkansas in 1838 and died in 1910 in Oklahoma, one of the most revered lawmen in that state's history.

Deputy US Marshal Bass Reeves spent his early years in Texas, owned by Col. George Reeves of the Eleventh Texas Cavalry, who later became a member of the Texas state legislature. When the Civil War broke out, Reeves accompanied the colonel to battle as a body servant. Following a violent argument during a card game, Bass threw a punch at Reeves, knocking him out. Fearing punishment the next day, Bass seized the opportunity to escape. In the dead of night and during the heat of the day, he made his way across the Red River into Oklahoma Territory and Indian country. The Creeks and Seminoles, themselves the victims of American exploitation from the Indian Resettlement Act of 1810, accepted him into their villages, where he learned their languages and served as a territorial scout.

Following the Civil War, Bass, now a free man, married Nellie Jennie in about 1870 and moved back to Van Buren, Arkansas, where he and Nellie purchased a small farm on which to raise their family, which eventually grew to ten children.

Bass Reeves came west as a body slave to Col. George Reeves of the Eleventh Texas Cavalry. *US Marshals Museum, Photographer: Jami Roskamp*

At the time, Oklahoma consisted of two territories: Oklahoma and Indian. The Indian Territory only had jurisdiction over its own tribes, while Oklahoma was controlled by federal laws. This arrangement benefitted robbers, gunmen, and other miscreants, since there were so few lawmen marshaling the Oklahoma jurisdiction. Criminals enjoyed virtually free rein and in one area west of the Missouri, Kansas, and Texas Railroad line, bandits and killers posted cards warning marshals to stay out or be killed.

That changed in 1875 when Judge Isaac Parker took on the role of federal judge for both the Indian and Oklahoma territories at the court in Fort Smith,

Arkansas. He began by appointing Daniel Upham to the US marshal post and optimistically ordered him to hire two hundred deputies. Upham immediately set about hiring as many deputies as possible, among them Bass Reeves, who by this time was well-known for his familiarity with Indian customs and his ability to speak their languages. Reeves also had the distinction of being the first black US marshal to work for Judge Parker. The marshals' territory—all of Oklahoma and western Arkansas—now stretched across an area of seventy-four thousand square miles.[19]

Reeves, with his six-foot-two, 180-pound frame, was the quintessential lawman. His skill with a weapon, his quick-thinking, and his fearlessness when facing hardened criminals became the standard for other lawmen to emulate. For weeks at a time, he rode the territory armed with his two Colt Single Action Army .45 six-shooters with the short four-and-three-quarters-inch barrels and his Winchester rifle, accompanied by several deputies, a cook, and a wagon with chains and other tools needed to safely transport prisoners.

The Seminoles had taught him tracking skills, so he wouldn't leave a trace of where he had been. He was the object of death threats, yet managed to arrest over three thousand criminals. He once rounded up seventeen prisoners and brought them into the Fort Smith courthouse to face Hanging Judge Parker. The sight of a huge black man riding into Fort Smith, hauling a wagon full of grumpy robbers, hardened killers, cattle rustlers, and gunslingers might have put the fear of God into the townspeople on the street.[20]

Reeves hunted down some of the most notorious outlaws of Western lore. Among them were Tom Story and Belle Starr, both accused of horse thievery. When Reeves accosted Story and presented the arrest warrant, the outlaw pointed his gun at Reeves but the marshal had his .45 Colts at the ready and fired, killing Story on the spot. When Belle Starr learned that Reeves had an arrest warrant out for her, she simply walked into the Fort Smith jail and turned herself in, saying she did not "propose to be dragged around by some federal deputy." It was the only time Belle Starr willingly surrendered to federal authorities.[19]

For all his knowledge of Indian languages, survival skills, and shooting expertise, Bass never learned to read. Once, out in the Oklahoma wilderness, two gunmen confronted Bass, pointed their guns and ordered him to dismount. Marshal Reeves willingly obeyed, but asked if they could do him one last favor before pulling the trigger. He handed one of his assailants a letter from his wife.

"Would you please read it to me?" he asked.

Somewhat confused and taken aback by his request, they glanced at the paper, averting their eyes just long enough for Bass to pull out his gun. Now he

This revolver filled one of Bass Reeves's holsters. His Colt Single Action Army with a four-and-three-quarters-inch barrel was favored by professional shootists. The gun shown here is well-worn from use—as much as a threat as from actual combat. *US Marshals Museum, Fort Smith, Arkansas/ Photographer: Jami Roskamp*

had the upper hand. One of the outlaws, seeing Bass with the pistol in his hand was so shaken, he dropped his weapon. Bass arrested the two and brought them up before Judge Parker.

Reeves was fearless, clever, and quick thinking. During one of his patrols into the wilds of Oklahoma he carried his usual handful of arrest warrants, one of which contained the names of the Brunter brothers, notorious outlaws bent on killing anyone who stood in their way. He located the gang and in his usual forthright manner, handed them a warrant for their arrest. They let out a chorus of guffaws, but to humor the marshal, they paused to read it. Again, in one disarming second, Reeves, known for being ambidextrous, drew both Colts, killed two of the brothers and arrested the third.[20]

Once again the piece-of-paper trick worked.

In a tragic quirk of fate, Marshal Reeves found himself facing Judge Parker and put on trial for murdering his cook, William Leach. In his testimony, Reeves stated that in checking his .44 Winchester rifle he discovered he had inadvertently loaded a .45 pistol cartridge into the magazine and it was wedged in place, blocking the magazine and locking the action. He dug it out with a knife, and as his hand returned the jammed lever, a .44-40 rifle cartridge in the magazine was levered up into the breech and his finger accidently struck the trigger as the lever snapped up into place. The gun went off, shooting Leach in the neck. Reeves was acquitted.[19]

Another tragedy affected Marshal Reeves more personally, yet it indicated his integrity and fairness no matter who had broken the law. In 1902, his son Bennie had murdered his wife, Reeves's daughter-in-law, for her affair with another man. Knowing what was in store for him, Bennie took off for the Oklahoma back country. The other marshals had no desire to go after Bass Reeves's son. After all, Bass Reeves was the most respected lawman in the territory. Reeves insisted on taking the warrant, saying it was his responsibility to bring his son in to stand trial. He returned with Bennie two weeks later. Bennie was convicted and served twenty years at the prison in Leavenworth.[19]

In spite of being unable to read or write, Bass Reeves never served a warrant to the wrong person. When it came time to write a report, he would dictate the information and sign with an "x." If he had several subpoenas to serve, he memorized the names in order.

Bass Reeves served under Judge Parker from 1875 until Oklahoma achieved statehood in 1907, the longest period of time for any marshal. Yet after thirty-two years of service, during which he made three thousand arrests, he was not ready to retire. He worked as a beat cop for the Muskogee, Oklahoma, police department for two years and his legend preceded him. In those two years no crimes were reported.[21]

Then, on January 12, 1910, Bass Reeves, the most feared and respected lawman in the Oklahoma territory, passed away quietly at his home.

The era of the Wild West was beginning to fade as well. Oklahoma had achieved statehood three years earlier. It wouldn't be long before US marshals used the automobile for patrolling and the telephone to send and receive information. Bricks, mortar, and paved streets had started to replace mud huts, wooden storefronts, and dusty trails.

Yet, with all the technological advances in weaponry, transportation, and communications, the qualities of integrity, fairness, and commitment better mark the true character of those who are charged to serve and protect. Bass Reeves, one of the first black men to patrol the Oklahoma territory, knew this, and lived it. His legacy is timeless; he set the standard for other lawmen to follow for decades to come.

NED HUDDLESTON, A.K.A. ISOM DART

Ned Huddleston's early background is similar to Bass Reeves. Both were black. Both were imposing figures at six-foot-two. Both were born into slavery—Huddleston in 1849. Both accompanied their masters to serve in the Confederate army during the Civil War.

That's where the similarity ends. During the war, Huddleston stole food for southern soldiers, but after he was freed following the war's end, he found work as a rodeo clown. He wandered into Texas and Mexico and made friends with a Mexican bandit known only as Terresa. They charged through Mexican country, rustling cattle, and driving the herds across the Rio Grande into Texas where the cattle were sold to unscrupulous ranchers.[22]

Over the years, Huddleston prospected for gold and broke broncos. In 1875, he rode to Brown's Hole (later known as Brown's Park) in northwestern Colorado, and eventually established his own group of outlaws called the Tip Gault Gang. Their mission statement was simple: horse stealing.

The venture proved successful until they went a step too far when they rustled horses belonging to local rancher Margaret Anderson. One night, as the gang sat around the campfire, eating beans and drinking, a troop of lawmen bore down on them, drew guns, and killed all, save Huddleston, who was elsewhere at the time.

Huddleston rode into camp later that night to find the bodies of his fellow gang members splayed out around the dying campfire. He set about digging graves to give the men a decent burial. Surrounded by blood, death, and the silent flap of buzzard's wings overhead, he took a few minutes to rummage through the saddlebags and pockets of his former comrades and came away with money, guns, and other valuables. Later that night, he escaped on foot. The next day he was shot at and wounded when he attempted to steal a horse for transportation. He wandered on, now anxious and frightened, but not too frightened to steal another horse and head for Oklahoma to lie low[23] and change his name to Isom Dart, which means "Village on the River."[24]

Ned Huddleston also came west as a slave and chose the owlhoot trail. He was snake-fast with a sixgun, an expert rider, and appreciated good horses—especially those belonging to other people. *Wikimedia Commons*

Dart returned to Brown's Hole and horse stealing. After setting up his base of operations at his old hideout, he discovered that cattle rustling might be a more advantageous career move. It wasn't long before he was arrested. On his way to the jail, the sheriff's horse reared, throwing the lawman to the ground, leaving him badly hurt.

Suddenly infused with a burst of decency, he did what he could to treat the sheriff's injuries and hoisted him onto the horse. The grateful sheriff arranged to have Dart acquitted.

This was enough to inspire Dart to try the honest life for a change. He ran for a position in law enforcement in Sweetwater County, Wyoming, in 1884 and won by a mere eight votes. A quiet period followed, but he ran again six years later and lost. He traveled south back to Colorado, and attempted to follow the straight and narrow when he bought a ranch in Brown's Hole.[25]

Dart joined forces with the Bassett family, a group led by Elizabeth Bassett, whose husband, Herbert, lacked the stamina to make good in the rugged West. Bent on survival, she and her daughters, Ann and Josie, had turned to cattle rustling, the only skill they knew to avoid starvation. True, this was a felony, but everybody did it. For the Brown's Hole folk, cattle rustling had turned into a way of life.[26]

Then, investors from the East, seeing a golden opportunity to establish a cattle-raising conglomerate, moved in with the plan to buy up smaller ranches and take over. They made a healthy profit in the early 1880s as they added to their cattle stock year after year. Yet, they didn't foresee the inevitable erosion that resulted from too many herds crowding the land. Add to that the bitter winter of 1886–1887 and some major cattlemen were wiped out. Matt Rash, a former trail boss for one of the large-scale operations, hooked up with the Bassett group and eventually became engaged to Ann Bassett.[27]

The Two-Bar Cattle Association, a group of cattle tycoons headed by Ora Haley, survived. The battles with the small ranchers continued, Haley blaming cattle stealing for his diminished returns. The Brown's Park Cattle Association, led by Matt Rash, tried to fend off the empire established by Haley but Two-Bar cattle often wandered into Brown's Park, merging themselves into the Brown's Park herd.

Then, in April 1900, a stranger rode into Brown's Park. As he shook hands all around, introducing himself as a horse buyer by the name of Tom Hicks, Ann Bassett cast a suspicious eye. Something told her this man was not a cowboy. Her intuition proved correct. Shortly after Hicks's arrival, Brown's Park ranchers—the ones more skilled at grabbing other people's cattle—found warning notes taped to their cabin doors telling them to get out or else. Brown's

Isom Dart poses in front of his ranch cabin. He was later killed by Tom Horn's long rifle shot as he stood in the cabin doorway. Horn had been hired as a range detective by the Wyoming Stock Growers Association.

Park natives ignored the advice until, one night, a gunman came upon Matt Rash and, without warning, fired three shots, killing him, and completed the job by killing his horse as well.

Ann Bassett's suspicions proved right. The horse buyer turned out to be hired killer Tom Horn. Brown's Park people felt certain that Ora Haley had employed him as a stock detective to protect the Haley herds. But no one ever knew for sure. A few months later, Isom Dart died when he suffered a shot to his head as he opened his cabin door. An empty .30-30 shell was found under a nearby tree.

They buried Isom Dart on Cold Spring Mountain, not far from his cabin.

Proving that hell hath no fury like a woman scorned, Ann Bassett, now bereft of her fiancé, Matt Rash, and good friend Isom Dart, exacted revenge on Ora Haley by herding hundreds of Haley's cattle over a cliff and into the Green River.[27]

CHAPTER 8

THE

CRAZIES

Longley, the Kid, and Hardin

NOT ALL THE Wild West's nineteenth- and twentieth-century outlaws needed a gang to back their play. Some built such a fierce reputation—both real and mythical—that facing them in the flesh made the blood run cold. The mention of their name caused a room to go silent. The lives of these crazies were also self-fulfilling prophesies. They stood as a challenge to any rank waddy with a belly full of rotgut whiskey and a loaded Colt in a greased holster on his hip. To notch a known man-killer on a gun fighter's reputation was to become one of the feared elite—for as long as he lived.

Of course, a double-barreled eight-gauge shotgun blast between the shoulder blades was a safer bet than sitting face to face across a poker table. To many, this fine distinction had little merit, and they earned reputations as yellow cowards for not challenging their targets face to face. Bob Ford shot Jesse James from behind; John Selman put a bullet into the back of John Wesley Hardin's head in an El Paso, Texas, saloon; and Jack McCall earned a dismal demise after he blew out Wild Bill Hickok's brains from back to front in Deadwood, South Dakota. All three victims knew they were living on borrowed time, counting the days and hours until some fool did them the favor of a quick exit.

WILLIAM PRESTON ("WILD BILL") LONGLEY

Following Bill's birth on October 16, 1851, the state of Texas became more dangerous. Nobody called him Wild Bill to his face in his lifetime. Because of his touchy disposition, such a liberty might earn you a .44-caliber ball in your wheelhouse. His debut time near Miller Creek in Austin County was a short stay before the family moved to the little town of Evergreen. His early years saw him fill out to a strapping six feet tall on a two-hundred-pound frame with ebony hair and a hard stare. His father's legacy instilled in the boy the widely felt Texas attitudes that one, he shouldn't step off the sidewalk for any man, and two, "sassy Negroes" weren't fit to live.

By the time he was fifteen and Reconstruction was sweeping the Confederacy out of Texas, black Union Buffalo Soldiers wielded law and order with vigor. Longley developed a virtual psychopathic loathing of the black soldiers who rode through Texas towns as if they owned them, rather than working in the fields "where they belonged." From the debris of war, he acquired a brace of J. H. Dance and Brothers .44-caliber percussion revolvers, produced as

Left: William Preston Longley's portrait shows he is working on that cold, dead stare many psychotic gunmen used to announce their presence and current temperament. *Wikimedia Commons*

Below: A Buffalo Soldier in garrison. These troops were used throughout the West, The Native Americans gave them the name "Buffalo Soldiers" because of their frizzy hair and dark color. Their assignment to former slave states made their lives difficult. *Wikimedia Commons*

Of all the handguns produced for the Civil War—that actually saw honorable service—these Confederate copies of the Colt Dragoon are considered the rarest of the rare. Only 475 finished revolvers were built by J. H. Dance and Brothers after beginning production in 1862. At the start of the war, Confederate soldiers were forced to use personal muskets, rifles, and their favorite, the double-barrel shotgun. Handguns were too expensive for the average sharecropper or clerk to afford, and their use was limited to officers who came from the plantation-owner class. Imports trickled in from England—which needed Confederacy cotton exports—through the Union blockaded ports. Union arsenals were raided and weapons were gleaned from the battlefield. The problem with this patchwork supply was ammunition. Too many calibers were required of the quartermaster for any single battle.

To fill in and compete against the industrialized North, small southern factories were encouraged to design and produce cheap, workable firearms. The J. H. Dance Company chose the Colt Dragoon to copy in .44 and .36 caliber, two of the most common battlefield pistol calibers. (Patents be hanged; this was war.) To give their revolver its own look and to simplify machining, the recoil shields on either side of the frame were left off, giving the gun a slab-sided look.

The pistols were prize possessions, but saw heavy use and, today, only one revolver in very good condition is known to exist.[28]

The Apache leader, Geronimo, with a Dance and Brothers percussion revolver tucked in his belt. Percussion revolvers were popular with Native Americans. The components to make them shoot were easier to get and cheaper than cartridges. *www. littlegun.info*

copies of the Colt Dragoon by the forge and factory on Fremont Street in Columbia, Texas.

Longley was blooded, heeled with a brace of pistols, and ready for life. He fell in with another young man in a horse-breaking venture. Soon, however, the touchy Longley got into a disagreement over a horse race and took out his ire by shooting up a local black street circus, killing two and wounding a few. Not placated yet, he later shot down three blacks in two gunfights and felt better. It was time to leave home and seek employment elsewhere. He ended up as a cowboy in nearby Karnes County.

That job ended when he killed another black soldier and took off. This time, the locals hunted him down and swung him by the neck from a tree branch. Stories conflict over how he survived the lynching, but after the posse left, he ended up on the ground flopping about, sucking in air as the noose loosened.

The Cullen Baker outlaw gang offered him a spot, but, as his luck would have it, on January 6, 1869, Cullen Baker, a former raider, bully, and murderer, was enjoying a roadside snack in the shade with a chum when a makeshift posse of four good citizens from a nearby town rode past, recognized them, and charged, guns blazing. Neither Baker nor his chum got off a shot. When the posse sorted through what was left of the former raider they found a typical arsenal: a shotgun, four revolvers, three derringers, and six pocket knives.[29]

This Dance and Brothers percussion revolver is an incredible rarity today. Only two are known to exist in this condition. It was a direct copy of the Colt Dragoon except for the recoil shields behind the cylinder, which have been milled off. Some of the early guns exploded during tests and the forge moved at least once as the war progressed.
Old South Military Antiques

Sobered after his truncated necktie party and Baker's bloody demise, Longley returned to Evergreen. Refreshed, he landed a job with a trail herd bound for Kansas. As usual, his attitude problem put him at odds with the trail boss, so he shot the man down and made it to Kansas on his own. Once there, Bill ventilated another soldier, but this time bribed his way out of jail before anyone could find a fresh rope.

Leaving his body count behind, he headed for Wyoming and hooked up with a larcenous quartermaster, a pack mule outfit, and a scheme to cheat the government. The quartermaster proved to be not worth his salt, so Longley canceled their partnership with a .44-caliber ball. The military tossed him into the guardhouse and later, as they waited to transfer him to Iowa State Prison, he escaped. On June 12, 1876, Bill lit out for Indian Territory until the hunt cooled off. He wandered through Texas and ended up back home in Evergreen where his once doting father and family wanted nothing to do with him.

He killed another man and, after escaping custody yet again, made his way down to Keatchie, Louisiana, and rented a plot of land for farming. By this time, he had replaced the Dance and Brothers percussion revolvers with Model 1873 Colt Peacemakers. Peace eluded him, however, when he found himself covered by shotguns in the hands of two lawmen from Nacogdoches, Texas, who had tracked him down. After chaining him up good and tight, they brought him back to Giddings, Texas, where his litany of senseless murders bought him a death sentence.

Longley protested that John Wesley Hardin only got a prison sentence for rubbing out more folks. This numbers game failed to produce any sentiment and, on December 11, 1878, after writing several letters to newspapers regretting his murderous ways, William Preston Longley stood on the gallows in his Sunday best suit with a bag over his head and shouted, "Let 'er rip!" Down he dropped—and landed on his feet. Rope trouble again, so two obliging deputies held his feet up off the ground while he strangled and twisted until he finally choked to death eleven minutes later. To make sure he was dead, three doctors checked his corpse and signed a paper to that effect.

HENRY MCCARTY, OR WILLIAM BONNEY, OR WILLIAM ("KID") ANTRIM— A.K.A. BILLY THE KID

Happy-go-lucky Billy the Kid with his dead-eye smile, the mentally toxic Bill Longley, and stone-cold killer John Wesley Hardin were as different as three gunmen could be and, yet, they shared the common savage quality that dried up the mouth and tightened the sphincter of any man they faced.

Life was both hard and cheap in the mid-nineteenth-century Wild West. If a kid survived childbirth—which most didn't—he faced a staggering set of role models: footloose cowboys lived in the dust and manure with their herds from month to month, criss-crossing bleak prairie and rugged mountains peopled by Indian bands, rustlers, thieves, and con men of every stripe, who killed rather than be thrust into a pitiless penal system. These associations warped judgments and dried up empathy. Power flamed from the muzzle of a gun. The war with Mexico and five years of Civil War had taught a generation lethal skills that became valuable in a world where posttraumatic stress disorder was called "tetched in the head."

Technology had leapfrogged ahead, creating an arms race between outlaws and lawmen that favored the gunslingers while the law struggled with small budgets and low wages. A plain Colt Single Action Army revolver cost just over twenty dollars in the nineteenth and early twentieth centuries. A Winchester rifle went for over fifteen dollars at a time when cowboys worked for thirty dollars a month. A box of one hundred .44-40 bullets cost $1.46 plus five pounds shipping at $1.73. Add to that the gun shop's markup, gun oil, grease, cleaning brush, and linen patches and a decent holster and gun belt with cartridge loops for $1.50, and packing a hog leg became a serious investment.[30] For the outlaw, spending money for day-to-day expenses was only a bank, a mercantile store, or—as later, in the case of Bonnie and Clyde—a gas station gum machine theft away.

Billy the Kid, like Longley and Hardin, had a split personality: jovial and convivial with his friends and loyal when sober and it suited him. He was born

Most towns had few amusements that did not involve downing copious amounts of questionable-quality alcohol. Role models were thin on the ground for growing boys. *Library of Congress*

The earlier Lightning Model Colt was one of the first successful double-action cartridge revolvers. It fired a .38 Long Colt bullet. The shooter simply squeezed the trigger to rotate the cylinder, cock the hammer, and release the hammer to fire the cartridge. Billy preferred the heavier .41-caliber cartridge fired by the Thunderer. Colt double-action revolvers had a bad reputation for breakage—called "the gunsmith's favorite"—but its speed getting into action made it a killing choice for both the Kid and pistolero John Wesley Hardin. Besides its speed, McCarty liked the small frame and particularly small bird-head grips for his tiny hands.

The Colt Lightning was a lot of gun in a small package. For small hands, the bird-head grip offered a solid handle when squeezing the double-action trigger. *Rock Island Auction Company*

The Colt Thunderer in .41 caliber packed a bit more punch than the .38 Long Colt, but had a bad reputation for breaking. For fast, aimed follow-up shots, it was the hot gun for its time. *Rock Island Auction Company*

into into a shanty Irish family in a New York slum in 1859. His father moved wife and the McCarty brothers—Henry was the oldest—to Coffeyville, Kansas, in 1862. The transition from urban slum to rural backwater was too much for the elder McCarty, and on his death, Henry's mother remarried and moved everyone in 1868 to booming Silver City, Colorado. The Kid (now known as Bill Antrim after his stepfather, whom he hated), a blondish, blue-eyed youngster with prominent front teeth, acquired the skill sets he would need to survive the great rage that boiled inside him.

Gambling and odd jobs kept him in pin money and bullets for practicing with borrowed guns to learn the mechanics of marksmanship, which in turn raised his self-esteem. Finally, his temper caused him to stab to death a burly blacksmith who was beating on a friend. He hightailed out of town and eventually out of Arizona to settle in New Mexico. His following footloose years are not well-documented, but he did manage to equip himself with the best tools of his trade: a Colt double-action Lightning revolver and a Whitney lever-action rifle.

Anything Billy the Kid needed to get the drop on an opponent was okay. One day in Fort Sumner, New Mexico, a Texas hard case named Joe Grant pushed through the door into the dark, cool, whiskey-smelling interior of Hargrove's saloon. Grant was hunting The Kid. He proceeded to make an apparently drunken nuisance of himself and took over the back bar. About then, Billy, James Chisum, and Barney Mason strode in, looking for shade and refreshment. Joe had met The Kid earlier and regaled him with friendly patter. Now, in his apparent drunken fog, he insisted that James Chisum was, in fact, his terrible brother, John Chisum, and pulled his Colt over some past real or imagined slight.

Billy stepped between the two men and did his best to calm the situation. He praised Grant's engraved revolver and asked to look at it. Grant handed over his hog leg and seemed to relax. Billy returned the gun and was all joviality again. With gun in hand, the suddenly clear-headed Grant leveled his Colt at Billy and dropped the hammer—which fell on an empty chamber with a loud click. A look of slack-jawed surprise froze on Grant's face as Billy's bullet punched through his forehead and blew brains out the back. Two following shots ventilated his chest. While examining Grant's pistol, Billy the Kid had turned the cylinder so the next hammer drop would land on one of three empty chambers.[31]

The Kid became firmly implanted in the Tunstall-McSween faction of the New Mexico range war with the Murphy-Dolans—called the "Lincoln County War." He had gathered around him a loose-knit collection of young tough cowboys calling themselves regulators, and had allied himself with Tunstall, a young English rancher who had befriended him. One day, Tunstall was herding horses and confronted a posse sent out by "Murphy's man" Sheriff William Brady. The sheriff's posse emptied their revolvers into young Tunstall and his horse, leaving their bodies to rot in the desert. This cowardly butchering of his best friend upset Billy, so he gathered some of his own posse of regulators and on April 1, 1878, rode into Lincoln. They selected a section of McSween's corral wall that paralleled Brady's morning walk to his office and waited. Along came Brady with deputies, George Hindman, Billy Mathews, and "Old Man" Pepin. A volley of gunfire blew away Brady and Hindman. The other two fled for their lives.

When Billy the Kid wasn't acting clinically crazy, he was cunning and manipulative. After the killings, he and his associates were surrounded in a ranch house. The Kid asked for a parley. In response, hired gunman Jimmy Carlyle stepped out in the open to negotiate, Billy killed him on the spot, and the rest of the posse ran away. Over time, The Kid's gang was whittled down by arrests and ambushes. The regulators continued to steal horses and rustle cattle for pocket money, but they were penny-ante outlaws. Many of the friends they

Rancher John Tunstall was partners with McSween. Together, they competed against the Murphy-Dolans faction, which had the backing of the politically connected Santa Fe Ring. Tunstall and his horse were assassinated on the road to Lincoln by a posse organized by Sheriff Brady, a Murphy-Dolan man. *Wikimedia Commons*

Pat Garrett, who was elected sheriff almost specifically to hunt down Billy the Kid. They were one-time friends on the trail, but Garrett saw considerable profit in taking on The Kid. He was eventually successful and celebrated in song and story. *Wikimedia Commons*

counted on for shelter and information in and around Fort Sumner gradually turned away and soon decided The Kid was no longer the carefree scamp they had admired and protected. Being hunted and the constant wariness therein had soured him.

The Lincoln County community reached out to a former buffalo hunter, Pat Garrett, who was in search of a steady wage, and hired him as sheriff. Garret had known The Kid, but now saw their past acquaintance as a future ticket to fame and fortune if he could put Billy behind bars or in the ground.

Garrett assembled a hunting party of Texas panhandle cowboys whose ranches along the Canadian River had been The Kid's stealing ground. Billy and his gang had holed up in an abandoned stone house at Stinking Springs. Garrett knew from the local people that Billy had been hunted to the end of his string. The posse surrounded the stone ruin. A brisk gun battle broke out ending in a Mexican standoff—neither side could end it without terrible casualties. A horse lay dead across the hut's front door and none of the rustler's horses in the building would jump across it.

Billy had claimed he would never be captured alive. When Charlie Bowdre, a longtime friend, stopped a bullet in the shootout, crying, "I've been killed!" Billy reacted with a manic outburst. He stuffed Bowdre's revolver back in its holster and shoved his friend out the front door, shouting, "They murdered you, Charlie! Kill some of the sons of bitches before you die!" Bowdre stumbled forward a few paces, his hands in the air, muttered, "I wish . . . I wish . . . " and fell dead in front of Garrett. What finally wore down the gang was the smell of breakfast being cooked by the posse. The surviving regulators trooped out over the dead horse and into custody.

The wheels of justice turned slowly in old New Mexico, plodding along dirt roads from court to court, one jurisdiction to the next. Eventually, secured in irons, The Kid ended up in a room adjoining Garrett's office on the second floor of the old Murphy-Dolan Store being used as a courthouse. He was guarded by sympathetic James W. Bell and a taunting bully, Robert Olinger, who couldn't wait to see Billy kick his life out at the end of a rope.

On the evening of April 28, 1881, Billy was alone in the holding room with Bell while Olinger and the other prisoners were at dinner over at the Whorley Hotel across the street. The Kid asked Bell permission to visit the privy in the yard. Bell accompanied him and waited holding the chain to the shackles and official jewelry.

All that is truly known from the time Billy the Kid left the outhouse is that Bell followed him back inside the courthouse and up the stairs whereupon Billy turned at the top of the landing armed with a revolver and plugged Bell in the

The engraved and gold-washed Colt Thunderer 1877 double-action revolver with solid German silver grips presented to Pat Garrett by his El Paso, Texas, friends for taking down Billy the Kid. *Rock Island Auction Company*

gut. Bell stumbled out into the yard where he died. Billy managed to free himself from the chains in time to see Bob Olinger from the second floor window. Having heard the shots, the deputy jogged across the street from the hotel. Olinger's pride was a double-barrel high-quality Whitney 10-gauge shotgun, which he had left leaning against Garrett's office wall.[32] Billy the Kid checked its loads, shouldered it, and laid the bead front sight on Olinger's upper works.

"Hello, Bob," Billy grinned and triggered both barrels. Olinger's facial identity disappeared, as did much upper body tissue and bone as eighteen large buckshot knocked him backward. The Kid, with a stolen horse underneath him, rode out of Lincoln and back into mythology.

There would be one more murderous ambush in The Kid's life. Garrett had been tax collecting when he heard of Billy's escape. Relentless and methodical, he began his pursuit. Too many hands were turned against the young outlaw and tips gradually placed The Kid holed up near Fort Sumner in or near the home of Pete Maxwell, a local stockman. Garrett, together with his deputy, "Tip" McKinney and a fellow stock detective, John W. Poe from the old Canadian River days, visited Maxwell on the night of July 13, 1881, and found the rancher in bed around midnight.

Poe and Kinney waited outside on the porch while Garrett went inside to sit on the edge of the bed and speak with Maxwell. Soundlessly, on bare feet, a figure moved past the two deputies in the dark. Possibly a Mexican servant? Inside, Garrett looked up to see the shirtless figure framed in the doorway. The figure asked in Spanish, "Who is this?" Maxwell blurted, "It's him!"

Garrett fell back on the bed and pulled his revolver. A single gunshot was deafening in the small room and the flash of flame blinding. A cloud of powder

Bob Olinger's ten-gauge Whitney double-barreled shotgun (bottom), which spoiled his day when Billy the Kid triggered both barrels from Pat Garrett's second floor office window. *Lincoln County Historical Society*

smoke rolled against the wall as Poe and McKinney clawed their way into the room past the fleeing Maxwell. A lamp was lit. The three law officers looked down on what remained of Henry McCarty, alias Billy Antrim, alias William Bonney alias Billy the Kid, for-sure killer of eight men and mythical slayer of twenty-one, one for each year he had lived.[33]

JOHN WESLEY HARDIN

Most men and women who lived and worked in the nineteenth-century Wild West never dropped the hammer on another human being even though the percentage of privately owned firearms was high. After all, guns put food on the table long before domestic meat production took root. But the outlaw breed rode the trails west with their own grim agendas, simmering from defeats in the Civil War, or financial failures, or stoked by the hardscrabble life in the half-settled wilderness. Childhood life was cheap where smallpox and cholera raced through whole communities, and where family life demanded large broods just to stay ahead of starvation and bad luck. Tough nurturing can turn any youngster sour.

Born in 1853, John Wesley Hardin came from a rich Texican heritage studded with ancestors who fought at the Battle of San Jacinto, where Texas won independence from Mexico. A Hardin signed the Texas Declaration of Independence; another Hardin served in the Texas Congress, and young John Wesley had been tabbed by his father to become a Methodist minister—the father's one-time ambition snuffed out by the needs of supporting his large family as a school teacher. In response to the Hardins' distinguished pedigrees, John Wesley knifed his first victim at age eleven during a schoolyard fight. His first murder came at age fifteen when he shot an ex-slave to death. When three soldiers came to arrest him, he shot and killed all three. Protected by the influential and extensive Hardin family, he was whisked out of the county to a rural backwater called Pine Ridge where he taught school.

John Wesley Hardin was a stone-cold killer who claimed forty white men as victims of his quick burn and faster draw. Still, only one death of a lawman put Hardin in prison. He was released after studying the law, became an El Paso, Texas, lawyer, and got shot in the back of the head at a bar while playing dice. *Sic semper pistolero. Wikimedia Commons*

After his sixteenth year, he cut ties with his illustrious family and headed out onto the owlhoot trail in the company of Bill Longley. Hardin's latest mentor and eventual rival, Longley also had begun his short and brutal life killing a black soldier. Their conversations were Hardin's impressionable introduction to the footloose life of the itinerant gunslinger. They eventually fell out. No room for two roosters in the same flock of chickens.

Hardin wasn't the kind of outlaw who stole money, rustled cattle, or made off with somebody else's horse. He worked for wages in cow camps across Texas and gambled some—once on a bowling match. He suckered his opponent into putting money on the pins and ended up shooting him when the loser came back with a shotgun. He tried to keep a low profile, even got married after escaping from the clutches of another passel of lawmen. But everything ended the same way: a leaking body on the ground and gunsmoke in the air.

Finally, as the trail of bodies got closer and closer to the last place he had slept, the Texas Rangers took up the chase with a four-thousand-dollar reward on his head. John Wesley decided to leave Texas for Florida. At last, the change of scene seemed to calm him. He prospered with his wife and two daughters. For three years, he became a businessman, buying and selling cattle and horses.

He opened a saloon and invested in logging interests. Then, in 1877, he took a train ride on business and was passing Pensacola, Florida, enjoying the view out the window when a posse of Texas Rangers led by Capt. John Armstrong leaped on him, beat him about the head with their pistol butts, and wrestled him into the coach's aisle. He never got the Colt revolver from his pants' waistband.

This Colt 1873 Peacemaker was used to beat on John Wesley Hardin, who was arrested on a train rolling through Florida by Texas Ranger Capt. John Armstrong. Hardin was traveling from his horse ranch where he had settled down to a peaceful life. *Texas Ranger Hall of Fame and Museum, Waco, Texas*

After reviewing the record and paddling down the river of blood that led to Hardin's trial in Huntsville, Texas, the prosecutors could only get one charge to stick. He killed Deputy Sheriff Charley Webb on Hardin's twenty-first birthday in 1874. For that crime, he received a life sentence. While he served his time, he studied for the Texas bar exam. His good behavior earned him his release in February 1894.

He hung out his lawyer shingle in El Paso, Texas, had business cards printed, and almost immediately began associating with felons—the people he understood and who needed his services. As advertising, he put a bullet hole in each of the business cards he handed out.

John Selman Jr., a police officer in El Paso, started making noises about arresting the arrogant Hardin. John Selman Sr. claimed he feared for his son's life and decided to act. On August 19, 1895, the elder Selman, a former law officer and gunfighter, pushed through the doors of the Acme Saloon where Hardin sat at the bar. Hardin rolled dice for drinks and said to the barman, "You have to beat double sixes." Selman raised his revolver, saw Hardin look up at him in the bar mirror, and put a bullet in the back of John Wesley's head. Hardin dropped, after which Selman stepped forward and further nailed him to the floor with two more shots.

With a jellied gob of his brain lying on the Acme Saloon bar top, John Wesley Hardin went to his reward the same way he had sent more than forty men to theirs.

CHAPTER 9

THE GOOD (BAD) MEN

Henry Plummer, Henry Newton Brown, Tom Horn, Wyatt Earp

I T IS EASY to point to the paragons of justice who selflessly pursued the outlaws: Bill Tilghman, Chris Madsen, and Heck Thomas (the Three Guardsmen); John Slaughter; Texas Rangers James Gillette and John Armstrong; the legendary William Butler Hickok; careful and confident Bat Masterson; and the many cow-town police officers paid out of dog license fees and road taxes. Boot-hill cemeteries are full of brave men who reached for their guns a second too late. The outlaws who lived to steal and the cold-eyed gunfighters who careened across the West from one murder to the next mostly ended up dancing on air at the end of a rope or making little rocks out of big ones in some heartless penitentiary.

There is a third group, however, who crossed back and forth between the worlds of law and lawless. These were the good bad men who hid behind a badge of respectability while they pursued their own agendas. Sometimes they made no secret of their goals or allegiances, kept alive by a ruthless reputation, part hero—part hellion.

A TALE OF TWO HENRYS

Henry Plummer

In 1852, at age nineteen, Henry left the rocky New England coast for the great possibilities of the vast, sparsely settled West. The Gold Rush of 1849 had exploded in California and by 1856 he'd taken root in Nevada City. By age twenty-three he had parlayed a pleasing personality and good will into prominent business as a mine owner, rancher, and bakery owner. He was elected sheriff, but when he sought higher office as a Democrat, he lost.

Beneath his affable veneer, a lack of empathy developed along with his shooting skills. He first killed a man named Vedder over his affair with Vedder's wife. The ex-sheriff was sentenced to ten years in San Quentin prison. He had many supporters who wrote the governor, but it was Plummer's contraction of tuberculosis that weighed heavily with the judge and he pardoned the popular citizen.

Whether it was the encroaching disease, or his festering character flaw, Henry Plummer packed his Colts and headed out onto the owlhoot trail. He was accused of robbing a Wells Fargo Office and then he killed a sheriff in Oregon. His brief crime wave ended in a gambling casino in Idaho where he worked and accumulated a nasty gang of cutthroats. Henry gunned down the head of the already active local vigilantes. Using his resume as a former sheriff, he became the local law backed up by his murderous thugs who called themselves the Innocents.

Henry turned in his old Dragoons and 1849 Pocket Model Colts for a pair of Colt 1860 Army revolvers and grew his organization. The Innocents became a huge gang, requiring secret signs and handshakes to recognize each other. They moved their headquarters to Bannock and Virginia City. One of Plummer's Innocents

During good times, Henry Plummer was a respected lawman, a ladies' man. and a pillar of the community. In bad times, he was a gang leader, a bank robber, and a killer who pushed the envelope of civic tolerance straight to being guest of honor at a necktie party. *Legends of the West*

One of the pair of Henry Plummer's 1860 Colt Army revolvers with three notches in the grip. The United States Navy ordered 900 fluted cylinder revolvers in May 1861 later issued to ships enforcing the Atlantic and Gulf blockade, making this gun a "Navy Army Colt" *Wikimedia Commons*

threatened to spill the beans about all the corruption and killings in the new sheriff's wake, so Plummer heated up one of those Army Colts, killing the blackmailer. But the word was out.

By 1863, the good citizens of Montana had formed their own vigilance committee—without Plummer—and began stringing up outlaws in wholesale lots, including some of the Innocents. Aware of the situation, Plummer chose to ignore the danger and continued business as usual playing sheriff.

He was amazed on January 10, 1864, when Montana vigilantes swept down on his jail, bundled him out the door and frogmarched him toward the brand new gallows he had been building with city funds. He wept and pleaded, offered an arm to be hacked off, offered to live like a hermit in the hills. He was going on and on about his tuberculosis when they dropped the trapdoor and he received a suspended sentence—about three feet off the ground: not the first lawman to take the long drop.

Henry Newton Brown

Early on, Henry Brown was a tumbleweed that blew on and off the straight and narrow to cross the owlhoot trail once too often. His unsettled life began in 1857 and went downhill from there. Orphaned early on, he was sent to live with his nearest kin, Uncle Jasper and Aunt Aldamira Richardson, in Phelps County, Missouri. By age seventeen, Henry had seen enough of pro- and anti-slavery brutality to last a lifetime. He packed his saddlebags and headed west. He worked as a cowboy in Colorado and then in Texas, which he had to leave quickly after killing a man in a gunfight. Trouble seemed to dog him as he drifted into New

Mexico just as a range war was starting between a faction headed up by attorney Alexander McSween and John Tunstall, who were battling a takeover by the Santa Fe Ring fronted by James J. Dolan; Maj. Lawrence G. Murphy, the Lincoln County Sheriff; James Brady,

Henry Newton Brown was another short, tough lawman who held the respect of his town with his pugnacious approach to enforcement. He was a two-gun terror and one day, on a whim, decided to rob a bank and doubled down by getting blasted to flinders escaping from his own jail. *Wikimedia Commons*

and a collection of gunmen. Brown settled into Tunstall's Rio Feliz ranch and shook hands with his new pard, who also used to be called Henry, but now wore the handle Billy the Kid.

In for a penny, in for a pound, Henry Brown was swept up into the conflict when Sheriff Brady's gunmen shot down Tunstall. In a rage, Billy joined up with the Rio Feliz hands into a band who called themselves regulators and, shortly after Tunstall's ambush, staged one of their own in Lincoln, the county seat. Brady was killed by a burst of rifle fire and the war heated up.

On July 15, 1878, Henry Brown found himself pumping bullets from his Winchester at a siege of gunmen ringing McSween's Lincoln home where the regulators had been bottled up. Amid blazing return fire and flames, the embattled cow hands fled as McSween was killed and his home was torched. Thus ended the Lincoln County War.

Tired of being on the dodge and getting out of New Mexico just ahead of two murder warrants, Brown settled into Tascosa in the Texas Panhandle. For the first time, he put on a badge and became either a deputy sheriff of Oldham County, marshal of Tascosa, or a constable on the police force, depending on the source material. Whatever the job, he got the boot a short time later due to his prickly temper and short fuse. He cooled off after drifting into Oklahoma, working as a cowhand in the Indian Territory until July 1882 when he put down roots in Caldwell, Kansas.

Caldwell was a hairy little cow town every bit as dangerous as Dodge City or Abilene. Law enforcement required a firm hand, so Henry Brown's speedy method of conflict resolution with the butt end of his Colt suited the town fathers just fine. He was appointed assistant town marshal and, in five months, swapped up to become marshal of Caldwell, Kansas. The new authority burnished off his rough edges and he became a model citizen.

To help him keep order, he hired Ben Wheeler, an ex-Texas lawman who had earlier taken up the owlhoot trail. The reformed bad man became his assistant and handled the messy situations while the marshal became a Methodist and a social success. Brown was short, quiet, and respectful beneath a square-jawed façade that promised quick and painful response to lawbreakers; he was aided by the pair of Colts he wore each day during his rounds.

As a token of the town's confidence in Henry Newton Brown's abilities in taming the crossroads of the Santa Fe and Chisholm cattle trails, the town worthies presented their marshal with a silver and gold mounted Winchester Second Model 73 rifle bearing a commemorative silver plaque.

This is the Winchester 73 rifle presented to Henry Brown by the folks in Caldwell who appreciated his law enforcement, but didn't care for his bank robbery and murder. They tried to hang him, but instead blew him in two with a double-barreled shotgun. *Kansas State Historical Society*

> Presented to City Marshal H. N. Brown
> For valuable services rendered In behalf of the Citizens of Caldwell Kas A. N. Colson Mayor Dec 1882

Within a year, Brown drilled a ball from that rifle into gambler Newt Boyce and also knocked off the renegade Indian, Spotted Horse. While taming Caldwell, Brown married the daughter of a local brick maker, Alice Maude Levagood, wedging himself even deeper into Caldwell's high society. The marshal and his assistant were living off the fat of the land, tipping hats to ladies and sharing stories with the movers and shakers of formerly dangerous Caldwell, when Ben Wheeler had an idea.

On a spring morning in April, Henry, Ben, and two cowboys, John Wesley and William Smith, told Caldwell's mayor they were heading into Indian Territory to track down a murderer. Instead, they spurred their horses to the town of Medicine Lodge, Kansas, where they strode into the Medicine Valley Bank with guns drawn. Nerves on edge, Wesley thought he saw a hostile move and plugged bank president Wylie Payne. At that, bank clerk George Geppert headed for the bank vault. Both Wesley and Smith fired into him. Before Geppert died, he managed to slam the vault shut and seal it.

Faced with failure, the four would-be robbers dashed out of the bank and galloped out of town. Across the street from the bank, a dozen cowboys were hanging out at a local stable when the hue and cry went up. The cowboys, without waiting to be deputized, swung into their saddles and pounded down the main drag into the dust of the escaping killers. Not familiar with the country around Medicine Lodge, the four rode full tilt into a box canyon with only one way in and out. Surrounded and facing more than a dozen blazing guns, the failed robbers threw up their hands.

Mobbed into the Medicine Lodge jail, the boys didn't have long to wait for Judge Lynch to hand in his verdict. As Brown sensed the gathering of vigilantes, he sat amid the tatters of his life and wrote his wife a letter:

Darling Wife: I am in jail here. Four of us tried to rob the bank here and one man shot one of the men in the bank. I want you to come and see me as soon as you can. I will send you all of my things and you can sell them. But keep the Winchester. It is hard for me to write this letter, but it was all for you, my sweet wife, and for the love I have for you. Do not go back on me. If you do it will kill me. Be true to me as long as you live, and come to see me if you think enough of me. My love is just the same as it always was. Oh, how I did hate to leave you last Sunday evening. But I did not think this would happen. I thought we could take in the money and not have any trouble with it, but a man's fondest hopes are sometimes broken with trouble. We would not have been arrested but one of our horses gave out and we could not leave him [the rider] alone. I do not know what to write. Do the best you can with everything. I want you to send me some clothes. Sell all the things you don't need. Have your picture taken and send it to me. Now, my dear wife, go and see Mr. Witzleben and Mr. Nyce and get the money. If a mob does not kill us we will come out all right after while. Maude, I did not shoot anyone and didn't want the others to kill anyone. But they did and that is all there is about it. Now, my darling wife, goodbye. H. N. Brown.

Anticipating the mob, the prisoners slipped out of their shackles and, when the cell door opened, they made a dash for the alley alongside the jail. Henry Brown reached the alley as both barrels of a shotgun almost blasted him in two. The other escapees were gunned down, but not killed. They were dragged to a nearby maple tree and swung up by the neck until they choked to death.

In the end, both Henrys had the world by the tail, but threw it all away. Plummer and Brown demonstrated the pull of the owlhoot trail and the ultimate risk of the outlaw life.

TOM HORN

Tom Horn was an enigma. Born in Memphis, Missouri, on November 21, 1860, he died one day short of his thirty-third birthday in the town of Cheyenne, Wyoming. During his passage through the West, he was a cowboy, miner, railroad employee, teamster, stage coach driver, lawman, army scout, range detective, Pinkerton detective, soldier, and drygulching bushwhacker for hire. To this day, he has passionate supporters and equally passionate scoffers who will swear he was nothing more than a yellow back shooter.

Horn stood six feet tall, was long and rangy, a record-breaking champion steer roper on the rodeo circuit. He also had the mild demeanor of a general store button merchant. His father worked him and whipped him on their Missouri farm until, at age fourteen, the big kid took off to Newton, Kansas, where he worked for the railroad; he then took a job as a mule skinner hauling freight for the Santa Fe. By 1876, he was savvy enough to get hired by the army

Here is Tom Horn braiding a rope in his jail cell and possibly reconsidering his career choices. He was a good man to some and a back shooter to others. *Wikimedia Commons*

Right: Horn adopted the Winchester Model 1894, the first rifle chambered for the hot, flat-shooting .30-30-caliber cartridge fueled by smokeless powder.

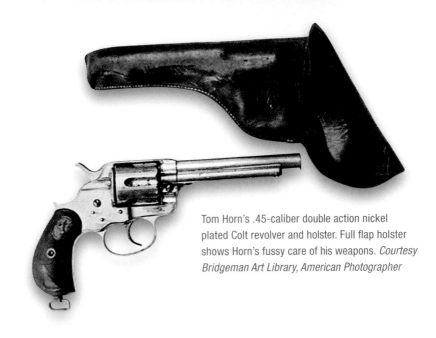

Tom Horn's .45-caliber double action nickel plated Colt revolver and holster. Full flap holster shows Horn's fussy care of his weapons. *Courtesy Bridgeman Art Library, American Photographer*

as a scout and slipped under the wing of legendary Apache scout, Al Sieber. He tagged along with Al as the army closed in on the Apache chief, Geronimo.

From Al and the Apaches he learned to track and to speak Spanish and enough Apache to hold up his end of a conversation, but his restless nature moved him along. He offered his gun to a faction of the Pleasant Valley War in 1887. But his education took a huge jump when he signed on as a deputy sheriff alongside Arizona's fearless and famous sheriff of Yavapai County, Bucky O'Neil.

Three years later, Horn joined the Pinkerton Detective Agency in Denver, Colorado. By 1890, he was recruiting gunmen for the Wyoming Stock Growers Association. More and more, his focus shifted to the elimination of rustlers and small-cow-ranch owners who stole beeves from the large company herds— mostly to feed hungry families. He developed a coldly effective signature announcing his work.

Rustlers working a red-hot running iron over a hog-tied steer to change its brand never knew Horn was around until one of them pitched over with a rifle bullet in his chest. Then, they heard the distant shot. Once the thieves scattered, Horn arranged the dead body with its head resting on a couple of rocks—like a casket's pillow—to be found later. For each hit, he received one hundred dollars.

To let off steam, Horn made trips to Denver to drink and enjoy solitary pursuits. But when the Spanish-American War erupted and Teddy Roosevelt called for an all-volunteer Rough Riders organization under the command of Leonard Wood, Horn got caught up in the excitement and volunteered. His experience as a mule packer was invaluable, but before he could head down to Tampa, Florida, and sail for Cuba, he contracted a stiff fever and spent his service in the United States.

A legendary man hunter and Pinkerton detective, Joe LeFors got Horn to sort of admit during a whiskey-soaked conversation that he might have shot the Nickell boy from three hundred yards with a Winchester .30-30-caliber rifle. *wyomingtalesandtrails.com*

Eventually, he made two discoveries that changed his life as he settled back in Wyoming as a killer for hire: he found a girl, Glendolene Kimmel, a local school teacher and part of a family who had an ongoing feud with a home-steader named Nickell. Apparently, Horn decided to eliminate the troublesome Nickell as a good-will gesture. The second discovery was the latest product of the Winchester Repeating Arms Company, the .30-30 rifle cartridge that debuted as a choice in 1895, chambered for the new Model 1894 Winchester rifle. This new flat-shooting, high-power, smokeless-powder cartridge was perfect for Horn's trade as rustler-buster.

Allegedly, in 1901, during one of Horn's rest and relaxation periods following a killing, Joe LeFors, another legendary man hunter, got Horn alone with a bottle in the US marshal's office in Cheyenne. Leslie Snow, a deputy and a hired shorthand writer, sat hidden in a side room eavesdropping. After swapping stories and passing the jug, LeFors got Horn on the topic of his latest ambush and its victim, the Nickell patriarch's fourteen-year-old son, Willy Nickell. The boy had been tending a hay wagon out in the middle of the prairie near the property gate when a shot picked him off as he climbed down and swung the gate open. Willy was trying to climb back up on the wagon when a second shot killed him.

Horn talked about spotting the distant wagon and driver on the Nickell land approaching the gate, and dismounting so he could stalk as close as possible. He stalked barefoot to leave no trail. LeFors asked, "What kind of gun have you got?"

The tall man in the middle of this swarm of bicycles is Tom Horn being escorted back to jail after his attempt to run on foot from the Cheyenne lockup. *wyomingtalesandtrails.com*

Horn: "A .30-30 Winchester."

LeFors: "Tom, do you think that will hold up as well as a .30-40?"

Horn: "No, but I like to get close to my man. The closer, the better."

LeFors: "Tom, how far was Willy Nickell killed?"

Horn: "About three hundred yards. It was the best shot I ever made and the dirtiest trick I ever done. I thought at one time he would get away."[33]

This shorthand confession became the cornerstone in Tom Horn's trial, regardless of whether or not Horn had mistaken the boy for Kels Nickell, the local troublemaker and the boy's father. The shooting happened at a time when feuds and vigilante justice had run their course. Horn became an example of the heartless gun for hire and was found guilty in a Cheyenne Court.

Before his execution, Tom Horn made one last bid for freedom. He broke out of jail with a train robber named McCloud. McCloud was lucky enough to find a horse while Horn struck out on foot, sprinting into the prairie, pursued closely by a deputy and a swarm of townspeople. Horn had snatched up a pistol on the way out of the jail, but apparently, this time new technology played a dirty trick. He had grabbed a Fabrique Nationale nine-millimeter semiautomatic pistol. As he struggled with it, the deputy swung his Iver Johnson .38-caliber revolver and Horn went down for the count.

Wyatt Earp at age seventy-five in 1923, enjoying his golden years, living off the gritty reputation he built over the decades of moving from town to town across the West, and spinning the yarns everyone wanted to hear. *Wikimedia Commons*

Returned to jail, he wrote his autobiography—like Cole Younger's similar tome—full of justifications and blameless rationales. On November 20, 1903, Horn was escorted to the scaffold; his arms and legs were strapped, he and stood on the trap, which was billed as a new humane execution invention. His weight on the trap opened a valve, allowing water to escape, and as the reservoir went down, the trap suddenly dropped. Horn, in effect, hanged himself. In eleven seconds, he was dead.

WYATT EARP

Wyatt Barry Stapp Earp died in bed in 1929 at the age of eighty, a beloved Western artifact, thanks to a mostly fictional biography based on Earp's dictation and embellished by author Stuart N. Lake. Earp had most of his teeth, a loving wife, and money in the bank. His status among the West's fearless, flinty-eyed lawmen was carved in stone. His moody silences and hard stare only served to underline a righteous past, alongside the likes of Bill Tilghman, James Gillett, Bat Masterson, and Heck Thomas. Good bad men came in all shades and degrees.

Few back in the 1880s would recognize the taciturn drifter who ran a faro bank at the Oriental Saloon in Tombstone and rousted drunks behind a deputy's badge as a man destined for greatness. Or, back in 1876, when he was hammered senseless by towering Red Sweeny over the affections of a dance hall girl. Or, further back in 1875, when he was arrested for horse stealing in Indian Territory. What gave Earp a leg to stand on in his early days of buffalo hunting and sweating in a section gang on the railroad, was beating out his half-brother, Newton Earp, for the job of town constable of Lamar, Missouri, in 1870. He tried to settle down, but his new young wife died three and a half months after their wedding. Disconsolate, he packed his traps and headed west.

Drifting down to Kansas with his brothers, James, Morgan, and Virgil, he tried gambling in Hays City, and then pinned on the badge of town policeman in Wichita. The low-paying job found him scrounging various small grafts, including failure to pass along fines levied on prostitutes to the city coffers. One day, while hauling out his hog leg to make a routine arrest, the revolver's hammer slipped and almost blew off his toe. Later, Wyatt was arrested for fighting and, finally, got kicked off the force by the town fathers.

The year 1876 found him in Dodge City, Kansas, where he worked as a policeman and later assumed the job of assistant marshal. He lasted four months before big Sweeny pounded him to a pulp. In 1879, he and his brothers set out for Las Vegas, New Mexico. On the way, his love of petty larceny resurrected the old gold brick scam (a lead bar triple gold plated and sold to the victim as solid gold) to pull in some traveling money. When he tried the con in Mobeetie, New Mexico, while working with John Henry "Doc" Holliday and Mysterious Dave Mather, the local sheriff ran them out of town.[29]

The boys split up. Virgil, Wyatt, and James moved to Tombstone, Arizona, a town built upon a huge silver strike. After acquiring a second wife, Wyatt dealt faro at the Danner & Owens Saloon and accumulated thousands of dollars in winnings, which fueled his mine claim interests. To get away from the boozy atmosphere of the spit-and-sawdust saloons, he rode shotgun guard on the Wells Fargo stage line. Morgan; another Earp brother, Warren; and Doc Holliday soon joined the rest of the Earp clan in the silver city. Wyatt failed to get appointed sheriff of Cochise County but signed on as a deputy when Virgil became deputy US marshal.

TOP ROW Will Harris - Luke Short - W. B. Masterson - Wm Tilghman
LOWER ROW Chas. Bassett - Wyatt Earp - Frank McLain - Neal Brown

One of the versions of this photo shows Bill Tilghman when he was a deputy marshal in Dodge. It is a who's-who of famous (and infamous) lawmen who comprised this tough cow town's city police force.
Wikimedia Commons

A long view of Tombstone, Arizona, perched on silver claims and its claim, "The town too tough to die." Without the O.K. Corral gunfight today it would probably be just a Dairy Queen and a gas station. *Wikimedia Commons*

Wyatt bought an interest in the Oriental Saloon to further augment his wages. James took a job behind the bar at Vogan & Flynn's Saloon, adding to his income by pimping for the local bordellos and bouncing drunks. All the brothers were making money doing what they did best—providing muscle and intimidation. Only a local band of cowboy cattle rustlers and stage robbers, the Clantons and the McLaurys, marred the otherwise rosy picture.[34]

These cowboys spoiled the Earps' moneymaking prospects in Tombstone by crowding the brothers at every occasion. In response, the Earp clan began their own campaign of intimidation and taunting, which quickly accelerated to physical confrontation. The town, the newspapers, and everyone took sides. Doc Holliday, the toxic, tubercular gunman, itinerant dentist, and gambler, threw in his lot with the Earps. On October 26, 1881, everything came to a head, and after a shouting match the two factions determined to meet in the street outside the O.K. Corral.

The symbolism of the gunfight was haunting. Wyatt, Virgil, and Morgan Earp, with Doc Holliday, strode down Allen Street in the chill morning air toward the corral, dressed in black overcoats, wide-brim black hats, and black stovepipe pants. They carried Colt revolvers in their waistbands,

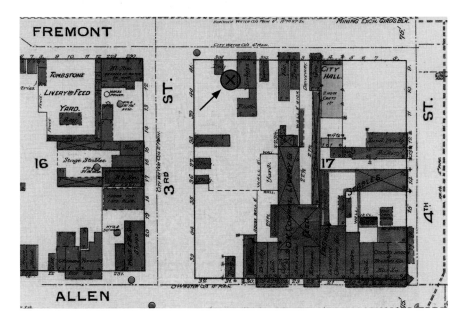

This insurance map of downtown Tombstone drawn up just two years after the O.K. Corral gunfight shows where all the shooting happened: at Fremont Street next to Fly's Photo Gallery. It was near, not in, the corral. *City of Tombstone*

except for Wyatt, who had custom-tailored pockets in his overcoat lined with waxed canvas for his Smith & Wesson .44-caliber American Model No. 3 revolver with an eight-inch barrel. Doc Holliday carried a sawed-off shotgun that Virgil had handed him and a nickel-plated Colt double-action .41-caliber revolver.*

Doc didn't like the shotgun. He was a frail man, and the recoil of a ten-gauge weapon punished him. Frank McLaury and Billy Clanton packed Colts under their jackets. The two groups began shouting at each other as the Earps and Holliday marched closer to the cowboys' stand three lots past the corral entrance nearer to Fremont Street.

Frank McLaury and Billy Clanton drew their Colts. Wyatt cocked his Smith & Wesson. Doc Holliday swept up the shotgun. Morgan and Virgil raised their

---

* The shotgun Doc Holliday carried was either a W. W. Greener, his personal Colt shotgun, or more likely a Belgian Eclipse Meteor ten-gauge, double-barrel weapon with no shoulder stock and the barrels trimmed back to eighteen inches—commonly referred to as a "Whippet" gun. Bill O'Neal, *Encyclopedia of Western Gunfighters.* University of Oklahoma Press, Norman, OK 1979.
Joseph G. Rosa, *They Called Him Wild Bill.* University Press of Oklahoma, 1979.
William B. Shillingberg, *Wyatt Earp and the "Buntline Myth",* Kansas Collection, Kansas Historical Quarterly, 1976.

Doc John Holliday lugged a sawed-off ten-gauge double-barreled shotgun held under his coat through the reach-through slit above his pocket. It must have been a big surprise to the cowboys. *Rock Island Auction Company*

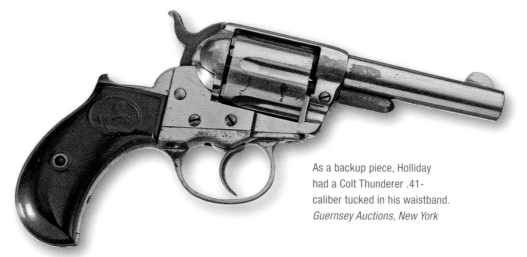

As a backup piece, Holliday had a Colt Thunderer .41-caliber tucked in his waistband. *Guernsey Auctions, New York*

Colt revolvers. From that moment to the end of the battle, seventeen shots cracked in the narrow street. Horses whinnied. Men shouted. Gunsmoke clouds roiled across the wagon-rutted road. Ike Clanton and Billy Claiborne, who had been watching from the sidelines, ran for the safety of Fly's Photo Gallery. Both McLaury brothers were gut shot. Tom McLaury clutched his Winchester, ripped from his horse's saddle scabbard. Billy Clanton had a broken wrist and a spreading red stain across his chest.

Morgan Earp squeezed his bleeding shoulder. Virgil Earp had a leg wound but was still on his feet. Doc Holliday lost a chunk of hide off his thigh and was limping. He'd chucked the empty shotgun and now had his smoking Colt in hand. Only Wyatt Earp stood untouched, sucking in the gunsmoke as he panned his Smith & Wesson across the killing ground.

Sheriff John Behan had the Earps arrested, but in the subsequent trial, they were acquitted. However, the Clantons and other factions who wanted to see the Earps dead, had deep pockets and held even deeper grudges. Virgil Earp was maimed in a shotgun ambush during his night rounds. Morgan Earp was shot dead through a window while he played billiards. Wyatt set aside his badge and went hunting with a posse of friends, including Sherman McMasters and Turkey Creek Jack Johnson.

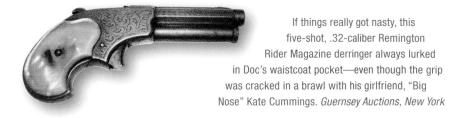

If things really got nasty, this five-shot, .32-caliber Remington Rider Magazine derringer always lurked in Doc's waistcoat pocket—even though the grip was cracked in a brawl with his girlfriend, "Big Nose" Kate Cummings. *Guernsey Auctions, New York*

In the train yard at Tucson, Earp found alleged assassin Frank Stillwell allegedly stalking the train that was taking Virgil and his family back to California. Though Stillwell had legitimate reasons to be in Tucson, Wyatt only saw his brother's assassin. In the dark between the tracks, Earp's double-barrel shotgun blast practically cut Stillwell in two. One by one, with his vigilante posse, Earp tracked down the others over time, leaving behind only bloody remains.

After the Tombstone incidents, Earp married a third time and, in 1896, refereed a prizefight between Tom Sharkey and Bob Fitzsimmons. Considering the rowdy crowd, he began the fight with a Colt revolver in his hip pocket, but was asked to remove it by officials. Following the fight, he headed for Alaska where he opened the Dexter Saloon in Nome. One evening, while dealing with a drunken patron, he drew a Colt from behind the bar. The local marshal gave him a backhanded beating and took away the gun.

Eventually, Wyatt headed south and began speculating in mine claims—and did a bit of claim jumping—until he took root in Los Angeles, living from one moneymaking scheme to the next. His two favorite profit-makers were prize fighting and horse racing, which was just then coming into its own as a big-money sport out west.

In his twilight years, Wyatt Earp became the darling of the silent film stages that popped up like mushrooms in the new suburb of Glendale, California—soon to be called Hollywoodland. In 1914, he was called upon to act as a consultant for Western movie scenes. He sat for hours talking about his adventures. Movie stars Tom Mix, Ken Maynard, and Hoot Gibson—all of whom were real cowboys and rodeo stars before becoming actors—were a willing audience.

In 1927, Stuart Lake, a World War I veteran who had been mustered out of the service with a crippling leg wound, hunted for a book subject to revive his writing career. He arranged to meet Earp and the two of them, the hungry pot boiler author and the self-created Western legend, found common ground. Lake jumped at the chance to write Earp's biography. At the behest of Lake's editor, the author's original 643-page manuscript containing 190,000 words

continued on page 130

Ned Buntline was a self-promoting pulp writer whose purple prose spun fictional tales of real heroes in action. In 1876, it is alleged (by Lake) that Buntline made gifts of a special Colt Single Action Army revolver with a twelve-inch barrel and detachable shoulder stock to five worthy and famous lawmen who once wore Dodge City badges. Among them was Wyatt Earp. The first mention of this gift was in Stuart N. Lake's iconic book, *Wyatt Earp: Frontier Marshal*. Both the gun's importance and Earp's postmortem reputation grew in direct proportion as he allegedly wielded the long-barrel six-gun in the name of justice.

Today, Buntline the author, Lake the author, the gun, the gift, and Wyatt Earp have all fallen under the probing gaze of hard-nose historians. These burrowing researchers have uncovered a trail of contrary evidence and conundrums in pursuit of the truth.

Ned Buntline was born Edward Zane Carroll Judson on March 8, 1821. His first story was published at age seventeen when he was serving as an acting naval midshipman. He was a natural, popular writer and churned out sea adventures for many national publications. He tried his hand publishing magazines under his "Ned Buntline" *nom de plume*, but they all folded. His works didn't veer into Western stories until Buffalo Bill Cody returned from his Wild West Show's European tour in 1869 with great fanfare and hooplah. Buntline met Cody, was impressed with the larger-than-life Western icon, and dashed off four pulse-pounding adventures, including *Buffalo Bill, King of the Border Men!*, which was immediately serialized by the Street & Smith's *New York Weekly*.

The extent of Buntline's literary career can be summed up in his rewrite of *Buffalo Bill's Last Victory*, or *Love Eye the Lodge Queen* into the stage play, *Scouts of the Prairie! Indian Deviltry As It Is!* In this production, besides the hammy scenery chewing of Buffalo Bill, Texas Jack Omohondro, and (mostly drunk) Wild Bill Hickok, Buntline took a role as the drunken Cale Durge,

This "Colt Buntline Special" was built in 1980. No Colt Single Action Army revolvers with a twelve-inch barrel as described by Ned Buntline were ever ordered from Colt according to their records. The gun is author Stuart Lake's fictional creation. *Rock Island Auction Company*

who embraces temperance but is killed off in the second act. Wiping tears of hysteria from their eyes, critics speculated Buntline's demise should have occurred early in the first act. Everyone who sat through a performance agreed that the play sent legitimate theater back to the Stone Age.

Meanwhile, according to the *Wichita Weekly Beacon*, Wyatt Earp was bounced out of their Kansas town with a vagrancy rap hanging over his head and moved on down the road to Dodge City, where, the *Beacon* further reported, on May 24, 1876, he had joined the Dodge City Police Department. At this point, his career as a lawman was hardly illustrious and his exploits were unknown outside of Kansas.

Another recipient of a Buntline special Colt was Bill Tilghman for his stellar work in Dodge. Tilghman was actually an army scout until 1877 when he arrived in Dodge and took a job as a deputy sheriff of Ford County. To make financial ends meet, he opened two saloons to augment his paycheck. He became city marshal in 1884.[29]

The cast of Buntline's stage play, *Scouts of the Prairie! Indian Deviltry As It Is!*: Ned Buntline, Buffalo Bill Cody, Giuseppina Morlacchi, and Texas Jack Omohundro. The critics were not kind. *Wikimedia Commons*

In any case, according to Lake, Buntline ordered five .45-caliber Long Colt Single Action Army revolvers from the factory. Each had a twelve-inch barrel, wood grips with "Ned" carved in them, a hand-tooled holster, and a detachable shoulder stock complete with a buckskin sling to hook around a saddle horn. The guns were presented to Wyatt Earp, Bill Tilghman, Bat Masterson, Charlie Bassett, and Neal Brown between May and July in 1876.

According to the Colt factory, no order for five revolvers with that barrel length was ever received—even though Colt did sell extra-long-barrel versions at one dollar an extra inch over the seven-and-a-half-inch standard Peacemaker. A Colt with a factory sixteen-inch barrel was available and had been shown at the Philadelphia Centennial Exposition in 1876.

It is possible that weapon inspired Lake to include its unique counterpart in the Earp saga. Regardless, none of the long-barreled Colts left the factory for sale until December 1877. Even more curious, no mention of the fabulous Buntline special or writings about Ned Buntline's gifts to the lawmen appears until Lake's biography was published in 1931.

Like Bat Masterson, who ordered six Colt revolvers from the factory during his years behind a badge, Earp preferred a shorter four and three-quarter-inch or five-and-a-half-inch barrel. And finally, writing in a letter to a friend about his days as a peace keeper, Wyatt admitted, "I never carried a gun only upon occasion and that was while on duty as an officer of the law."[*]

---

[*]Although Colt displayed some long-barreled, single-action revolvers at the 1876 Centennial, it was not until December 1, 1877, that any left the Hartford assembly plant for actual sale. Besides, five guns were not involved in this shipment, nor were they sent to Ned Buntline or even to a New York dealer. Instead, this order consisted of four sixteen-inch, .45-caliber single-actions, assembled with the now rare semiflattop frame (not "regulation style"), shipped to B. Kittredge & Company of Cincinnati, Colt's main Western agent.[48] These guns, advertised with a "long carbine barrel," sold for five dollars above the standard price.[35]

continued from page 127

was streamlined to 150,000 words to reflect a more manly action hero lawman with a long-barreled gun, who was both a man killer—and a lady killer.[34]

When Earp died in 1929, he was certain his refined version of the manly life he had led throughout the West was safely enshrined in Lake's work in progress, *Wyatt Earp: Frontier Marshal*. Earp had reinvented himself so many times; it was important to him which final facts were left behind.

CHAPTER 10

BANDITS
INTO THE
TWENTIETH
CENTURY

Butch and Sundance

ROBERT LEROY PARKER "Butch Cassidy" and Harry Longabaugh "the Sundance Kid" are everyone's idea of the fun-loving, irrepressible pals who were part of the closing days of the Old West. They galloped out of the Robbers' Roost—an outlaw B&B—in Wyoming's rugged Hole-in-the-Wall country to rob banks and trains. Their gang, the Wild Bunch, was a pick-up group of whoever was at the Roost when a job was

Harry Longabaugh and Etta Place were an item. She was a former school teacher and he was a free spirit with a reckless streak of larceny. *Wikimedia Commons*

The Wild Bunch in San Francisco around 1900: Seated, Harry Longabaugh "Sundance Kid," Ben Kilpatrick "Tall Texan," and Robert Leroy Parker "Butch Cassidy." Standing, Will Carver and Harvey Logan "Kid Curry." This is during one of their spending-spree trips to enjoy the amenities of big cities. These good times were fading fast. *Wikimedia Commons*

planned, but that attracted hard cases like Harvey Logan "Kid Curry," who had a brutal murder streak. It wasn't long before these fun-loving fellows attracted the attention of the Pinkertons and equally hard cases, such as man hunter Joe LeFors.

Butch and Sundance had become friends, and regardless of their notoriety and time spent in big-city vacations all duded up and frittering their money on good food and gambling, the law was catching up to them. Both Butch and Sundance had served time in prison and had no desire to repeat the experience. By the 1890s, detective agencies like the Pinkertons crossed county and state borders in pursuit, used the telegraph, telephone, and the web of trains to move men and horses anywhere they were needed virtually overnight.

By 1903, Sundance and his girlfriend, Etta Place, a former school teacher, arranged to meet Butch down in South America. They would all get a fresh start in a country that lagged behind the United States in technology. Sadly, all their attempts at legitimate enterprises down south came to nothing. They were thieves, not businessmen. Etta returned to the United States following an appendicitis attack and the boys, left to their own devices, returned to the owlhoot trail, robbing banks and miners' pack mule trains in Bolivia.

Even the smallest, least-technologically adapted communities eventually see a pattern where their disappearing treasure is concerned and, in 1908, the Bolivian Army sent out patrols. One day, the horsemen were halted by a boy who had spotted two gringos with pack animals at a local restaurant in his village. When the soldiers arrived, the two men, dining *al fresco*, were separated from the rifles and ammunition on their pack mules. A pitched battle erupted. As darkness came, one of the men ran for the animals as the other provided covering fire. The barrage of rifle fire from the troops cut down the first man who was dragged back into cover by his companion. The battle raged again with more troops joining the first patrol.

In the morning, the troops advanced on the silent cluster of bullet-pocked barricades and behind a table, they found Sundance shot to pieces and dead from a single bullet wound in the head. Cassidy was gone.

Later that year, William Thadeus Phillips married Gertrude Livesay in Adrian, Michigan, after which they moved to Arizona. Phillips served as a mercenary in the Mexican Revolution of 1910 and later established a business equipment manufacturing company in Spokane, Washington. Phillips prospered and traveled to Wyoming where he visited various Hole-in-the-Wall locations and relatives of Robert Parker.

In 1929, the Depression cost him his manufacturing plant and he wrote and tried to publish a book titled *The Bandit Supreme*, a biography of Butch Cassidy, but found no takers. Revealing an unexpected larcenous streak, he even planned the kidnapping of a wealthy industrialist for ransom, but the scheme never came off.

Finally, William Phillips died of cancer in 1937, an inmate of the county poor farm at Broadacres in a suburb of Spokane.[29] On his death, the Parker relatives swore that he was indeed, Butch Cassidy. The last of the noteworthy outlaws had played out his string.

A .44-caliber Colt Single-Action Army that belonged to Butch Cassidy and saw hard use, like fording a river or using the barrel to twist barbed wire strands. *Guernsey Auctions, New York*

CHAPTER 11

OUTLAWS RIDE TOWARD A BLOODY SUNSET

IT WAS NOT as if someone pulled a switch when the nineteenth century rolled over to become the twentieth century and the old owlhoot trail magically changed. The original muddy, wagon wheel-rutted, horse-manure-strewn path had twisted through crusty wilderness from one tent town to another, each smelling of new lumber and old beer, of unwashed union suits and oiled leather, of blood and gunsmoke and fresh-turned earth.

The new road to perdition's door followed by the next outlaw generation was paved with hot asphalt, the hot breath of V-8 engines, the ripping drumfire of submachine guns echoing down village streets and concrete canyons, of diamond-hard molls, of beer and booze and bulletproof vests. The Stetson's crease became the fedora's snap and everyone packed heat and a flask, dressed to kill in white spats and shiny shoes.

When World War I ended in 1918, it had already laid its heated hands on every global culture. Prohibition had turned Americans into lawbreakers. The war gave them the tools they needed to succeed. The bucking chatter of an automatic gun scything across a line of running men no longer held any mystery.

The Combination Saloon in sunny Utah is typical of the quickly assembled amenities at the end of track as the railroad pushed through and spread its web of prosperity. A couple of snorts of Who-Hit-John with companionable friends at the end of the day was welcome. *Utah Historical Society*

The hosing stream of hot lead hissed overhead, lashed down into helpless positions, or cut the legs from under running men. To hold down the Vickers or Browning machine gun triggers and watch troops bowled over changes a man. *Wikimedia Commons*

Nor did the trench shotgun pumping round after round of buckshot into screaming targets wearing gray overcoats and coal-scuttle helmets. Grenades that once obliterated machine-gun nests decimated saloons that bought their beer from the wrong bootlegger.

Killing technology had flourished during the war years and warehouses filled with murderous surplus offered the next generation of outlaws—both veterans and eager students—arsenals for the taking. Unions rose up against draconian

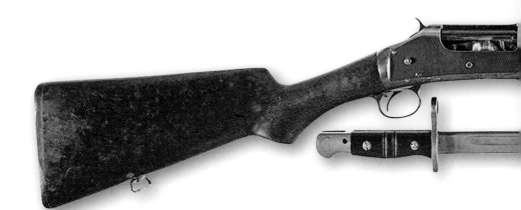

Above: The trench shotgun was created around a Winchester Model 97 with its barrel shortened. It featured a bayonet attachment, perforated hand guard, magazine extended to hold more than three shells, and a shoulder sling for carrying. *Rock Island Auction Company*

Left: J. Edgar Hoover created the Bureau of Investigation to bring various crimes common to all the states under federal jurisdiction. He led a cadre of lawyers and accountants to hunt down criminals across all borders with the help of local police to provide manpower and firearms. His Federal Bureau of Investigation supplanted this organization. *Wikimedia Commons*

labor rules. The stock market blossomed and the twenties roared. Life was short. Get it while you can. Don't have the cash? Use the new layaway plan. Never give a sucker an even break.

The Great War had returned a generation of young men from France who had killed up close—smelled the sweat up close—with the latest technology available from factories at home. Then, in 1929, Wall Street collapsed, banks closed, factory payrolls dried up, and property foreclosures widened the gulf between the super-rich and the new dirt poor.

Judging an outlaw became a matter of degree. Against whom was he outlawing? A .38 Colt revolver pressed against the base of the skull grossed more spending money than a pick and shovel, so why not? Weapons could be stolen, bought from underground stockpiles that had been filched from armories, or purchased legally in many states. Anyone off the street could buy a Thompson

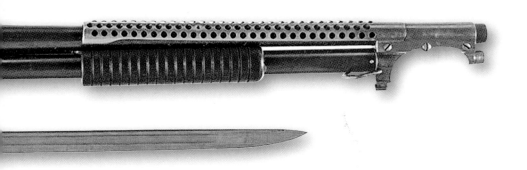

submachine gun with a twenty-round stick magazine or one-hundred-round drum magazine starting at $250.

Police were still fragmented into state, county, and town jurisdictions with virtually no coordinated communications except by telephone. Many communities did not have private lines and shared their telephone time with two or three other neighborhood families on party lines. This made it difficult to alert the county sheriff that a fleeing felon was barreling down Rural Route B if Wanda Fleuglemeyer was busy dictating her crumb cake recipe to Opal Simms.

Stingy budgets based on local taxes and fees often meant officers bought their own uniforms and shared firearms from one shift to the next. Money to buy ammunition for revolver practice down at the city dump, or to build a makeshift range in the city hall basement, was also scarce. Most quickly recruited deputies had only hunting guns, but were not trained in dealing with game that shot back.

After the war, the army had been reduced to barely garrison strength, good for parades and horse cavalry drills. There was no national police force, except the Bureau of Investigation, championed by young lawyer J. Edgar Hoover. These investigators were primarily law school graduates with no police experience and were not allowed to carry weapons until they became agents of the Federal Bureau of Investigation in the 1930s.

As it had been in the Old West, local police trained on the job and the low pay did not attract the best and the brightest. Often, they were men working a second job to feed a family and had no stomach for confronting killer outlaws fleeing a bank heist. They mostly brought in traffic ticket fines paid by flappers and their sheiks, scorching the rural roads in Stutz Bearcats and Marmon Speedsters—if the rural cops were fast enough to catch one.

Speed was another outlaw weapon. While the local laws gave chase in their four-cylinder coupes, Ford Model Ts and secondhand Overlands, the outlaws cranked up Henry Ford's big V-8 engines inside sedans built like

The Ford "Fordor" V-8 sedan was the perfect vehicle for the outlaw trade. It was fast and built like a tank. Five people and four machine guns with extra drum magazines and accompanying sidearms fit inside with comfort, and big windows provided a 360-degree field of fire. *Volo Auto Museum*

bank vaults—some with added steel plates around the gas tank and under the streamlined metal. These gunships carried 360-degree firepower stowed in compartments originally designed to ship jars of moonshine.

Over time, the outlaws themselves began to change. As law enforcement became more formidable, gangs split up—or were shot to pieces by rivals or the law—and solo stars found themselves breaking rocks in soulless prisons, waiting their turn for a seat in the electric chair. Reputations waned with age and their job titles, in the new gangster hierarchy of organized crime, slipped down to cannon fodder and hit men. Like the punch-drunk fighter who carries the champion's spit bucket to the boxing ring, they became curios of another age.

But all that lay in the future. Back when outlaw monikers and gang names were still enough to chill the blood and dry the mouth, another war was brewing as the nation stepped out of the 1910s and into the 1920s. Many entrepreneurs were carving up the country into alcohol-soaked fiefdoms as Prohibition clamped down on the manufacture, sale, and distribution of alcoholic beverages. This period began as the boys came home from war looking for work and found a market for their more deadly skill sets. A time of mayhem, murders and, mergers had begun.

CHAPTER 12

AL JENNINGS

Two-Gun Outlaw and Movie Star

ALPHONSO J. "AL" Jennings first saw the light of day in an abandoned Virginia school house on November 25, 1863, as both the Union and Confederate armies closed in. His resourceful father had settled the family there in order to go back to the plantation house that had been set up as a surgery center and help tend to Confederate wounded.

While nursing her newborn, caring for his four siblings, and making the battered school room livable, Jennings's mother agonized over her husband's fate. Returning home, she baked trays of apple popovers and passed them out to troops straggling by on the road. One of those ragged soldiers was Judge Jennings, coming home with the rest of the defeated Confederacy. Al Jennings had arrived at a time when the country was torn apart by hatred and suspicion. Now, he had to grow up surrounded by the residue and ruin of conflict.

For two years the family survived, moving from place to place. Eventually they settled down in Marion, Ohio, staying to help fight a postwar cholera epidemic. Jennings's father hung out his lawyer shingle once again. Eventually, Al's touchy attitude fired up a petty argument with his father and, packing a few belongings, young Jennings ran away from home, hopped a freight train, and rode the rods under a boxcar west to Cincinnati, Ohio.

While trying to earn money shining boots in the street, he met a cowboy cattle rancher named Jim Stanton. Curious about the boy's defensive chip-on-the-shoulder attitude, he offered Al a job as a herder for thirty dollars a month and living expenses. He also offered to fit the boy out with a saddle, a small horse, and any tack he needed. Al Jennings rode west with Stanton to be a cowboy. Part of that education included the mechanics of a Colt .45 revolver and its required shooting skills.

Al felt at home with the cowboys and read aloud to them at the night campfires from classic adventure books that Stanton had provided him to keep his education going. And then, one day, a dispute arose over ownership of a calf with a blotched brand claimed by the nearby XO ranch. Stanton defended his claim, but the XO owners claimed Stanton was a rustler. One afternoon, a Mexican *vaquero* rode up to where Stanton was working, kneeling by the branding fire. Without a word, the gunman pulled his Colt and shot Stanton in the back.

When Stanton's cowboys found his body, they set off to track down the murderer and exact gun justice. Al searched with them for days until they found the *vaquero* riding into a ranch's corral where he had found a job. The cowboy posse approached him, walking their horses. Al stayed by the fence and watched them say a few words and then draw their guns. The Mexican made his play, but was shot from the saddle. No arrests were made and the posse left as quietly as they had come.

Once again, Al Jennings was on the move. No longer a skinny stripling, Jennings had filled out to become a short, compact, red-headed young man. His life on the plains had given him stamina, judgment, and practical skills to go with his book learning. He drifted up to Colorado and then heard about the imminent Oklahoma Land Rush.

The government had decided to open up the Indian Territory to settlement and its borders were crowded already with land-hungry homesteaders waiting for the army's cannon shot that signaled the gallop for ranchers, nesters, town builders, and entrepreneurs. For Al, it meant a family reunion.

In the town of Woodward, Oklahoma, Al's father and his two brothers, John and Edward, were already practicing law. Al arrived in time to help with a case over disputed cattle pasturage. The opponent's lawyer was firebrand, Temple Houston. Ed Jennings had the stronger case and won, but Houston wouldn't let it go. Al's father, J. D. F. Jennings, a wily politician, begged the boys to back away, but the feud boiled over and after a bitter confrontation, shots rang out. Ed Jennings was dead and John was wounded by Houston. Al stayed true to his promise to Judge Jennings and, though he raged for vengeance, blaming his seething Southern blood, he left town, planning to deal with Houston another day.

Up to this point, the story sounds like a reenactment of Wyatt Earp's life. The good man run afoul of bad luck, puts on a badge, becomes a lawman, but has a brother killed and another wounded, and vows vengeance on their murderers. Jennings took a job as a cowhand for the Spike-S Ranch in the Creek Nation. The owner was a rustler and a front for a gang of Long Riders, the elite of Oklahoma's bad men. Like the Hole in the Wall Gang, they occasionally planned and executed train and bank robberies to keep a little jingle in their pockets. Angry and lacking in love for his fellow man, Jennings fell in with them. Like Earp's vendetta ride to avenge his brothers after the Tombstone fiasco, Jennings parked his principles on a high shelf, buckled on his pair of .45 Colts, and rode off on the owlhoot trail.

The Long Riders with whom he rode were not particularly murderous, nor were they that good at planning their jobs. Jennings discovered right away they needed direction. His legal education and attention to detail improved their results. They were also religiously bound to repay the locals who helped them with cash and baubles to keep everyone in the Oklahoma Hills friendly and close-lipped when the marshals came sniffing around. Still, their scores were not huge and often they had to pass the hat among the train passengers when the express car failed to yield enough riches. Their swag also included a bunch of bananas.

After each robbery, the gang scattered to meet again in a month to dig up their haul and split the take. In 1897, on his way to such a dig, Al caught the curiosity of some heavily armed men when he stopped at a rural store for some soda bread and cheese for breakfast. As he rode away, at a distance of about two hundred yards, the men opened fire on him with rifles. His horse dropped dead. In a fit of rage, Al tore his Winchester rifle from its saddle scabbard and charged, running at the firing men, blazing away as fast as he could pump the rifle's lever. His bullets flew thick and fast and when empty, he dropped the rifle and went for his Colt revolvers. Jennings had filed the triggers off his guns and fanned the hammer with the palm of his hand, ripping a cascade of hot lead at the bewildered back shooters.

They fled, some dropping their guns as they ran. Al stomped up onto the porch of the store and stormed inside, flushed red and seething. "You want an outlaw?" he shouted into the deserted store. "I'll give you one!" He smashed open the cash drawer, scooped out what he could clutch in one hand, stomped outside, and leaped aboard one of the skittish horses tied to the hitching rail. Raking his spurs, he galloped off, leaned down, snatched up his Winchester, and rode off into the Oklahoma hills.[36]

The Jennings Gang rode up to the nondescript bank of Cache, Oklahoma; six hard cases led by Jennings tied up their horses at the hitching rail to the rear of the building. It was a sunny, hot day in 1908 as they filed inside. Suddenly, a bank customer leaped out the open side window and took off running across the square. The gang burst from the bank's front door, guns blazing. Gunsmoke bloomed in great clouds from all the revolvers and two arriving lawmen were disarmed and pushed aside as the gang members mounted up. More gunshots were sprayed at random as townsfolk fled the carnage and then, in a clatter of hooves, the gang galloped down the street and away into the prairie.

In the wake of the confusion, a voice called out, "That was good!"

Back through the dust and gunsmoke, Al Jennings trotted his horse into the

square in front of the bank. "You think you got all that?" he asked the young man standing behind a rectangular box with a crank protruding from its side.

"Yessir, pretty sure it's all there. Looked good to me."

Early silent movies were filmed with hand-cranked cameras. This 1898 Prestwick camera made in England is typical with feed and take-up reels in removable wood boxes. *Internet Encyclopedia of Cinematographers*

This Colt has been modified for fanning the hammer with the palm of the hand by filing off the front of the trigger guard and the trigger. Great speed, much noise, little accuracy. *Rock Island Auction Company*

"How about you?" Jennings asked the director holding the megaphone.

"Looked fine. Who was that fellah who jumped out the window? I don't have that in my script."

Jennings laughed as the rest of his gang straggled in holstering their empty revolvers. "He was in the bank t' make a deposit, I reckon, and when he saw us come in with our hog legs in hand, he took it t' be the real thing, grabbed his money off the counter and was damned lucky the winder was open or he'd a' broke his head."

"When you gonna need us?" asked Bill Tilghman, sitting heavy on a big gelding, sweat running down from his gray hair. The sun glinted off his marshal's badge. Next to him rode Quanah Parker, former Comanche war chief, who now entertained presidents in his lavish home on the reservation. To his left, Sheriff Frank Canton, formerly of Wyoming's Johnson County War bloodbath, reined in his bay mare. He spat into the dirt before he spoke.

"This movie bank robbin' is hot work. We got time for a snort?"

As the cameraman moved his camera, tripod, and film magazine box into the bed of their spring wagon, the fleeing bank robbers and pursuing posse dismounted and walked their horses to the folding canvas watering trough set up next to the production tent beyond the Cache, Oklahoma, town square that formed the very real set. The first shots of Al Jennings's *The Bank Robbery* were in the can. Produced by Heck Thomas and Bill Tilghman, this first plotted Western movie ever shot in the United States was on its way into the film history books.[36]

His anger had completely obscured the bullet wound in his ankle that left a trail of blood oozing from his stirrup. Jennings, however, was a survivor and hooked up with his Spike-S Ranch outlaws for one last big score on which to retire—ninety thousand dollars carried by a Rock Island train. Following an elaborate plan, on October 1, 1897, the robbery was a success until they blew the safe in the express car. Jennings used two sticks of dynamite, but accidently left three more sticks lying on the express car floor. The resulting detonation blasted the car to flinders, but left the safe virtually intact. The blast alerted every marshal and vigilante within one hundred miles that the Jennings Gang was nearby.

After several close calls, the remnants of the gang made their way back to the Spike-S Ranch. On November 30, 1897, a final ambush caused the gang

to scatter when Winchesters fired .30-30 steel jacket bullets backed with smokeless powder and .45-90 buffalo slugs. The gang escaped, but the countryside had turned against them, and they could no longer find safe houses or friendly havens. The marshals bagged Jennings a week later, and after two years of court appearances and legal battles staged by his brother, John, his sentence was reduced from life in prison to five years. He was freed on technicalities in 1902 and received a presidential pardon from Theodore Roosevelt in 1907.

In 1911, Jennings went straight into politics—the closest career he could find to his former work—and, in 1912, won the Democratic nomination for county attorney, but lost the 1914 election. While campaigning, he wrote his autobiography, *Breaking Back* with Will Irwin, which was turned into a silent film produced by Bill Tilghman in 1914, with Al Jennings playing himself for the cameras. His book writing also included a volume covering his relationship

Al Jennings (center) testifying in a congressional committee investigating the Teapot Dome scandal that rocked President Warren Harding's corruption-riddled administration. *Library of Congress*

with a fellow felon and later Ohio State Penitentiary inmate, William Sidney Porter, a short story writer with a popular pen name. The book was *Through the Shadows with O. Henry*, published in 1921.

His crusading activities in Washington put him in front of a congressional committee helping put away some of President Warren G. Harding's crooked cronies caught in the Teapot Dome oil scandal of the early 1920s. The old outlaw lived a long and vigorous life, and he saw another Hollywood movie version of his life, *Al Jennings of Oklahoma*, released in 1951 with Al played by Dan Duryea—a red-headed actor. Jennings died on December 26, 1961, at the age of 102.

CHAPTER 13

THE GREAT WAR (1914–1918)

Quantum Leap for Weapons Tech

THE GREAT WAR had been over for almost two years. General John Taliaferro Thompson and his assistants from the Auto Ordinance Company had set up their samples and demonstration tables facing an empty firing range at Camp Perry, Ohio, beneath a crisp overcast sky. Their audience, a mix of military officers and civilian contractors with their wives, plus the usual clutch of subordinates, gathered, whispering, well behind the red flags that marked the firing line.

Since 1915, Thompson had been working to create a weapon that could put great firepower in the hands of a single soldier. The war in Europe had begun to bog down into fortifications and trenches where ground gains were measured in blood-soaked yards. German Maxim and British Vickers belt-fed, water-cooled, heavy machine guns had chewed through ranks of advancing troops over the artillery-blasted moonscape that stretched from France to Switzerland. To counter these fixed trench positions, soldiers needed a flexible, portable gun platform to clear the ground ahead. They needed to sweep the enemy aside as with a broom—a trench broom.

As a West Point graduate, Thompson was no amateur. His application of a walking weapon of terror offered advancing and defending troops a chance of survival. One man had the firepower of ten. He also knew his audience had seen wonder weapons demonstrated before. They were here because it was their duty to witness these bragging geniuses and winnow out the mad designs from the truly brilliant.

Thompson was anxious to prove his design as he stepped to the table and hefted his fanciful Annihilator, stripped of buttstock and front sights. He seized the grip beneath the barrel, clutched the other grip just behind the trigger, tucked his elbow in against his side, and swung the muzzle down range.

With a yammering blast, a flower of flame burst from the muzzle, propelling a gray rolling cloud of gunsmoke into the field. From the gun's breech spewed a cascade of hot, empty brass cartridge cases in a shining arc. Fearing the weapon was exploding out of control, some of the audience retreated. Others cupped their ears. The sound, described later in the press, resembled someone "tearing an enormous bed sheet." At a rate of 1,500 rounds per minute, the scythe of .45-caliber pistol rounds stitched a path of destruction across the field, letting the imagination paint in the ranks of screaming dying soldiers.

And then it stopped as the last shell casing from the magazine followed its mates to clink into the pile on the gravel at the edge of the firing line. The roiling cloud of gunsmoke rolled away across the imaginary no-man's land. Military officers nearest to Thompson and his terrible gun edged closer examining the new trench broom and visualizing five or ten American soldiers, each with such a weapon.

Thompson's innovative track record had already helped establish the .30-06 rifle bullet and the .45 ACP (Automatic Colt Pistol) bullet as US military standard ammunition, but championing the submachine gun was too radical a departure for

Thompson and his 1921 Tommy Gun at yet another military trial. While its firepower was awesome, the army brass was not convinced that such a terror weapon was needed. *Wikimedia Commons*

Above: This belt-fed prototype Persuader submachine gun is what Thompson developed into the 1921 finished model with the Blish blowback design and other refinements. *Wikimedia Commons*

Right: Firing the Thompson produces considerable fireworks at the muzzle and breech and ejects a torrent of empty shells. The recoil pushes up the muzzle from shot to shot, forcing the shooter to lean forward and have a firm grip on the fore end. *Wikimedia Commons*

army brass. Even unofficial demonstrations and successful tests by the Springfield Armory failed to win official recognition. The army had chosen to adopt the fifty-round capacity Lewis Machine Gun, chambered for the .30-06 US rifle round. The big gun cost double the price and weighed twice as much as the submachine gun—but it had been combat-proven by the British.

The American light machine gun that had gone briefly to France in 1918 was John Browning's Automatic Rifle. The BAR was a compromise light machine gun (LMG) with only a twenty-round box magazine firing the .30-06 US rifle bullet. This amount of ammunition was insufficient to sustain covering or suppression fire, and the size of the mechanism needed to handle the long cartridge at full automatic mode caused a brutal repeating recoil. The BAR was usually fired using a muzzle bipod, or from the hip as walking fire. Anything, however, was better than the French LMG issued to American doughboys in 1918. The

The Lewis Gun was a slow-firing, rotary-drum-loaded machine gun that was clumsy to lug about, required an extra soldier to carry loaded drums, and was air cooled. Its primary service was mounted on airplanes and it fired the US .30-06-caliber rounds. *Wikimedia Commons*

This Browning Automatic Rifle (BAR) is the full combat model with muzzle bipod and the basic twenty-round magazine. The BAR was a combat compromise—too heavy, low ammunition capacity, and a crew of two—but it lasted through World War I, World War II, and Korea. *Rock Island Auction Company*

Chauchat (pronounced "show-shah") was considered by the world's armorers to be the worst LMG ever designed.

When crates of Thompson submachine guns were to be battlefield tested in France, delays caused the shipment to arrive on the New York dock on November 11, 1918—the day the Armistice ending the war was signed by Germany and the Allies. Two years later, the weapon's sales had not improved as the army downsized after the war to end all wars, and was not in the market for a hand-held machine gun. The war department was busy unloading racks of BARs, crates of Winchester Model 1897 twelve-gauge trench shotguns, and the Browning .45-caliber Model 1911 pistols that had also become standard issue in the military. National Guard armories and state and local police took a few— but even at government cost, or for free, civilian budgets could not justify the cost of ammunition ripping through these fully automatic and semiautomatic weapons. The guns also required a lot of practice to be effective.

The Thompson—manufactured by both Colt and Auto Ordinance—cost about $200 on the civilian market (roughly $2,613 in 2013 dollars), but was available over the counter in sporting goods, mail order, and hardware stores. Every civilian market was tapped to thin the inventory of five thousand of the Model 1921 guns. In a nod to the Wild West of the nineteenth century, the Thompson was advertised in a print ad as the ideal gun to defeat cattle rustlers. A cowboy in wooly chaps is shown on his front porch spraying a band of shadowy riders with a hundred-round drum of bullets slung under his personal submachine gun.

Curiously, this nod to the outlaws of the recent past became a harbinger of the present and near future. The roar of machine guns began to echo off cities' concrete canyons and rolling rural plains as the outlaws of the twentieth century made their last stand.

Harkening back to yesteryear, this ad touting the ability to gun down hordes of rustlers and black-hat bad guys by threatened ranch owners hoped to appeal to the rich and well-heeled protecting the family jewels. *Library of Congress*

The "Thompson Anti-Bandit Gun" was sold through civilian distributors as the ultimate protection against the depredations of the unlawful or unruly. The determined-looking policeman hefting the Thompson was the poster child needed to convince potential buyers this was a serious threat to yegs, footpads, muggers, and anarchists. *Wikimedia Commons*

CHAPTER 14

BAD GIRLS

Outlaw Women

GUNMEN IN THE nineteenth and twentieth centuries—no matter how scandalous their reputation or disgusting their demeanor—carried an air of danger and a promise of adventure that some women found irresistible.

Their lives started out innocently enough; few women (or men) were born into the outlaw world. Many turned to a life of crime during their impressionable adolescent years and nearly all their lives ended in untimely deaths, imprisonment, or anonymous solitude.

BELLE STARR, "LADY DESPERADO"

Belle Starr was born Myra Belle Shirley in Carthage, Missouri (some claim it was in Arkansas), in 1848 and enjoyed an uneventful middle-class upbringing, educated in music and the classics. The family moved to Texas following the Civil War and thereafter Belle fell in with certain men with unsavory reputations, including Cole Younger of the notorious Younger gang, but it was another brigand who eventually won her heart.

In 1866, she married outlaw Jim Reed and in between raising two children, operated a livery stable while her husband hid out from the law. In 1874, Reed died, killed by a member of his own gang. Belle sold the stable, left her children with relatives, and headed to the Dallas, Texas, area where she worked as a faro dealer in the town's gambling halls. In her spare time, she tore through the Dallas countryside, stealing cattle, horses, and cash, while decked out in a velvet skirt and large plumed hat, armed with her .36-caliber Manhattan revolver.[37]

By the late 1870s, Belle had moved to Galena, Kansas, and hooked up with Bruce Younger as his common-law wife. Later, she crossed into Oklahoma Indian Territory. She made friendships easily and soon organized her own band of cattle and horse thieves.

During that time, she entered into a common-law marriage with Cherokee Indian Sam Starr. The two continued their life of crime for several years before they were apprehended for horse thievery and sent to the Detroit Federal Prison. After serving their time, they returned to Oklahoma but, once again, Belle was widowed in 1886 when Sam died in a gunfight with an old enemy.

Belle turned herself in to authorities in 1886 after she had been accused of horse thievery. At her trial at the Fort Smith courthouse, she pleaded not guilty, proved her innocence, and was acquitted.[19]

Belle immediately took up with the bandit Jim July, a Creek Indian who was arrested for robbery in 1889. She rode part way to Fort Smith with July where he would face charges. Halfway there, Belle turned

Belle Starr at Fort Smith, Arkansas, in 1886. Her outlaw activities and short fuse made that big revolver on her hip a good idea. She surrendered at Fort Smith rather than be arrested by Bass Reeves. *Wikimedia Commons*

Inset: The .36-caliber Manhattan Navy revolver was Belle's choice. A Colt copy brought out in 1857 after Colt's patent expired. *Courtesy Manhattanfirearms.com*

to return home. She was riding along a lonely stretch of road when a gunman lurking in the bushes, lifted his gun and fired, hitting her twice in the back. She fell to the ground and died. Authorities never found her killer.[38]

PEARL HART: FROM STAGE COACH ROBBER TO VAUDEVILLE

Born in Canada in 1871, Pearl Hart eloped at sixteen, divorced, and then hooked up with Dan Bandman, a gambler and dance-hall musician. The couple

Pearl Harte, all decked out with a Winchester and a Colt Lightning revolver with pearl bird-head grips, poses for a tourist photo after her brief fling at stagecoach robbery executed shanks mare (afoot). She hiked back home in time to be arrested by a bemused sheriff. *Arizona Historical Society*

moved to Phoenix in 1892 and Hart went on to Globe, Arizona, while Bandman was off fighting in the Spanish-American War.

Her life of crime began in 1899 when she met Joe Boot, a German American with little ambition other than to find ways to avail himself of other people's valuables. Short on cash and horses, but long on optimism and self-confidence, Joe and Pearl (dressed as a male desperado) hiked several miles to the nearest stage road and halted a coach on the Globe-Florence route. Joe brandished his scattergun at the frightened passengers who handed over a total of $421, but Pearl found it in her heart to return $1 to each one for a meal when they reached their destination.

Flush with their swag, Pearl and Joe walked the several miles back to their cabin, where they were met by the local sheriff, arrested, and later sentenced to thirty-five years in prison. Eighteen months later, Pearl announced she was pregnant, and to avoid an embarrassing political situation, the warden released her.[37]

Now known as the Arizona Bandit, Hart parlayed her experience and reputation into a traveling show. She rode the circuit dressed in baggy pants, boots, and a cowboy hat, brandishing a rifle and a brace of pistols, telling outrageous stories about her colorful, albeit brief, career. Not everyone believes this. It's also thought that she may have simply married a rancher, settled down, and lived well into her eighties, trying to forget that long walk of so many years before.[39]

LITTLE BRITCHES AND CATTLE ANNIE

These two women with a colorful-yet-short history have been ignored for the most part in the annals of the Wild West. Neither had the skills to sustain a life of crime, but what they lacked in careful planning they made up for in sheer cussedness.

Jennie Stevens, later known as "Little Britches," was born to a God-fearing family in Missouri in 1879. Years later the family moved west, settling in Oklahoma/Indian Territory.

In her early teens, she read about the exploits of the infamous Doolin Gang. The stories so fascinated her that one night she ran off, hoping to join the outlaws. When she lost her horse, she was forced to return home to her angry father. She married in 1895, later committed adultery, and once again found herself back home.

But by that time, the outlaw life was in her blood. She met fellow gunslinger aficionado, Anna McDoulet, also known as "Cattle Annie," at a dance and the two hit it off. That night, they also made the acquaintance of Doolin Gang cohorts and sat enthralled as the gunfighters spun yarn after yarn about the glories of banditry.

The two women followed the Doolins for a brief time before setting off on their own—dressed in suspendered pants and baggy shirts, toting .45 Colts, and riding astride their horses in an unladylike manner. They engaged in horse thievery and sold whiskey to the Native Americans.

Jennie, now called Little Britches, was arrested and taken into custody. The sheriff who had captured her stopped in a restaurant on the way to the prison. Jennie saw a chance to escape out a back door, removed her dress, grabbed a horse, and rode off. The horse belonged to a deputy marshal.

She and Annie were found later, and during the capture attempt, Little Britches grabbed her Winchester rifle, mounted her horse, and fired several shots at the marshal and his deputy as she attempted an escape. Cattle Annie had tried to climb out a window but was caught and handcuffed. One of the marshals shot at Jennie's horse as she rode off. The animal fell, but Little Britches, undaunted, continued to fight viciously before she was subdued and taken to jail. Both women were sentenced to a women's prison in Framingham, Massachusetts, and both served less than a year.

Cattle Annie and Little Britches had a tangled relationship with the Doolin Gang and put up a big rumpus when they were captured. *via John Young, Hubpages*

It's uncertain how they spent their final days. Jennie, as before, returned to her parents and some accounts say she married. Cattle Annie is said to have married once or twice after her release, but all stories indicate that both women lived out their lives in quiet obscurity.[40]

BONNIE PARKER: POET AND KILLER

No one who knew Bonnie Parker as a child and teenager could have predicted her tragic and violent death. When she was born in 1910 in Rowena, Texas, the days of the horse-riding gunslingers were drawing to a close and it was only a matter of time before the bandits used autos for getaways and machine guns as threats. Years later, Bonnie would find both quite useful in her chosen profession.

Bonnie was the second of three children. Following her father's death in 1914, the family moved to West Dallas near her mother's relatives. Bonnie studied hard in school, made the honor roll, wrote poetry, and read romance novels. At sixteen, she married her high school boyfriend, Roy Thornton, but the couple fought constantly, yet Bonnie tried to keep the marriage intact while waitressing in a Dallas café. Roy wound up in prison three years later and Bonnie lost her job when the café closed.

Then, she crossed paths with the handsome and rakish Clyde Barrow, but their romance had barely started when he landed in jail. She smuggled a pistol into his cell, he escaped, was recaptured, and found himself in an Ohio prison farm.

Following Barrow's release, Bonnie and Clyde went on a low-rent crime spree, robbing filling stations, grocery stores, and small-town banks. In April 1932, Bonnie was captured during a robbery attempt and jailed. Clyde murdered a storeowner and fled. After they met up following Bonnie's release two months later, there seemed to be no way of stopping the pair. Bonnie was hooked on the outlaw life. It set her heart racing as the two traveled

Bonnie Parker did not really smoke cigars, nor was she bright enough to cover the license plate on their getaway car. *Wikimedia Commons*

Blanche Barrow was an unwilling recruit into the Barrow gang, following her jailbird husband, Buck Barrow. She was mostly a whining hysteric, but fiercely loyal to Buck. When he was fatally wounded, she stayed with him, facing arrest, and later wrote a book about their adventures. *Wikimedia Commons*

across Texas, Missouri, New Mexico, and Oklahoma. She shot at anyone who got in their way, including a number of law officers.

They lived briefly with Clyde's brother, Buck, and his sister-in-law, Blanche, in a small bungalow in Joplin, Missouri, until their rowdy behavior caused neighbors to call the police. The four took off and engaged in numerous bloody gunfights with the law until Buck was killed and his wife taken prisoner.[41]

One brutal murder took place on Easter Sunday 1934. Two police officers stopped when they saw the outlaws' car by the side of the road. Henry Methvin, a recruited gang member, misunderstood Clyde's order to take the approaching officers—meaning to kidnap them—and Methvin shot them both. Bonnie ambled over to one of the bodies and, with her sawed-off shotgun, aimed two more shots into his noggin, amazed that his head "bounced like a rubber ball."

Their next and last killing of a police officer happened in Commerce, Oklahoma. The all-out manhunt meant that the fugitives had to keep constantly moving, driving back roads, always on the lookout for Texas marshals, local sheriffs, anyone in a marked or unmarked vehicle.

But they could outrun the law only so long. On a sunny day in May 1934, Bonnie Parker and her lover were gunned down on a rural Louisiana back road. Officers fired a total of 184 bullets into the pair. Bonnie's last words were a terrified scream ripped from her throat when bullets began slamming into their

Here's the pair clowning for the Kodak camera and telling the rest of the world where to go. Their lives on the road were squalid and nerve-wracking, so Bonnie lived off the publicity while Clyde simmered and fed off her shallow excitement. *Wikimedia Commons*

car. As one of her poems predicted, it was "death for Bonnie and Clyde."[42]

"MOMMIE DEAREST" AND THE BARKER BOYS

The two-story lakefront cottage in central Florida was a perfect place to spend a relaxing getaway vacation. Ma Barker and her boy Fred thought so too, until that day in January 1935 when fifteen FBI agents drove up, surrounded their hideout, and opened fire. As the feds pumped over two thousand rounds into the house, Fred and his devoted mother grabbed their submachine guns and blasted away from the second floor window. [43]

Determined not to go down without a fight, they fired round after round but, in the end, were no match for Hoover's men. Four hours later, when the lawmen ran out of ammunition, they stopped and listened for sounds from the upper floor before entering the house. A trail of blood led to an upstairs bedroom where they found mother and son lying next to each other, their bodies riddled with bullets. A Tommy gun lay nearby.[43]

Agents also found enough weapons to start a small-scale revolution: two shotguns, two .45-caliber automatics, a .380 automatic, a Winchester rifle, a large quantity of ammunition, bulletproof vests, and over fourteen thousand dollars in cash.

Ma Barker, born Arizona Donnie Clark in in 1873, grew up in Ash Grove, Missouri, attending church and playing the fiddle. But she had a rebellious nature, and longed for a life more exciting than that of a Midwest housewife. Nevertheless, she married George Barker, a local farmer, and bore him four sons—Herman, Lloyd, Arthur, and Fred, whom she loved fiercely. As far as she was concerned, they could do no wrong, even if the authorities disagreed.

The Barker house by a lake where Ma Barker with her son, Fred, sought peace. It later became a shooting gallery. A gun collection arrayed on the front steps demonstrates the variety of Ma's and her boy's toys during the outlaw spree she encouraged. *Federal Bureau of Investigation*

Ma Barker, looking like the nice lady who always bakes cookies for the Sunday church bean feed. She died in hail of bullets with a Thompson submachine gun cradled in her arms. *Wikimedia Commons*

By the time the Barker sons reached adulthood, all four had served a number of prison sentences for petty crimes. No matter how often they were arrested and sent to jail, their mother angrily defended them to her husband and neighbors. After the family moved to Oklahoma, George, unable to control his wife and sons, finally abandoned the family. Fred and Arthur were serving time. Herman had committed suicide in 1927 when he was stopped at a police roadblock.

Arizona, now known as "Kate," settled in a cabin near Tulsa and waited for her remaining boys to be released. She was overjoyed when Fred was paroled and brought his friend Alvin Karpis, a former inmate, to her cabin. They talked of joining forces as the Barker-Karpis gang and set up plans for a crime spree. Shortly thereafter, Fred and Alvin engaged in a series of armed bank and store robberies. After the boys shot and killed a local sheriff, their lust for wanton violence and murder couldn't be quenched. As a harborer of murderers, Ma Barker was on the lam as well. She'd finally attained the dangerous life she always craved.[44]

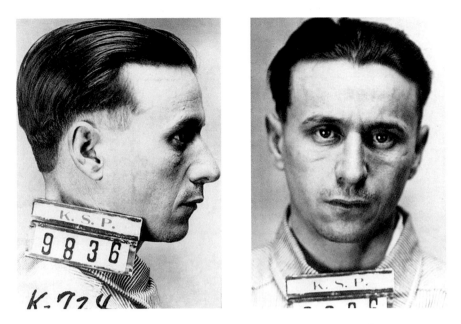

Fred Barker's mug shot. Ma's boys all earned chin numbers before they were finally tracked down. Fred ended up perforated with FBI bullets next to his equally punctured mommy. *Wikimedia Commons*

In September 1932, Arthur was freed and ready for serious mayhem. The gang moved to St. Paul, Minnesota, and, in order to avoid arrest as they pursued their criminal activities, they found a police officer willing to look the other way for some compensation. Ma lived apart from the gang, primarily because she had an intense dislike for any girls they courted.[45]

For the next three years, Fred, Arthur, and Alvin plus a few other hangers-on stormed through the Midwest, holding up banks, murdering lawmen, robbing payrolls, and kidnapping. One of their kidnap victims was William Hamm of Hamm's Brewery whom they released after receiving the hundred-thousand-dollars ransom.

On January 8, 1935, Arthur was arrested in Chicago. Eight days later, the feds descended on the Florida home where Ma Barker and Fred were living, posing, improbably, as a married couple.

Lloyd Barker was released from prison in 1938. The following year, Arthur was shot trying to escape from Alcatraz.

While Ma Barker served as the mastermind of the Barker-Karpis operation, she did not participate in the crimes themselves. But in the eyes of Hoover, the fact that she supported and encouraged her boys justified her death at the hands of the law.[43]

BEHIND EVERY MAN . . .

Kathryn Kelly grew up poor in the Mississippi farmland, but she did have one skill. She knew how to fire a gun. The attractive, dark-haired woman, like her counterparts who followed their men into crime, made friends with gamblers and bootleggers, who provided the thrill of living on the edge.

In Memphis, she met George Kelly, a small-time bootlegger. She supplied him with the proper tools and taught him the one skill that he needed to move up in the world: firing a Thompson submachine gun. Day after day, under Kathryn's watchful eye, he practiced target shooting, yet he never shot and killed anyone. His only victims were the tin cans that fell to their death along a wooden fence.[15]

The couple's crime of choice was kidnapping. In 1932, they seized Howard Woolverton, a banker from South Bend, Indiana. They released him after receiving a promise that the fifty-thousand-dollar ransom would be delivered, but it never arrived. Woolverton later revealed that the Kellys had called him several times demanding the money, but he ignored their calls and eventually the demands stopped and they went away.

After figuring out their mistake, they made sure their next kidnap victim, Oklahoma oilman, Charles F. Urschel, was held for nine days, then released after the Kellys received a two-hundred-thouand-dollar payment. They made one last rookie error: the Kellys forgot that although their victim had been blindfolded,

George "Machine Gun" Kelly's mug shot. He was a polite, inoffensive prisoner whose reputation as an expert tommy gunner was largely the creation of his wife, Kathryn, who steered him through many of his criminal escapades. *Wikimedia Commons*

Facing the music in court in Oklahoma City court, October 1933. Kathryn and George Kelly were both sent to jail—but her sentence was commuted. *Granger Images*

he could hear quite well and listened carefully as they discussed future plans. Once released, Urschel told FBI investigators what he had overheard. This gave the authorities enough information to track down the pair and arrest them two months later.

George and Kathryn Kelly received life sentences. He died in 1954 and in 1958 Kathryn's sentence was commuted.[46]

Very few outlaws were without some female companionship. They needed the devotion and support of a helpmate, and if that helpmate had the shooting skills needed for a successful career in crime, so much the better. In return, their lady loves received the excitement they so desperately craved.

CHAPTER 15

IT'S ALWAYS BEEN ABOUT
FIREPOWER

GENERAL WASHINGTON'S MUSKET-WIELDING band of insurgents relied on buck 'n' ball to volley fire into British ranks. Road agents' pepperbox pistols inspired fear along the Natchez Trace. Colt six-shot Walker revolvers revolvers allowed seventy American soldiers to stop five hundred Mexican troops. Smith and Sharps breechloaders delayed the Confederates storming into Gettysburg. The Henry repeating rifle gave platoon firepower to a squad at the Second Battle of Bull Run.

On July 1, 1898, Americans were pinned down by Spanish fire from San Juan Hill in Cuba. And then, above the sharp cracks of the Spanish Mauser rifles, rose a strange drumming sound. Chaos exploded across the face of the Spanish trenches and chopped at the hilltop blockhouse as a blizzard of heavy bullets tore into the Spanish fortification. Lieutenant Colonel Theodore Roosevelt leaped to his feet. "It's the Gatlings, men! It's our Gatlings!"

In the Great War that rapid fire—trebled in volume—raked the German trenches from belt-fed and box magazine machine guns and pump-action trench shotguns until the war to end all wars choked into silence on November 11, 1918.

Each of these leaps in military firepower volume trickled down to civilian use—especially into the hands of outlaw bands. Post–Civil War raiders overwhelmed a town's defenses long enough to rob a bank, or intimidated a train engineer and express car defenders long enough to dynamite an iron safe. Surprise, planned tactics, and a noisy, smoky crash of firepower usually carried the day. Supplies of the latest weapons technology were always available to outlaws—stolen or bought outright with stolen funds—following military necessity that drove manufacturers to seek new solutions and win production contracts.

The nineteenth-century Industrial Revolution and the advent of mass production created a need for innovative engineers, inventors, chemists, and fabricators on a huge scale to satisfy the growing, increasingly mobile population. Transportation by canal and then the railroads brought raw materials to factories and delivered the output to the field. Military contracts drove the constant search for greater weapon sophistication. The end users for these evolutionary combat designs, besides the original military purchasers, have been outlaws and civilian law enforcement.

A flurry of activity was obvious following the Civil War. Colt, Smith & Wesson, Winchester, Remington, and a rush of new manufacturers hurried to fill the void created by the end of that bloody conflict. The transcontinental railroad, the great western migration from the ruined South, and immigrants from the overcrowded North created a natural market. As noted earlier, virtually every traveling settler carried a firearm of some sort in the wagon bed, coach luggage, or saddle bag.

A Gatling gun on display in a museum. It was a huge pepperbox gun whose barrels were turned and fired with a crank, fed .45-70-caliber cartridges by gravity from a hopper. *Wikimedia Commons*

Lieutenant Colonel Theodore Roosevelt at the center of his Rough Riders and regular infantry command that took Kettle and San Juan hills, ending the Spanish-American War—with the invaluable aid of his Gatling guns. *Wikimedia Commons*

The Great War of 1914 to 1918 offered up a virtual buffet of innovative weapons designs as firepower dominated the battlefield, while tactics only grudgingly inched forward from the Napoleonic Ideal. The conclusion of that brutal slaughter returned to the United States thousands of crippled, shell-shocked, and jaded young men along with steamship loads of state-of-the-art killing machines.

War surplus was a glut on the market. Returning army and navy troops were mustered out to civilian life. Military training bases closed. Warships, armored cars, and tanks were shipped to desert storage depots. People who had served the war effort at home were exhausted. Worst of all, less than a year after the soldiers returned home, Congress passed the Volstead Act, which prohibited the sale or manufacture of alcohol.

Thanks to anti-saloon zealots and religious leaders, America had been sliding toward a ban on the manufacture, sale, and imbibing of all alcoholic beverages for more than a decade and, in 1919, the door slammed shut. As one door closed, another opened. The local speakeasy or blind pig—camouflaged saloons—welcomed thirsty lawbreakers where a snort of the "real stuff right off the boat" could be had served in a coffee cup—at least until the cops battered down the door.

Professional outlaws, holdovers from the bad old days, and the aspiring jobless who had dropped the hammer on a few Germans in France, now became part of Prohibition's illegal work force. Need to protect a truck convoy loaded with kegs of beer or cases of homemade hooch? Make a phone call and twenty guys show up. Need a rival beer baron knocked off to send a message? Many of the old curly wolves were still around, willing to be cannon fodder if success and survival meant a steady job. And there were the killers with the cold eyes and steady hands, the guys who were trusted never to turn yellow in a tight spot.

The big difference now was scale. While roving outlaw bands still knocked over banks and payrolls, the smart money was on organization. A payroll heist, gambling, prostitution, all these income sources were dwarfed by beer and whiskey distribution. The illegal booze businesses required lots of bodies, as well as hierarchies of leadership who could buy off politicians, corrupt judges, and put money in cops' pockets to look the other way.

With the country becoming awash in illegal alcohol, law enforcement found itself undermanned, under gunned, and unprepared to battle crime that was fueled by huge sums of money and increasingly more sophisticated organizational structure. Marshals, sheriffs, and deputies in the Wild West had always found themselves struggling to catch up with the gangs and bandits who had the sympathies of the rural folk who knew what it was like to be shoved off their land or wiped out by bank failures.

But now, Prohibition had turned large numbers of Americans into deliberate law breakers, cooking mash, fermenting beer, stirring bathtubs of homemade gin with canoe paddles—whole families risking fines and jail time—flaunting a Constitutional amendment. Growing criminal organizations not only tapped into the nations' freshly acquired thirst, they became cash-on-the-barrelhead distributors for distilleries run by mom-and-pop families who went to church every Sunday, entered Granny's apple pies in the county fair, and flew the flag on the Fourth of July. Besides, most of the gangster killings shot up other gangsters. So, as long as civilians went unharmed, many lawmen looked the other way.

During the 1920s, while organized crime flourished, independent gangs of outlaws kept the trade alive outside the big cities and avoided turf war blood

Busting up a brewery was heavy work unless you wore a suit. Every raid drew a crowd—
some observers waited downstream for floating kegs that still had a top and a bung in place. Other
observers wept openly. *Wikimedia Commons*

baths. Solo leaders surrounded themselves with crooks they understood: former
juvenile hard cases, penitentiary escapees, disenchanted army vets, or techni-
cians with a love of craft who could make a Thompson sing like an opera star.
Disenchanted younger members of rural families discovered that corn was more
valuable fermenting in a pot still than dripping butter from a cob. Raids by local

These police officers staged this photograph showing modern tactics at a road checkpoint by covering this approaching car with a Thompson. Reality was more like a pair of bored deputies toting family shotguns. *Wikimedia Commons*

law that busted up the stills and beer vats created fan clubs for the gangs who bought the farmers' illegal production with hard cash.

Too many gang recruits came from local lads locked up alongside hard-time criminals who taught the rudiments of the owlhoot trail. One of those lessons was that packing a gun confers power; the bigger the gun, the more power.

Boosted in authority by the amounts of money raised by gangs defying Prohibition, the outlaw-turned-gunman flourished in cities and rural areas. Gang control of illegal alcohol eroded law enforcement and became its own culture. In Chicago alone—the hub of internecine criminal warfare—four years of assassinations resulted in 215 murders, yet no convictions were secured by the legal process. The frustrated police during this same period shot and killed 160 criminals in running gun battles—eliminating the value of the code of silence evoked by the underworld when it came to legal prosecution.[47]

Add to this carnage the open emergence of the *Unione Siciliana* (equated with the Mafia) and their continuing blood vendettas brought over from Sicily and inflamed by booze distribution turf wars. The gun had become judge and jury, forever linking what had begun during nineteenth-century

continued on page 170

The new owlhoot trail led straight through Cromwell, Oklahoma, a square mile of spit-and-sawdust saloons, the rankest brothels, and flophouse hangouts of the worst drug-snorting, liquor-swilling, murderous outlaws west of the Mississippi— all surrounded by profit-pumping oil rigs. The quickest way to get rich in Cromwell was to be a federal Prohibition agent and collect look-the-other-way payoffs with both hands. Wiley Lynn was reported to be that sort.

On November 1, 1924, good old Wiley was taking the air with his two favorite hookers, Rose Lutke, a local brothel madam, and one of her employees, Eva Cator, and Eva's John for the evening, an army sergeant on furlough. All were three sheets to the wind, and Wiley, in an apparent drunken haze, ripped two pistol shots into the sky to celebrate.[29]

Stepping into the street from Ma's Cafe came a figure everyone recognized. A year ago, he had arrived as the new deputy US marshal and, without so much as a howdy-do, began shutting down seventy of the worst of the slop chutes and bug parlors. In a year's time, he had arrested sixteen hardened criminals and chased more than five hundred would-be outlaws from the district.

This Halloween night, his gun, a nickel-plated, engraved Colt Single Action Army .45 was in his hand as he walked straight up to Wiley and pinned the agent's gun hand against his body. As the marshal's deputy ran up to take away Wiley's

Colt Single Action Army, .45 caliber, ca. 1882, owned and used by Bill Tilghman while in Dodge City

Tilghman's Colt .45-caliber Single Action Army revolver displayed at Dodge City's Boot Hill Museum. Outlaws were not the only shootists who liked a pretty gun. The silver and engraving add a civilized touch to a very uncivilized occupation—on both sides of the badge. *Boot Hill Museum/ Gerry Souter*

gun, the marshal holstered his Colt and took his eyes off the prisoner. The suddenly sober drunk pulled a snub-nosed hideout .45-caliber revolver from his coat pocket and fired twice at point blank range.

Bill Tilghman, gray in his twilight years, accepted one last marshal's assignment in 1924 to clean up Cromwell, Oklahoma. He's packing his engraved Colt .45—an old friend—and a Winchester 73. *Wikimedia Commons*

Seventy-year-old Bill Tilghman, one of the Three Guardsmen who, along with Heck Thomas and Chris Madsen, had cleaned the criminals out of Judge Isaac Parker's Fort Smith district, fell back dead with two bullets in his chest. Wiley climbed into the waiting automobile and drove off with Rose Lutke. The gunman was eventually acquitted since no Cromwell resident in his right mind would testify for the prosecution. But men like Bill Tilghman were never without friends.

Wiley was eventually gunned down by Oklahoma State Crime Bureau Agent Crockett Long. One month after Tilghman's death, printed fliers were distributed throughout Cromwell warning its unsavory denizens to get out. And then, one night, a large group of men wearing white sheets to look like the Knights of the Klu Klux Klan (a very popular social club in 1924) paid Cromwell a visit with kerosene-dipped torches. When the sun rose next morning, most of the town's houses of ill repute were nothing more than smoldering stains on the Oklahoma prairie.

Bill Tilghman was a nineteenth-century lawman who had crossed into the Golden Age, lived through the Great War years, and ran out his string in the Roaring Twenties with grace and purpose. From town marshal of Dodge City to US marshal in Indian Territory, he was elected sheriff of Lincoln County in 1900, state delegate to the Democratic Convention in 1902, and appointed special US representative to Mexico by President Theodore Roosevelt in 1904. On reading a requested personal report from Tilghman, Roosevelt was so impressed with his bully choice, he said, "Tilghman would charge hell with a bucket of water."

Fascinated by the burgeoning silent film industry, Bill invested in Al Jennings's short movie, *The Bank Robbery*, and went on to write, produce, and direct his own film, *The Passing of the Oklahoma Outlaws*. At age seventy, Tilghman could have retired to his nationally praised Oakland Farm, where he raised purebred horses, Jersey cattle, and Poland hogs. Instead, he accepted the deputy marshal job in that contemptible little Oklahoma backwater. He was a lawman from his Stetson hat to the soles of his boots. When warned that his age had slowed him a bit, he replied, "It's better to die in a gunfight than in a bed."[48]

continued from page 167

western expansion with the hard, cynical edge of modern urban culture. In effect, the owlhoot trail became a highway.

Outlaws feared relentless lawmen such as Tilghman, Chris Madsen, Heck Thomas, Joe LeFors, and Texas Rangers such as James Gillett, John Armstrong, and later Frank Hamer, who tracked down Bonnie Parker and Clyde Barrow. Even Hoover, founder of the Federal Bureau of Investigation, for all his faults and eccentricities, was a single-minded man hunter. Efficient law enforcement had struggled to establish itself in a growing country based on liberty and freedom. A uniformed police force was considered an occupying army, enforcers rather than protectors.

Back in England, it was 1829 before the first metropolitan police force was created by Robert (Bobby) Peal. New York City followed in 1845 with the New York Municipal Police Force. Their patrolmen wore a copper badge of authority and came to be known as "coppers" or "cops" while their London counterparts were dubbed "pealers." Both forces were unarmed at the start, but criminals had no such limits.

In 1857, the Baltimore police were the first force to arm patrolmen who were combating gang and labor riots. Their weapon of choice was the Colt 1849 Pocket Model percussion revolver. In other cities and villages, officers bought their own sidearms, often as cheap as possible. By 1895, Theodore Roosevelt, then New York's police commissioner, standardized the Colt Police Positive revolver in .32 long-caliber and set up a training program for all officers and patrolmen. By 1901, the caliber was raised to the .38 Long Colt.

The 1849 Colt Pocket Model packed a .36-caliber ball ahead of its powder load and a percussion cap, and made for a small package for a policeman to carry in uniform or plain clothes. The Colt was popular and reliable. *Rock Island Auction Company*

The twentieth century marked the apogee of the independent outlaw. City, state, and federal agencies began to consider law enforcement to be a science as well as a practical application of the five senses. The Bertillon method of facial measurements to determine a suspect's criminal potential or involvement in a crime had been replaced by fingerprints. Blood typing had become more sophisticated. Photographs were circulated in newspapers and sent across the country by wire photo over telephone wires. One-way and then two-way radio broadcasts linked squad cars to communication centers. But new training classes that looked like college courses really improved the quality of officers on the streets from detective to patrolman.

These changes did not take place overnight. Grinding examples of poor training and inadequate facilities hounded law enforcement from the small towns to large cities. Two examples can serve as tragic true tales of languishing law enforcement as quoted from Joe Dyment's article in the 1957 issue of *Guns* magazine:

> [A] lieutenant on a big city police force appeared at a gun repair shop with his service pistol wrapped carefully in a hotel dinner napkin. Trouble? The gun was cocked. The officer had cocked it in anticipation of trouble which had not developed and he did not know how to uncock it without pulling the trigger.
>
> Then there is the one about the officers who were called to dispose of a large dog that had bitten several children in a school yard. The policemen approached within a few yards and commenced firing. They ran out of ammunition. The dog, no longer amused, went home. The police followed, and the scene was repeated. Nobody knows (or will tell) how many shots were fired, but all agree that the dog was not hit. The dog catcher was called, finally. He caught the dog.[49]

Roosevelt's adopting the Colt New Police Positive in .32 Long-caliber was hardly a man-stopper, but its cost was manageable for the force. Faced with a foaming madman, you had six tries to bring him down. *Caldwell Auctions*

With incompetence and graft reaching into the lowest and highest levels of political life and law enforcement, gangs found an open invitation to take their cut of the pie. Outlaws had always been a part of survival in the immigrant and underemployed population, usually sorting out according to nationality through social clubs and neighborhoods where everyone spoke the same language. Irish, Jewish, Italian, Polish, and African American bonds drew the underprivileged and opportunistic together as if the cities were walled up into feudal fortresses without walls, but with brutally defined borders.

G-E model 4MC2B1 control unit and Automatic Electric Co. monophone hand set installed on dash of Ford 1938 automobile. For use with model 4G1B1, 15-watt crystal-controlled ultra-high-frequency mobile transmitter. 1938.

This patrol car sports a roof liner-mounted speaker for "Calling all cars!" announcements, plus a telephone handset on the dash for talking back to headquarters—and eventually between individual cars. *Wikimedia Commons*

Where once the weapon of choice for the aspiring footpad, yegg, or pimp was a cudgel, a bar of soap wrapped in a sock, a brass knuckle-duster, or a push-button flick-knife, advancing technology offered a virtually unlimited choice of affordable firearms. The Sears, Roebuck & Company catalog contained twenty-two pages of guns and ammunition. It included everything from an "A. J. Aubrey Self-Cocking, Automatic-ejecting .38-caliber revolver with a three-and-a-half-inch barrel for $3.75" to a "Forehand & Wadsworth New Double Action, Self-cocking Revolver in .38-caliber with a two-and-a-half-inch barrel for $1.45. For Home or Pocket."[30] In Chicago, during the late nineteenth century, it was possible to rent a gun for an hour and return it to get your deposit back.[50]

Compare these prices with the cost of a typical restaurant dinner at New York City's Alice Foot MacDougal's Cortile (open internal courtyard of a stately building) in 1929 that included: "Chicken a la King, Hearts of Lettuce with French dressing and pear stuffed with cream cheese and nut" for $2.25. Out in the sticks, you could fill up at Cooper's Cafeteria in Champaign, Illinois, with "veal loaf with

An FBI training course teaches the basics for handling the difficult Thompson submachine gun. It was just one of the firearms proficiency programs required. *Federal Bureau of Investigation*

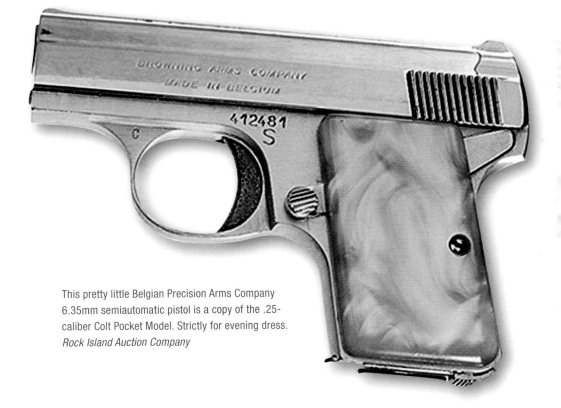

This pretty little Belgian Precision Arms Company 6.35mm semiautomatic pistol is a copy of the .25-caliber Colt Pocket Model. Strictly for evening dress. *Rock Island Auction Company*

tomato sauce, mashed potatoes, cabbage salad, apple pie and a second cup of coffee" for twenty-five cents in 1922.[51] The price of a ten-minute adventure with a hooker ran an average of three dollars. So, an outlaw looking for a good time in the mid-1920s could eat, shoot, and get laid for less than ten bucks.

Many of the cheap belly guns, or pocket guns, were reverse-engineered knock-offs of the major manufacturers: Colt, Smith & Wesson, Remington, Iver Johnson, and Harrington & Richardson. The advance from old black powder-fueled cartridges to the more powerful smokeless gun powder overstressed the knock-off handguns, shredding the digits of penny-wise, pound-foolish desperados.

Successful outlaws of the twenties were not afraid to test a new technology if it gave them an edge over their rivals or the law. While they might be short of book learning, they possessed two necessary drivers to achieve their goals: animal cunning and blind ambition. Like any good entrepreneur, to fill in the gaps in their own knowledge, they hired smart people and specialists.

In the atmosphere of anything goes in the 1920s, where a nip of gin from a pocket flask could earn a couple of nights in the pokey, and folks in the know were shoving their savings into the soaring stock market, the risks and rewards winked at both the law of the land and the law of averages. Normally law-abiding citizens learned it was better not to ask too many questions when someone offered you a sure thing.

Another phenomenon that fueled the hot and fast lifestyles of the Jazz Age and later kept hope alive during the Great Depression were the movies. The silent-film era whetted the public's appetite for escapism and harmless thrills just as the penny-dreadful paperback books teased the imagination of nineteenth-century readers. The hyperbole of yellow journalism, as practiced by the turn-of-the-century press, combined with the advent of dramatic action-filled stories on the screen, complete with sound after 1927.

Movie versions of real outlaws came to life, illustrated with blazing guns and glamorous, luscious molls. James Cagney played tough killers who loved their moms, as well as courageous federal bureau agents who idolized Hoover. Humphrey Bogart could play a Dillinger lookalike in *Petrified Forest* or a tough private eye in the *Maltese Falcon*. Edward G. Robinson's big break came with the role of Rico, the half-mad Capone-esque outlaw in *Little Caesar*. Mickey Rooney stepped easily into the lookalike role of *Baby Face Nelson*.

Like the potboiler writers of the penny dreadfuls, screenwriters offered up killers and robbers with sympathetic backgrounds. They were required by the box office to show that every mother's boy had a kind heart even as he tucked a Thompson submachine gun under his arm and laughed as he turned movie good and bad guys into movie Thompson submachine gun carnage.

THE THOMPSON SUBMACHINE GUN—AN UNLIKELY ICON

As outlaw weapons go, the Thompson was a handful. But its arrival was a natural evolution from Richard Jordan Gatling's drum fire that saved American lives

In *The Petrified Forest*, Humphrey Bogart gave a John Dillinger look-alike performance as a wanted outlaw holed up with cabin full of hostages as the cops close in. Bogart was another good bad guy that made the 1920s and 1930s so interesting. This is a still from the 1955 TV remake. *Wikimedia Commons*

on the slope of Cuba's San Juan Hill in 1898, the Browning and Vickers water-cooled, belt-fed guns that raked no-man's land in 1918, and failed attempts like the French Chauchat or the Colt potato-digger.

While the Gatling was the breakthrough gun of the 1860s, it was only a reworking of the 1830's pepperbox multibarrel pistol. The fast-shooting Gatling used gears and cams to rotate the barrels and sequence the sliding breech bolts for loading, firing, and ejection while gravity fed cartridges into the breech from the magazine. The Gatling's hand crank speed determined its semiautomatic shots-per-minute. The Thompson was new from removable shoulder stock to muzzle brake.

It is heavy for a hand-held weapon. The basic 1921 gun sans shoulder stock and magazine weighs eight pounds, thirteen ounces. A shoulder stock adds one pound, thirteen ounces. Latch on a hundred-round drum magazine weighing eight pounds, eight ounces, loaded with .45-caliber lead bullets and you are hefting nineteen pounds, two ounces. Its trigger pull requires ten pounds of pressure to trip the firing mechanism, whereas a typical sporting rifle needs only about four pounds. In the Thompson's favor, it can be field stripped for cleaning or repairs in about thirty-five seconds, and reassembled in one and a quarter minutes in total darkness without the aid of tools.

When Thompson was considering the fully automatic firing mechanism, he eliminated the full blowback—using the energy of the firing cartridge to drive back the bolt, eject the case, and initiate the spring-driven auto-reload sequence—as primitive. Gas-operation using a piston was too complex, and any other patented system that might require a licensing fee, too expensive. His search introduced him to US Navy Cmdr. John Bell Blish, who had created a design based on a friction-delayed blowback action using the adhesion of two inclined dissimilar (steel and bronze) metal surfaces (wedges) pressed together.

Blish's observation came from watching the firing of large naval guns using threaded breeches of dissimilar metals that were sealed by the pressure of the

A Cutts Compensator screwed into the muzzle is for the testosterone-deprived. It channels gas pushing behind the bullet up through the slots, keeping the muzzle from rising with each recoil kick. *Wikimedia Commons*

exploding shot. Scaling this principle back to a hand-held weapon required a small pistol-caliber bullet to achieve the needed short lock time. The .45 ACP round developed for the Colt Model 1911 semiautomatic pistol was ideal. In the final iteration of the Thompson mechanism, subsequent designers improved on Blish's patent, turning the gun into a less expensive-to-produce direct blowback gun in time for mass production during World War II.[52]

Another innovation that improved handling under full automatic fire is the Cutts Compensator that extends the ten-inch barrel length by two inches. This muzzle brake, added in 1926, consists of a steel chamber fastened to the muzzle with saw cuts across the top for venting gas upward as it enters the chamber behind the exiting bullet, forcing the barrel downward, countering the recoil caused by the breech lock's spring return to battery after each shot.

These Thompson submachine guns are the 1921 model with twenty-round "stick" magazines in place. A favored firing position was tucked in against the body and walk short bursts into the target. *Wikimedia Commons*

CHAPTER 16

THE SHELTON AND BIRGER GANGS

Rural Roughnecks

ABRISK WIND RUFFLED the grass beneath a high overcast sky as Elmer Kane strode across a bleak field with his partner, Henry Mundale. They, in turn, were flanked by their keepers, two quiet men dressed in rumpled suits and fedora hats, who had driven them to the location that morning. Ahead of them, closely watched activity was turning their livelihood into a weapon of war.

Elmer and Henry were aviators. On the previous day, November 11, 1926—Armistice Day—they had been piloting their two Curtiss JN-4 Jenny biplanes from their last barnstorming gig in Sparta, Illinois, when Elmer's plane was damaged while making a landing to hunt up some gasoline. The World War I surplus "aeroplanes" were two-seater training aircraft used to instruct American and British combat pilots who were then sent to France. By the war's end Curtiss had built more than six thousand of the durable aircraft whose success was instrumental in putting the Wright brothers' antiquated designs out of business.[53]

Kane and Mundale were finishing their field repairs of the aeroplane when three men drove up and offered to give them a lift to the nearby town of Benton to fill their gasoline cans. The drive ended at a filling station where the gas was pumped into the cans though a chamois filter to screen out bugs and other debris that could fatally clog a carburetor at an altitude of five thousand feet. That chore completed, the sedan was driven to the home of West City mayor, Joe Adams, who had guests that included Carl and Bernie Shelton and other members of southern Illinois's notorious Shelton gang.

Over a convivial lunch, the two aviators finally received the bill for all this service and good will. Instead of their usual moneymakers—performing aerial stunts at county fairs, or flying locals and farmers above their town and property for a small fee—one of the planes would fly over the nearby Shady Rest Inn, owned by Shelton arch rival Charlie Birger, and bomb it. The pilots would spend the night at Gus Adams's house—Joe's brother—and take off in the morning. In the meantime, the Sheltons would prepare the aerial bombs. Kane and Mundale's payment would be a thousand dollars and a new car.

That night, as the two pilots tried to get some sleep at Gus Adams's house, a car drove by and a burst of gunfire stitched across the home, blowing out windows, puncturing the walls, shattering glassware and china. The car kept on going. This visit was just a wakeup call from the Birgers, signaling that they were keeping an eye on the Sheltons. If there had been any doubt as to completing this dive-bombing exercise, that .45-caliber curtain-raiser erased it. The dawn patrol was on.

The closer Kane and Mundale got to the aeroplane parked on the barren field, the more they saw. The Sheltons' homemade bombs were simply sticks of dynamite laced together with copper wire and a small bottle of clear liquid tied into the package. Both men swallowed hard as they realized why the Shelton gangsters loading the bombs into the plane seemed so nervous. Their fear, as they handed each bomb up to Ray Walker, a Shelton gunman and the bombardier in the plane's front seat, came from handling the small glass bottles of nitroglycerin that would shatter and trigger the explosives.

Finally, Kane slipped on his leather flying coat, helmet, and gauntlets and climbed up from the wing root to the Jenny's rear seat. Mundale went to the biplane's propeller, took hold, and walked the prop though a half revolution to prime the carburetor. Kane shouted, "Contact," as he engaged the battery and Mundale kicked and gave the prop a spin. It caught on the first try and exhaust sputtered from the engine's pipe. The Shelton men hung onto the Jenny's tail and wings—it had no brakes—and made jokes in poor taste for their cohort belted into the plane's front seat, surrounded by bundles of dynamite and nitro. The take-off was a bumpy one and everyone held their breath until the jouncing, rattling aircraft was airborne and circling onto the heading that led to the Shady Rest Inn.

Kane reduced his power by blipping his engine off and on. He banked into a turn that would carry him down in swooping circles to arrive above the rooftops of their target. Walker had to lean out of the cockpit into the sixty-mile-per-hour slipstream each time to drop one of the dynamite bombs and clear the plane's bottom wing. Kane dipped his wings down as his final circle's radius approached the inn. Walker dropped the bomb and Kane hauled back on the stick. With a snarl, the aeroplane grabbed the sky and lifted up. The bomb floated down—surprisingly on target. Walker and Kane watched the bomb strike the inn, and fail to explode. The thud of the bomb bouncing off the shingles stirred the hornet's nest of Birger gunmen and they piled out of the inn pointing at the biplane and cocking their rifles and Thompson submachine guns.

Kane felt the wing braces strain as he flung the Curtiss into a tighter circle to avoid the cone of gunfire reaching up from the inn. He snapped into a chandelle, reversing course, and bore in for a second run. This time, Walker held the last two bombs. Once again, his aim was good and they tumbled down toward the inn. On the ground, Birger gunmen scattered. The Jenny shot across the rooftop chimneys and Kane pulled the stick into his stomach. The second bomb was another dud, but the third exploded with a great display, detonating against the roof of the structure used for staging cockfights.

Arcs of submachine gun fire followed the biplane as it clawed for altitude, but not a single shot touched its canvas skin. Kane flew to an airfield at DuQuoin, where the elated Walker disembarked. Kane then flew onto a third small field where Henry Muldane waited with the second Curtiss aeroplane, their new automobile, and one thousand dollars in cash.

Sadly, all did not come up roses for the intrepid pilots. The automobile they were given turned out to be hot. It was stolen from in front of a movie theater nine days before the air raid. When the police found it in February 1927 in Cedar Falls, Iowa, the boys were arrested and charged with transporting a stolen car across state borders. They, of course, denied all knowledge that it was a stolen car as they were carted off to begin their sixty-day jail sentence. Fortunately for them, there was no law on the books that forbade dropping aerial bombs on roadhouses.[54]

The colorful escapades of the Shelton brothers and other notorious gangsters are the stuff of legends in southern Illinois. Carl, Earl, and Bernie

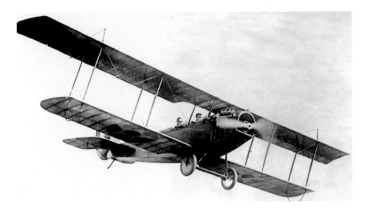

A Curtiss JN-4 Jenny as might have been seen by the lads at the Shady Rest as it winged overhead on a bombing run in the middle of the Shelton-Birger war. *Wikimedia Commons*

grew up quietly in the early 1900s in Wayne County farm country, the sons of Ben and Agnes Shelton. Shooting was part of the family's daily routine. When dinnertime rolled around, Ben would grab his rifle and head for the woods to bring home the main course.[54]

As young men, the brothers learned that, done right, crime often did pay. In the early 1920s, after serving time for participating in a holdup followed by a stint in the army during World War I, Earl opened a booze joint, road house, and gambling den in East St. Louis, Illinois. Soon after, he brought Carl and Bernie into the family business and it wasn't long before the three became the kingpins of Midwest rum runners. Their success drew local hoodlum wannabes like flies to manure and, along with them, came an arsenal of weapons that was more of a dog's breakfast than a tactical force of arms. Krag-Jorgensen 1898 .30-40-caliber carbines were popular alongside Winchester Model 1894 rifles, long-barreled shotguns, Springfield .03 rifles, Winchester 1905 Model 35 automatic rifles and—the king of the hill— a collection of Thompson sub-machine guns sporting one-hundred-round drum magazines. Pockets and waistbands bulged with a mixed bag of revolvers and Colt semiautomatic pistols. Carl Shelton favored a hefty Colt .45 revolver, nickel-plated with aged yellow ivory grips.[55]

For the next several years, it was nearly impossible to keep track of shootings, framings, score-settlings, back-stabbings, negotiations, and which lawman was on which outlaw's payroll without a diagram or scorecard.

The Ku Klux Klan had gained a foothold in southern Illinois in 1919 following the passage of the Volstead Act. The KKK saw this as an opportunity to rid the area of Catholics and foreigners, the groups most likely to turn to bootlegging, since alcohol was ingrained in their culture. It therefore launched an all-out campaign against anyone who set up a moonshine operation. By 1923, they had become a force to be reckoned with and hired S. Glenn Young, a former revenuer, to help them clamp down on the vermin that sought to destroy the morals of the good people of Williamson County.[56]

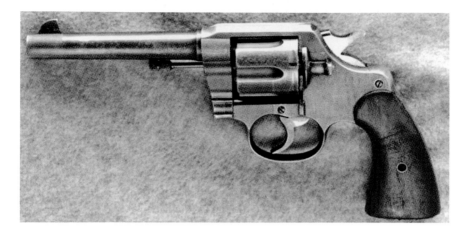

Carl Shelton carried a reliable .45 Long Colt revolver with ivory grips and full nickel plating. *Wikimedia Commons*

The Sheltons' first order of business was to drive out the KKK and Glenn Young. Young himself had an itchy trigger finger and, while serving as a revenue agent, had been under investigation by the federal government for conduct unbecoming an officer. His eventual dismissal by the government left him free to work for the KKK as the group gathered white Anglo Saxon Protestants together to storm the citadels of evil.[54][55]

In 1924, Young and his wife were victims of a drive-by shooting when five men in a car pulled up and fired with pistols and shotguns. Both survived, but later Young was killed by Deputy Sheriff and anti-Klansman Ora Thomas in a shoot-out reminiscent of the Old West when both drew their pistols and faced off in a hotel in Herrin, Illinois. Thomas came out alive but suffered gunshot wounds minutes later when one of Young's henchmen opened fire.[55]

As Thomas lay dying in hospital, Klansmen broke into his room and beat on his bandaged face. Thomas died that night.[57]

More bloody battles followed until, finally, the Sheltons, fearful for their lives, quietly departed for Florida and points south to expand their bootlegging enterprise and establish a shipping route.

Liquor jars filled cavities under seats and beneath the floors of sedans, coupes, and trucks. Drivers chose lesser-known routes to avoid big cities where federal tax agents—revenuers—might spot them. When they arrived in southern Indiana, they were met by heavily armed escorts for the remainder of the journey into Illinois.[57]

One of the Sheltons' best customers was Charlie Birger, who had engaged in several bootlegging, gambling, and killing escapades in his early years

Bootleggers in the 1920s were nothing if not creative. One whiskey manufacturer took a strip of metal and attached wooden blocks resembling cow's feet to the bottom of his shoes. As he walked through the woods, he'd leave bovine imprints, thus deceiving the revenuers in their search for criminals operating illegal stills. Authorities believed he got his inspiration from a Sherlock Holmes story in which the villain shod his horse with hooves resembling those of a cow. According to the *St. Petersburg Evening Independent*, on May 17, 1922, the shoe was found in Fort Tampa near where a still had been located. The shoe was sent to the prohibition department in Washington.[58]

A revenue agent demonstrates the shoe modified to look like cow footprints to avoid leaving a shoe trail to an illegal alcohol still in the woods.
Wikimedia Commons

and became an expert pistol shot thanks to his army training. Although his expertise helped him wipe out a number of enemies, it was alcohol manufacturing that first landed him in jail in 1923. After his release in 1925, he opened the Shady Rest, a tourist camp and barbecue stand in Williamson County, near Harrisburg. Birger offered entertainment for the whole family. Mom and the kids could enjoy a tasty chicken dinner at the restaurant and later visit the small menagerie out back. Meanwhile, Dad entertained himself watching the action in the dog- and chicken-fighting pits, tossing down a few bottles of homemade brew, or playing a few hands of poker.

Although Birger bought his liquor from the Sheltons, usually he'd dilute it for his wholesale customers. At one point, he offered Carl a partnership in his slot machine operation and Carl took him up on it. As the adage goes, "There is no honor among thieves," and eventually, Shelton got word that Birger was short-changing him on the profits but decided to let that and other possible betrayals pass for the time being.[57]

Rumors began circulating that the KKK was planning to fix the Herrin City elections held on April 13, 1926. The night before the polls opened, Birger

Birger's car at the Shady Rest Lodge decorated with his gang of rural outlaws, all armed to the teeth with a motley collection of semiautomatic, automatic, bolt-action, and lever-action rifles, pistols, and revolvers. Charlie Birger is center on the running board. *Franklin County Historic Preservation Society/Photographer: Dave Cooper*

and the Sheltons, along with friendly law enforcement officials, met and assembled a collection of submachine guns, shotguns, rifles, and pistols to prevent irregularities. The next morning, the Shelton/Birger faction arrived in town and faced off against KKK fanatics. It wasn't long before gunfire filled the air and, toward the end, the gangsters' overheated machine guns jammed, and unable to fight any longer, they fled, leaving dead bodies on both sides in their wake. This was the last time the Birger supporters and the Shelton entourage played on the same side. The KKK men decided their lives weren't worth the fight for clean government and departed soon after, leaving the field wide open for bootlegging.[57]

Now that their common enemy was out of the picture, Shelton's grudge against Birger intensified. Charlie had started to offer near beer as part of his stock and counted on Shelton as one of his customers. It only seemed fair, since he was buying Shelton's whiskey. Shelton thought Birger's product was not up to his standards, and his resentment about the slot machine operation turned into full-blown hostility. Moreover, both men coveted the same southern Illinois territory. Neither was about to give up.[57]

There followed a number of shootings in which some of Shelton's men were gunned down, but no one was ever convicted. By late September 1926, all bets were off. The war escalated, with henchmen and any lawmen who could be bought choosing sides.

The Sheltons set themselves up with an armored truck to use when venturing into Birger territory and initiated a machine gun attack on the Shady Rest. They shot at Art Newman (a Birger aide) and his wife as they approached in their car, then departed to also shoot up Shaw's Garden, a property Birger had his eyes on. Their work done, the brothers headed for East St. Louis to lie low until things cooled down.

The vandalism continued. Birger wrecked Shelton's roadhouse. The Sheltons returned and finished off Shaw's Garden by setting fire to it, and then planted dynamite hoping to draw Birger to the scene. Birger, wise to Shelton's way of thinking, never showed up.

Then came the aerial bombing of the Shady Rest.

In December 1926, Mayor Adams, who had given Carl Shelton free rein in his town, was gunned down at his home by unknown assailants. His widow stated that she felt certain Charlie Birger had hired the killers.[54][57]

The Sheltons' troubles with Birger were only beginning. In 1927, Birger revealed to authorities that the Sheltons had committed the Collinsville mail

Charlie Birger carried this Thompson submachine gun whenever facing crowds of Sheltons in heavy gunfire situations. It is stripped down to a waist-level, point-and-shoot weapon with a drum magazine. *Franklin County Historic Preservation Society/Photographer: Dave Cooper*

Birger's henchman, Art Newman, had no problem humiliating himself if it meant one less Shelton in his life. During a particularly bloody period between the Birger and Shelton gangs, Newman and his toadie, Fred Wooten, heard that Earl Shelton was being treated at St. Mary's hospital for a bout of malaria. Art and Fred saw an opportunity they couldn't pass up—a Shelton bedridden and helpless. They decided to pay him a visit.

Knowing the sight of two men heading toward Earl's room might look suspicious, they adorned themselves in garments worn by the fairer sex. For the occasion, Art selected a fetching mink fur cape that draped across his hulking shoulders; Fred chose a slippery silk frock over which he draped a sealskin coat to hide his biceps. A pair of fashionable, concealing cloche hats completed the *haute couture* costumes. As the two *faux femmes* tottered down the hall arm in arm in fashionable pumps, Newman reached into his handbag for his only accessory—a sharp hunting knife.

Just then, they spotted Earl's wife and another woman leaving Earl's room. Thinking that the women might be headed to a meeting with Carl, the would-be assassins reversed direction and followed the ladies; if they could wipe out Carl Shelton, so much the better. Unfortunately, that trail led nowhere.

The boys thought they'd play dress-up again the following night, but Art was detained by police on another matter. As luck would have it, Earl left the hospital shortly thereafter. They'd missed their chance. One wonders if, over the years, Newman and Wooten didn't kick themselves time and again for not sticking—so to speak—with Plan A.[54]

robbery of January 27, 1925, a crime that had remained unsolved. During the trial, Birger, Art Newman, and others presented testimony solid enough to convince the jury in spite of the Sheltons' repeated denials.

The Sheltons received twenty-five-year prison sentences, but, to Birger's dismay, were released on bond in May 1927 after one of the witnesses admitted to perjury in the trial.[55]

Carl, Earl, and Bernie Shelton decided to shift the family business to gambling and established themselves in Peoria. Clyde Garrison, king of the town's illegal gambling operations, decided he needed more muscle following an attempt on his life, during which his wife was killed. For the next several years, the Sheltons helped protect Garrison's gambling and prostitution empire, and then, in 1940, Garrison stepped down to let Carl Shelton take over. Some believe Garrison's relationship with the corrupt mayor of Peoria had deteriorated. Others think that Garrison realized he was no match for Carl Shelton's skills in dealing with politicians and decided it was best to back off. From then on, the Sheltons monitored the town's prostitution ring, slot machines, and any other illegal interests.

Things went well in Peoria until the people elected a new mayor who vowed to rid the town of its sin city reputation. Peoria County was still wide open, so the Sheltons continued to use their only marketable skills to keep the rackets alive.[59]

The brothers didn't count on enemies in Chicago and St. Louis moving in to eliminate their operation. One of these was Charlie Harris, a former employee of Shelton who believed he'd been betrayed by Carl when, years earlier, it appeared his boss had given him counterfeit money to make a whiskey buy, resulting in Harris's arrest. Harris's bitterness hadn't let up and he saw his chance to get even by making friends with local farmers who had grown tired of the Sheltons' protection racket.[60]

By the late 1940s, Carl Shelton had so many enemies he took great care to keep his traveling plans and his whereabouts secret. Yet, even he must have known he

Running out his string, Charlie Birger walks up the thirteen steps to the gallows at Benton. He earned the dubious distinction of being the last man to be executed by hanging in the state of Illinois. *Franklin County Historic Preservation Society/Photographer: Dave Cooper*

Birger with bag on head waiting for the trap to drop. He made a short farewell before the black bag was slipped over his head and the trap was sprung. *Franklin County Historic Preservation Society*

was living on borrowed time. On a sunny October day in 1947, armed with his .45 Colt revolver, he climbed into his jeep and headed down a winding country road toward town, ironically to make arrangements for the drafting of a will. Two of his henchmen following in a truck recalled hearing horns honking—one long and two shorts. As Carl reached a small bridge, a barrage of gunfire rang out. He collapsed, and though mortally wounded, he managed to get off five shots before falling onto the ground. No one was ever convicted of the killing. Bernie Shelton was shot outside a tavern the following year. Earl survived several attempts on his life, but eventually moved to Florida and died in 1986. And so ended the Shelton empire.[54 61]

If there is a gun that is the antithesis of the 1873 Colt Single Action Army revolver, it is the Colt Model 1911 semiautomatic pistol. While the Colt SAA invites the hand to caress its curves and settle into the grip with a lethal curvaceous authority, the Model 1911 challenges the shooter to master its angular brutality. The Colt SAA is greased lightning sculpture, and the Model 1911 is coldly efficient industrial design hacked from a steel ingot. Both are icons. Each perfectly reflects its era.

The single-action revolver is for the short sharp fight. The semiautomatic pistol punches out seven rounds, takes three seconds to slap in a fresh magazine, and is in business as long as targets keep coming. When the automobile replaced the trotting horse, the Model 1911 joined the Thompson submachine gun and the Browning Automatic Rifle as a lead-spitting equalizer with a large punch from a small package that fairly dripped testosterone. There were other semiautomatic pistols that preceded it: the toggle-bolt Borchardt with the strange, coiled clock spring bolt return of 1893; its direct descendent, the sweet-pointing,

The Colt .45ACP Model 1911 semiautomatic pistol was a major leap in technology and became a standard design that continues today. *Wikimedia Commons*

Charlie Birger landed in a courtroom in 1927 when, along with Art Newman and Ray Hyland, he was convicted of engineering the murder of Mayor Adams. Newman and Hyland were sentenced to life imprisonment. Several appeals by his lawyers followed, but to no avail. Charlie Birger climbed the steps to the gallows on April 19, 1928, the last man to be executed by hanging in the state of Illinois. In his final statement before the hood was placed over his head, he said: "I have nothing against anybody. I have forgiven everybody . . . I have nothing to say. Let her go."[55]

hard-kicking 1908 Deutsche Waffen und Munitions fabriken (DWM) Luger; or the elegant 1896 Mauser broom handle C96, the Steyr Mannlicher M1894; and even Colt's own M1900. But these handguns all relied on 7.63mm and 7.65mm cartridges, all roughly .30-caliber that lacked raw stopping power. The Colt 1900 semiautomatic pistol chambered a new .38ACP round that traveled at a higher velocity than the .38 Long Colt standard service cartridges. DWM also developed a round for the Luger specifically to solve the low-velocity problem, the 9mm Parabellum ("for war"), which would become the world's most universally used cartridge.[62]

With the United States embroiled in the turn-of-the-century Philippine Insurrection battling the fierce Moro tribesmen, the army begged for stopping power. Colt 1892 Double-Action revolvers firing .38 Long Colt cartridges were their back-up guns to the fast-firing, slow-loading Krag Jorgensen .30-40 rifle. Often, six revolver shots were not enough to stop a sword-wielding berserk Moro warrior. The press claimed the Moros were "hopped up on drugs" that deadened pain, but that was a face-saving myth.[63]

Colt's Model 1900 was the precursor of the Model 1911. This Colt chambered the .38ACP-caliber round that delivered higher-velocity stopping power than the .38-caliber Long Colt. *Wikimedia Commons*

It is hard to imagine a more awkward looking pistol than the Borchardt 1893 with its toggle-bolt cocking system, but it worked even though a quick draw was out of the question *Wikimedia Commons*

A soldier prized his DWM 1908 Luger as a true refinement with its natural point and the 9mm Parabellum cartridge. The cocking system owed much to the Borchardt, but the workmanship and accuracy were exceptional. *Wikimedia Commons*

These warriors had the same spirit as the later Japanese soldiers in World War II with their code of Bushido—death before surrender. Crates of old .45-caliber Colt Single Action Army revolvers were dug out of storage depots and shipped to the Philippines, but their black powder smoke and slow reload time reduced their efficiency.

This immediate demand for a fast-shooting, hard-hitting, quick-reloading handgun stimulated John Browning to create a semiautomatic pistol for Colt, based on the Model 1900. The army held handgun trials in 1907 and quickly eliminated the designs that did not hold up to combat conditions of weather, terrain, and hard use. After five years of changes and resubmitting designs, only the Colt .45 ACP semiautomatic pistol emerged in 1911.

At one point near the end of the tests in 1910, the Colt fired six thousand rounds over two days with no malfunctions. When the pistol got too hot to handle, it was dunked in water to cool the gun down. The remaining competitor, built by Savage Arms Company, had thirty-seven malfunctions. The Colt Model 1911 pistol went on to be the military's standard sidearm for more than four decades.

Many of today's automatic pistols follow the pattern of the Austrian Glock 17—all lightweight polycarbonate and sleek simplicity designed for two-handed shooting. The Colt and its lookalikes survive because there is an admirable antique quality to their turn-of-the-century complexity. The grip is fat, designed for classic one-handed shooting. It is all bumps and knobs from the hammer to be cocked, to the compressible grip safety and the magazine release button. The Model 1911 weighs almost two and a half pounds empty. And the outlaws of the 1920s and 1930s collected them by the crate.

The C1896 Mauser broom handle became a fixture with many armies as a reliable pistol with a full automatic/shoulder stock version for the not-faint-of-heart. It is an elegant weapon that served all over Europe for fifty years. *Wikimedia Commons*

Designing the 1894 Steyr Mannlicher looks like an exercise in solving one problem after another with no cares about the look, feel, or performance of the final result. *Wikimedia Commons*

CHAPTER 17

HYMAN LEBMAN

Gun Maker to the Stars

GUNS ARE AN outlaw's tools, much like a hammer and screwdriver rest in well-worn hangers on a carpenter's belt. Once an outlaw explored his or her trade, certain tools were preferred for the job of intimidation, firepower, carry-weight, availability, and readily available ammunition. While some guns are easy to conceal, such as the .380 Colt semiautomatic pistol that Dillinger carried in his hip pocket when going to the movies, other firearms required a greater commitment. Slung under a long coat and held in place by a shoulder sling, the stripped-down Thompson submachine gun was justified when its one hundred rounds turned a Clark Street garage into a bullet-riddled, corpse-strewn abattoir.

Some guns, however, didn't exist for certain needs and the outlaw either modified an existing weapon, or struggled along with choices off the rack. Know-how and the ability to mill and drill to fine tolerances canceled out most psychotic gunslingers' handiwork. Enter the professional gunsmith.

Hyman S. Lebman's gun repair and saddle shop at 111 South Flores Street in San Antonio, Texas, smelled of oiled leather, gun oil, sawed hardwood, and hot steel. In the days before the National Firearms Act, passed on July 26, 1934, forbidding the sale or ownership of fully automatic weapons without a federal license, Hyman welcomed visitors who plunked down ready cash for as much machine gun as they could handle. While he sold boots and saddles on the main floor and cheaper guns upstairs arranged in large, empty whiskey barrels, his reputation rested in his basement workshop and how much machine gun he could jam into the smallest package.

The Lebman Baby Machine Gun went viral in the outlaw world where spray-and-pray gunmanship damaged property, chewed through crates of ammunition, and hacked down dozens of lives every year. Lebman's son, Marvin, a retired lawyer, claimed that Dad "hadn't done anything, but sell guns to men in nice suits and hats." In further defense of his old man, Marvin went on to say:

> This was an open business that had doors that were open (to everyone). And we were half a block from City Hall, half a block north of the police department; across the street from the sheriff's office. We did more work with policemen that we did with anyone else.[64]

Considering his proximity to San Antonio's halls of justice, the mind stumbles over Hyman's opportunity to glimpse mug shots of some of his clientele. Be that

The hot Lebman Baby submachine gun relied on the durability of the Colt semiautomatic pistol to withstand the heat and stress of full automatic fire. *Wikimedia Commons*

as it may, the men in "nice suits and hats" beat a path to Lebman's open business to purchase his lethal masterpiece with blood-drenched stolen cash.

Hyman was always on the lookout for new or lightly used .45 ACP Model 1911 Colt semiautomatic pistols. Also snapped up were Colt semiautos in the new .38 Super caliber that launched a light 130-grain bullet at over 1,200 feet per second. These specimens were stripped and tweaked to handle a higher rate of fire than one shot per trigger pull. Next, the sear and firing pin were modified to allow the bolt to keep on loading, firing, and then ejecting the empty cases as long as the trigger was depressed. The result was an amazing cyclic rate of one thousand rounds per minute.

Controlling this lethal fire hose of hot lead proved frightening in its early development. One day while testing a version of the Baby, Hyman's pistol screamed through a magazine load and the barrel swung up sharply from repetitive recoil. The ragged end of the burst stitched through the basement ceiling near where Marvin was standing upstairs. After almost—at the very least—gelding his son, Lebman added a two-inch Cutts Compensator to the Baby's muzzle. Together, with a forward-hand grip from a Thompson submachine gun mounted beneath the barrel, the .45- or .38-caliber buzz saw could be reasonably managed. Since the eight-round grip magazine would be used up in hiccup, he installed a removable eighteen-round magazine in the .45 ACP version. The smaller .38 Super cartridge-packed twenty-two rounds into the same space that extended about nine inches below the base of the grip.

The FBI confiscated this Lebman Baby, which features the front hand grip and a Cutts Compensator from a Thompson submachine gun installed on the pistol to help control full automatic fire. *Federal Bureau of Investigation*

While outlaws were a small percentage of his customers, their notoriety more than eclipsed run-of-the-mill transactions. One day in 1933. a young well-dressed man accompanied by a pretty woman and a young boy entered his shop. With them was a heavyweight man of a rougher cut who had little to say. The short, dapper young man with a trimmed mustache and breezy manners introduced himself, Jimmy Williams, his family, and their friend, "Chuck." He and Chuck were new oilmen with a field to protect against poachers. They had driven down from Indiana and needed firepower. Hyman explained he was awaiting a shipment if Williams could come back in a few days. Williams agreed and over the next week stopped by the store every day.[65]

Lebman and Williams—though his wife occasionally called him "Les," which tipped off Lebman that "Williams" was probably an alias—discussed guns and got along famously, especially concerning the Baby machine gun in development.[65] He led Williams through a trapdoor in the shop to the basement that had been converted into a workshop firing range. The concrete grotto was cool and the tang of burnt gun powder suffused into the concrete walls, one of which was perforated with bursts of gouged divots that criss-crossed the trowel-smoothed surface.

Work benches were crowded with works in progress on guns, holsters, and boots. Empty brass cartridge cases crunched underfoot. Along another wall,

beneath open beams, hung aluminum dummies of firearms, each labeled with the make and model, used as guides for designing wrap-around holsters.[66] Lebman hefted one of his sample Babies and ripped off a burst at the already devastated soft stucco back wall, blazing through a twenty-two-round magazine in a few seconds.

Obviously impressed, the shorter of the two—Jimmy Williams—ordered five .38 Super-caliber Babies. Hyman invited the party to his home for dinner. So it was that Jimmy Williams (a.k.a. "Baby Face" Nelson); his wife, Helen; their son, Ronald;

continued on page 198

Lester Gillis alias "Baby Face Nelson," alias "Jimmy Williams" was Hyman Lebman's convivial dinner guest along with the "Williams'" family and Charles Fisher. They discussed firearms, family, and kids while Nelson thought about robbery and mayhem. *Wikimedia Commons*

Standing on the corner of 63rd Street and Western Avenue on Chicago's southwest side, Edward "Spike" O'Donnell was talking to a beat cop. It was the chilly morning of September 25, 1925. Maybe the prominent south side bootlegger—and Capone rival—was thinking about going into the warmth of Weiss's Drugstore behind him. Maybe he turned toward the door. Whatever he did motivated Frankie McErlane, riding in the first of a short caravan of cars approaching the street corner, to test his new toy earlier than expected.

The coleader of the Capone ally, McErlane-Saltis Gang, leaned out the open rear window, leveled his Thompson submachine gun at unaware Spike, and squeezed the heavy ten-pound trigger pull. The gun came alive, recoiling with each exploding shot, gushing a fire hose arc of hot lead that bucked the muzzle upward. O'Donnell felt himself pelted with brick fragments as the bullets chewed across the store's façade above his head. The caravan of cars picked up speed as he crawled and scrabbled back toward the store's doorway.

In a moment, they were gone. In the silence, a tableau of dog walkers and store shoppers who had sought cover on the street began to reanimate and, out of habit, looked around to see who didn't get back on their feet. Spike O'Donnell felt his person and discovered he was unpunctured, uncrippled, and just sprinkled with bits of brick. He had just survived Chicago's first assassination attempt with a Thompson submachine gun.[67]

Edward "Spike" O'Donnell was a rival of Al Capone. Frank McErlane, an ally of Capone, was out cruising with his Thompson when he spotted O'Donnell, a regular clay pigeon for Capone's hit men. *Mario Gomes*

Scarface Al Capone had a daily routine that included breakfast in Anton's café, which was part of his Hawthorne Hotel headquarters above Chicago's 22nd Street. On September 20, 1926, he sat in his customary seat with his bodyguard, Frank Rio, at the end of a row of fifteen tables facing the front door, when a series of shots erupted outside. Rio stood up to look out the plate-glass window and saw the head end of an armada of cars that had stopped outside the café. The shots had been bait to draw out curious Capone associates. Rio grabbed Capone's arm and dragged him off the chair to the floor.[69]

For the next few minutes, the parade of eight cars rolled slowly past the café, and from each flamed a withering blast of Thompson submachine gun bullets exploding across the building's façade. Patrons and waitresses screamed and dove for the

Frank Rio had been a tough little thief who secured his bodyguard job with Capone through unquestioning loyalty. He was always there when Al needed a ball bat to crush a head, or other odd jobs. *Wikimedia Commons*

Anton's Café became the Hawthorne Café after the shooting and still later was the Towne Café until the hotel burned down. *Mario Gomes*

floor. China shattered, glassware fragmented, plaster disintegrated, light fixtures burst, and window glass shards ripped into the room like shrapnel. Debris and plaster dust rained down on the cowering diners. As the last car passed, it paused and a man wearing khaki overalls jumped down from its running board, knelt in front of the café, and shouldered his Thompson. Methodically, he hosed the muzzle back and forth across the jagged hole where the front window had been, chewing through the machine gun's one-hundred-round drum magazine. When it clicked empty, he returned to the waiting car and the motor entourage drove off down 22nd Street.

Inside what remained of Anton's Café, coughing, weeping shell-shocked diners and serving staff began to stir. Many bled from glass cuts and metal shard wounds. All were dusted with plaster and bits of blasted food and china dishes.

Frank Rio helped Al Capone to his feet, both with shaking knees. Aside from cuts and bruises, no one in the café had been seriously injured or hit by one of the over one thousand rounds of .45-caliber bullets poured into the confined space. Outside, local kids crunched through broken glass, searching for souvenir ejected cartridge cases that littered the sidewalk.[70]

Hymie Weiss's mug shot. Al Capone had a genuine fear of Earl J. Wojciechowski, aliases "Hymie the Pole" and Hymie Weiss. He hated Hymie's bug-eyed stare. *Wikimedia Commons*

continued from page 195

and the gunman, Chuck Fisher, enjoyed a good meal with a convivial host. They had been sent to Lebman by Nelson's mentor, master bank robber Eddie Bentz, and Dillinger associate, Homer Van Meter.[66] Baby Face also paid cash for four .45 ACP–caliber Model 1911 Automatic pistols and two Thompson submachine guns at three hundred dollars each.

When the feds finally did descend upon Hyman Lebman's gun repair, saddle, and machine gun outlet store, they could not touch him since all his

With glass fragments in his hair and plaster dust layering his custom-tailored suit, Capone had some thoughts on the gents behind the tommy gun raid—and Earl Hymie Weiss led the list. "Weiss will never kill me by any such silly stage play in broad daylight," Al said. "He might as well come after me with a brass band."

One month later, on October 11, 1926, Hymie Weiss and four associates parked on State Street in front of Holy Name Cathedral and hurried across the trolley tracks to a meeting in Weiss's office above Schofield's Flower Shop. They never made it. From the second-floor bay window of a nearby boarding house, a now familiar hammering chatter cut through the street noise. A virtual rain of slugs plowed into the five men and they screamed, lurched, collapsed, spun, and slumped as the bullets tore into flesh and pinged off the busy street. Hymie lay on his back, his obscenely grinning face splashed with arterial blood coughed

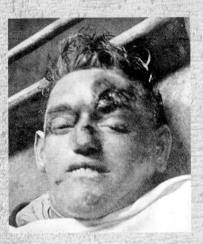

up when a dozen jacketed slugs eviscerated him and caved in his forehead. The shooters were never caught, but a couple of blocks away, police found a smoking-hot Thompson submachine gun attached to an empty one-hundred-round magazine.[70]

Hymie Weiss on a morgue slab. Still creepy in death, his grin was more rictus than amusement of the moment. *Wikimedia Commons*

activity happened in the pre-NFA days. Protected by his politically well-connected family, he continued his trade into 1970, but quit gunsmithing under pressure from the feds. Eventually, he succumbed to Alzheimer's disease and died in 1990. In a curious twist, many of the guns he modified provided FBI hunters with traceable paths to thefts and illicit sales, sending Hyman's happy customers variously to prison or to the electric chair.

It was a lovely Sunday with a high blue sky on July 1, 1928, as Frank Uale—also known as Frankie Yale—drove his tan Lincoln home, answering an urgent phone call about his ailing wife. Al Capone's former mentor and boss of the Brooklyn *Unione Siciliana* had no fears—until he saw the tail behind him. He mashed the gas.[68]

It is doubtful that he actually heard the blasting roar of the submachine gun as its magazine pushed a load of .45-caliber bullets into the weapon's hot and smoking breech. The automobile that had overtaken him now motored off, leaving behind a gray diaphanous cloud of gunsmoke rising above the mess of bloody rags that had once been Frankie Yale. To his other distinctions was added the title: first New York City victim of the Thompson Submachine gun.[68]

Frankie Yale was a popular hit man who iced former Chicago gang boss, Big Jim Colosimo, and worked his way up the *Unione Siciliana*. Also a reputed member of the Saint Valentine's Day Massacre gun team, he was Capone's original mentor. *Wikimedia Commons*

CHAPTER 18

THE GREAT DEPRESSION AND THE OUTLAWS' LAST HURRAH

WHEN THE BOTTOM dropped out from under the American economy with the collapse of the high-flying stock market, the outlaw economy dropped right along with it. A limbo occurred between the 1929 stock market crash and Franklin Delano Roosevelt's March 23, 1933, signing of the Cullen-Harrison Act, which legalized the manufacture and sale of alcohol, and the December 5, 1933, passage of the Twenty-First Amendment, which repealed Prohibition. With two strokes of the pen, Roosevelt crushed the big-city bootleg booze market and cut off major customers to rural whiskey still operators. Small-town banks had begun to fail, buried in bad mortgages and loans against future crops.

Farmers living on thin margins auctioned off their livestock and homesteads to meet their obligations. On top of this financial burden, decades of soil abuse and over-tilling came home to roost as great clouds of topsoil blew across the plains, alighting on rooftops and laundry lines as far as Chicago and points east.

It wasn't long before outlaws, used to a fat five-thousand-dollar bank heist to keep them in bullets and gasoline, had to settle for hand-to-mouth two-hundred-dollar grocery store robberies. Their victims also faced plummeting tax revenues as job losses soared. The drop in revenues caused salary cuts and maintenance cuts to public service such as police at state and local levels. Faced with growing poverty and diminishing options, many young men and middle-aged former wage earners, who now had holes in their shoes and lint in their pockets, strayed over to the always beckoning lures of the owlhoot trail.

Farm families migrating toward California with all their belongings heaped on a suffering old pick-up truck read about the exploits of these homespun bandits. At least someone was hitting back at the foreclosing banks and the harassing police. And hitting hard, if any of the newspaper reports were correct; these boys had more guns than good old Jesse James.

A Minneapolis labor riot in 1934 required police containment in fierce hand-to-hand battle. Falling wages and demands for union organization pitted workers against company owners in a class war. *Wikimedia Commons*

The 1929 stock market collapse brought crowds to Wall Street in a panic. Investors wanted to sell off their plummeting stocks or try to save them by answering margin calls as corporations shut down factories. *Wikimedia Commons*

The US Army that was drafted, double-timed through training, and shipped to France in 1917 and 1918 was a tragic collection of eager amateurs. The European allies saw United States involvement in the war as a political victory rather than as a military advantage. The Americans were to be scattered among the depleted French and British units wherever cannon fodder was needed to bulk up the line for attack or defense. American pilots flew French and British aircraft. Americans manned French and British tanks and were shipped about the battlefields in French boxcars designed for forty men or ten horses. What the American doughboys had going for them were guts and high morale that had not been bled out of them by three years of strategic and tactical incompetence.

They also had the superb Springfield .30-06 rifle, the Colt Model 1911 .45-caliber semiautomatic pistol, and the water-cooled Browning belt-fed heavy machine gun. What they did not have was a light machine gun to arm shock troops as ossified trench tactics shifted toward mobility and maneuver. Americans struggled with the French Chauchat machine gun and the Hotchkiss M1909 Benet-Mercie, a twenty-seven-pound, gas-operated shoulder weapon using

John Browning in his lab with his Colt-Browning Automatic Rifle. It was really neither fish nor fowl in combat: too heavy for a rifle and too little ammunition in a twenty-round magazine to effectively furnish fire suppression, it was rugged and hung around for fifty years. *Wikimedia Commons*

venerable thirty-round strip clips of 8mm Lebel cartridges, and usually bolted to
something solid to control its jitterbugging recoil.

The army approached American inventor John Browning with the need
for automatic fire on the move and he produced a sturdy hunk of firepower,
designed to survive the ghastly conditions of trench warfare. This Browning
Automatic Rifle fired the long Springfield .30-06 rifle cartridge at five hundred
rounds per minute from a detachable twenty-round box magazine in full
automatic or single-shot mode. Unfortunately, the compromise in weight-saving
came at the expense of ammunition capacity. At full automatic, the BAR churned
through twenty rounds in a few seconds, requiring bandoliers or bulging pockets
loaded with extra magazines. Usually, a BAR was manned by a crew of two:
one shooter and his partner lugging the extra ammunition. Walking fire also
became a fading idea under combat conditions. The hip-fired weapon's sixteen-
pound weight combined with the recoil of the gas piston and linkage required
considerable strength to control the hosing bullets. A bipod was retrofitted
to the muzzle end of the barrel, forcing the shooter to lie down, or otherwise
prop the bipod on the edge of a trench to cover a specified field of fire. The BAR
functioned best as a rifle squad support weapon and served through the end of
1918 and later in World War II, Korea, and the early days of Vietnam.

The outlaw motor bandits of the 1920s and 1930s loved the BAR. In an attempt
to keep the post–World War I market going for the big gun in civilian and law
enforcement hands, Colt offered a stripped-down model called the Monitor. The
BAR's muzzle bipod was lopped off, replaced by a Cutts Compensator screwed
into the muzzle to reduce recoil, and the twenty-four-inch barrel was shortened to
eighteen inches plus the four-inch Cutts extension. A pistol grip was added behind

A demonstration for the brass at Camp Simms in Congress Heights, southeast of
Washington, D.C., using their one thousand-yard range. The BAR is shown firing
from the shoulder in the offhand (standing) position. This required a husky soldier.
Wikimedia Commons

Firing a Colt Monitor BAR shows off its streamlined shape with trimmed barrel, Cutts Compensator, pistol grip, and wide forward grip for better control. This model saw action on both sides of the law. *Wikimedia Commons*

the trigger group for greater fire control. Tricked out with these alterations and trimmed to thirteen pounds, the Monitor achieved the weapon's original walking fire combat requirement.

After the war, a civilian could wander into an Ott-Heiskell Hardware Store and buy a fully accessorized BAR—complete with six magazines—off the rack for three hundred dollars. After 1931, well-heeled outlaws could scoop up a black market Monitor—fresh from a burglarized National Guard armory—for the cost of one good bank heist, about five thousand dollars.[71] With its limited magazine capacity, what was the gun's appeal over the iconic Thompson submachine gun?

The post-war 174-grain .30-06 bullet proved to be a selling point that elevated the BAR's value to both outlaws and law enforcement. This replacement for the army's .30-40 Krag round—that went to Cuba in 1898 and proved to be a dud compared to the Spanish 7mm Mauser—was developed in 1905 and introduced in

1906. The .30-06 metal-gilded, boat-tail, Spitzer (pointed) 174-grain bullet driven at high velocity of 2,640 feet per second with a maximum range of 5,500 yards outclassed every pistol round.

When the .45 ACP-caliber cartridge, used in the Model 1911 semiautomatic pistol and the Thompson submachine gun, failed to penetrate police car auto bodies and many bulletproof vests, the gangs stepped up to the BAR and its hot .30-06 Springfield M1 bullet. In 1926, the M2 Ball cartridge with the black-tipped, metal jacketed armor-piercing round became available. This slug ripped through car doors, engine compartments, gas tanks, and bulletproof vests of the period.

When FBI agents were finally allowed to carry weapons, Hoover ordered Monitor BARs to be distributed to FBI offices around the country to counter the expanding arms race. For police departments who could not afford the big automatic guns and found their .38 special revolver ammunition bounced off steel-bodied cars and the vests coming into vogue during Prohibition, Smith & Wesson responded. The 38/44 Heavy Duty cartridge took the 158-grain bullet with its 750 feet-per-second velocity and amped it up to 1,175 feet per second with 460 foot-pounds of energy at the muzzle. The hot bullet penetrated both doors of a sedan and fatally surprised vest-wearing gunmen in shoot-outs.[72]

The arms race continued to accelerate with no end in sight as the outlaws battled lawmen in the streets and on the country roads. Ordinary citizens, trying to make it through each day, developed a fatalist sense of humor.

Two men were walking down a city street when suddenly bank robbers opened fire on arriving police. One man looked over his shoulder, startled, and then relaxed, saying, "It's only gunshots! I thought it was a backfire!"

The heavy-duty .38 Special–caliber round required a beefed-up revolver frame to absorb the heavier gas pressure. This Smith & Wesson 38/44 Heavy Duty revolver filled the bill, allowing police to carry a sidearm that was effective against automobile steel. *Rock Island Auction Company*

CHAPTER 19

THE TAWDRY TEAM OF
BONNIE
AND CLYDE

HOT GUNS, HOT CARS, and hot sex were trademarks of Bonnie Elizabeth Parker and Clyde Chestnut Barrow, the outlaw pair whose rampage throughout the Midwest from 1932 to 1934 splashed across national newspaper headlines. They met in 1930 and immediately spotted each other's reckless streak. Slender, boyish, and ambitious, Bonnie wanted out of her dead-end life in steamy, run-down West Dallas, Texas. Clyde looked like a small, slightly effeminate country ferret with his hair parted down the middle and "aw shucks" taste in food and clothes. But that country boy nurtured a deep passion for fast cars and faster guns. He paid for his early recklessness with a case of itchy fingers during a two-year stint in Eastham Prison Farm while Bonnie waited for him. In prison, a large homosexual claimed him and used him night after night until Clyde beat the man to death with a club. When he got out of jail in 1932, his boyishness had been replaced by a snake-mean temper. He scooped up Bonnie and they set out to show the world who they were.

As robbers, they were strictly small potatoes. In the big cities, gangs such as the Karpis-Barker bunch; Dillinger, Van Meter, and Pierpont; Baby Face Nelson's crew; and Pretty Boy Floyd's slick hit-and-run capers each netted thousands of dollars. Clyde and Bonnie robbed the proceeds from gum machines in gas stations and the daily receipts out of cigar boxes at fruit stands. Whenever they stayed under a snug roof and enjoyed the luxury of flush toilets and fresh water baths, they often paid their bill with handfuls of gum machine silver coins—a

Bonnie and Clyde lived
each day on the edge.
Wikimedia Commons

Mug shot of Buck and the
six-hundred-dollar reward
for Joplin bloodbath.
Wikimedia Commons

dead giveaway the police and the tabloids pounced upon. While they did hit the occasional bank for a big score, they couldn't walk into a building to case the premises first. Early on, they were chased out of hideouts in running gun battles and left behind photos of themselves taken with Bonnie's folding Kodak and poems she was always revising. Many photos showed them posing together in front of a stolen Ford V-8 and the license plate is clearly visible in the frame. Bonnie's love of publicity cost them dearly in blood and treasure.

The hot guns mostly came from National Guard armories, which were literally firearms supermarkets to the outlaws of that era. Clyde and teenager W. D. Jones; or Buck Barrow, his older brother; or his friend, Henry Methvin, often came back to the hideout du jour with armloads of Browning Automatic Rifles, shotguns, or a buffet selection of rifles. They lugged cases of ammunition and crates of Model 1911 Colt semiautomatic pistols into their temporary shuttered bunkers. Once, while cleaning the cosmoline storage grease from one of the Brownings, Clyde accidently triggered a burst. The sudden stuttering growl reverberated down the street and soon thereafter the gang was packing up their arsenal once again as a net of local cops approached.

Crossroads store and gas station—Bonnie and Clyde's typical robbery of cigar box tills and gum machines—were slim pickings to stay on the move between bigger scores. *Farm Security Administration*

Bonnie and Clyde in front of the license plate on their getaway car. Time after time, they unwittingly gave police clues to their transportation and whereabouts for the chance to appear in the newspapers and magazines. *Wikimedia Commons*

Clyde with a Krag rifle and Whippet cropped-down autoloading shotgun. *Wikimedia Commons*

Clyde was always careful to steal only the latest Ford automobiles powered by the famous high-performance flathead V-8 engine for their jobs, getaways, and long motor trips across the Midwest. Four-door sedans were preferred to accommodate four or five passengers, plus all those guns, baskets of food for dining in the woods, towels for bathing in creeks, and first aid supplies as various members stopped lead bullets, shattered glass, steel shards, and the occasional exploding gas tank. Clyde was so impressed with the quickness and durability of the Ford Fordor Model B V-8 Sedan, he wrote a personal letter to Henry Ford.

> Mr. Henry Ford
> Detroit, Mich.
>
> Dear Sir:
> While I still have got breath in my lungs I will tell you what a dandy car you make. I have drove Fords exclusively when I could get away with one. For sustained speed and freedom from trouble the Ford has got every other car skinned, and even if my business hasn't [*sic*] been strickly [*sic*] legal it don't hurt anything to tell you what a fine car you got in the V8.
> Yours truly
> Clyde Champion Barrow.[73]

When Barrow wasn't cleaning his arsenal of weapons, he spent hours modifying them for any contingency. He stripped the BARs to their basic elements, trimming excess weight. Semiautomatic Remington and Winchester shotguns had their barrels and shoulder stocks hacked off for ease of use when shooting from car windows. In one case, he lopped the long barrels and stock off a sixteen-gauge shotgun and created a zippered sleeve holster he could wear strapped to his leg and practiced speed-drawing the gun like a Wild West gunslinger.

Bonnie carried a .38-caliber snub-nose revolver taped to her inner thigh when they were on the road. Clyde taught her to shoot all the guns—especially the chopped and trimmed-down Brownings. She only weighed about ninety pounds, but managed to brace the gun against her hip and trigger automatic bursts with surprising accuracy.

In Joplin, Missouri, together with W. D. Jones, Buck Barrow, and Buck's wife, Blanche, they rented a stone house built above a two-car garage on April 1, 1933. Bonnie and Blanche went shopping for clothes and trinkets and their food was delivered. The shades were drawn day and night, but sounds of raucous parties could be often heard outside. Eventually, their furtive comings and goings and their incessant watchfulness aroused their neighbors' suspicions. The police suspected the renters driving cars with Texas license plates were bootleggers.

On April 13, Clyde and W. D. Jones were outside in front of one open garage when two police cars motored slowly past. Sensing trouble, the two outlaws

Bonnie's .38-caliber Colt revolver, which she often taped to her inner thigh, is pictured just below one of the .45-caliber Model 1911 semiautomatic pistols Clyde stole by the crate from National Guard armories. *Wikimedia Commons*

Joplin, Missouri, hideout house exterior at the top of a hill with both garages filled with two getaway cars. An arsenal was upstairs, crowded in with Bonnie, Clyde, Blanche, Buck, and W. D. Jones. It quickly became a shootout crime scene. *texashideout.tripod.com*

hurried inside and pulled the doors closed. The cars swung onto the driveway, blocking both garages. Plainclothes and uniformed police spilled into the street with guns drawn. At that moment, they discovered they had poked a hornet's nest.

An explosion of rapid shotgun fire ripped from the garage as the gang ran downstairs to pile into the Ford V-8 sedan. Jones tried and then Buck succeeded in releasing the hand brake of a cop's car that was blocking the driveway and it rolled clear down onto the street.[74] Policemen, who had already taken casualties, hunkered down as bullets hammered into their cars and spanged off the concrete. Blanche, gripped by panic, ran shrieking into the street, past the startled cops, and down the block. The Ford burst out next, guns roaring, gears clashing, and squealed sharp left. As it passed Blanche, who was pounding down the pavement at a high lope, arms reached out and swept her into the car.

The police who could still regain their feet let the car full of insane gunmen go and, with great caution, approached the vacated house to find Clyde's arsenal, Buck's Marmon auto, his pardon papers and marriage license, and the remnants of twelve days of peace and quiet. There was also an unfinished poem in Bonnie's handwriting titled "Suicide Sal."

With the Ford punctured by bullets, wind blowing through shattered glass, and four passengers in various stages of shock, Clyde flattened the gas pedal and tried to clear his head. Behind him, their identities were being telephoned to local police agencies and the word that the Barrows were on the loose would galvanize every farmer who had a goose gun or a squirrel rifle. Soon, makeshift posses were scouring Missouri and nearby back roads for the shot-up Ford. The smell of reward money was in the air.

For three months, the Barrow gang ran, pausing only to steal new Fords and rob mom and pop shops, scratching to get by. They replenished their arsenal at

W. D. Jones with Bonnie and Clyde's armory. On the hood ornament is an 1892 Colt .38. On the grill is a Colt Single Action Army revolver and a Colt Police Positive. On the ground is a Krag-Jorgensen .30-40 carbine, the quick-draw Whippet shotgun, and a Browning shotgun. *Wikimedia Commons*

a convenient National Guard armory, stuck up some Iowa gas stations, cleaning out gum and soda pop vending machines, and looked for a place to cool off for a week or so. They drove into the Red Crown Cabin Camp outside of Platte City, Missouri, and rented two brick cabins joined by a pair of garages.

Once again, their lifestyle and thoughtless rookie habits betrayed them. The cabin camp manager looked on with growing suspicion as Clyde counted out their bill payment in vending machine swag: shiny quarters, dimes, and nickels. This time, however, when the local Missouri police were alerted, they figured the Barrows were in town and called up reinforcements from Kansas City.

Unfortunately, the massing of police cars and uniforms did not escape the notice of W. D. Jones as he bought bandages, salve, and disinfectant at a local store. His warning when he returned to the cabins that evening arrived just before the vanguard of law officers began setting up their perimeter around the

Red Crown Cabins, the motor lodge that was almost a death trap. W.D. Jones went out for medical supplies and saw the rural cops lining up their cars to attack the outlaw gang. *Wikimedia Commons*

pair of cabins. Police machine guns were set up behind steel shields; officers with shotguns, rifles, and pistols fanned out. A steel-plate-reinforced automobile joined them, rumbling to a halt facing the cabins' front and garage doors.

As hammers cocked and bolts slid into place, there was a breath of silence, and then came a knock at the door. "Officers! We want to talk to you!" boomed a voice.

"As soon as we get dressed," Blanche answered sweetly.

Gun barrels moved up to the cabin windows and then Clyde shouted to Bonnie, Buck, and Jones, "Let the bastards have it!"[75]

The Barrows' trademark crash of gunfire slammed into the machine gun shields and went whining off into the woods. The heavy bark of Browning Automatic Rifles stuttered across the armored car, slicing through its steel plates, catching the police inside by surprise as armor piercing rounds caromed around the interior. The driver clashed gears into reverse just as a bullet severed the horn cable setting off a raucous screech. Taking the incessant squall as a call to cease fire, officers stopped shooting and began reloading.

At that moment, Buck Barrow, a Colt .45 automatic in each hand, dashed from the garage blazing away. Bonnie and Blanche followed him running behind a mattress. Following them, a Ford Model B four-door sedan rushed out with Clyde on the running board. The girls dropped the mattress and began firing pistols as the car stopped for Buck. He stumbled when a bullet hit him in the head and collapsed.

Jones climbed from behind the wheel to help the girls drag Buck inside and Clyde jumped into the driver's seat. They roared away as slugs punctured the trunk and roof and finally shattered the rear window, sending a piece of glass slicing into Blanche's left eye. Her constant screams pitched up an octave as the car faded into the night, leaving the lawmen to once again lick their wounds and hope for another chance.

After a frantic flight, Clyde swung off the road onto the grounds of a former amusement park and rolled to a stop in the stygian dark where the only sounds were chitters of night insects, heavy breathing, and soft moans of the wounded. Meanwhile, for miles around, roadblocks slammed shut on every road and lane and vigilantes stalked through the trees. Their campsite would be undiscovered for four days.

Eventually, a local vigilante found their still-warm campfire and bloody bandages. They had left the site to steal another car and returned. Buck's head wound and Blanche's cut left eye had kept them pinned down. It wasn't long before a virtual army of lawmen and locals closed in as W. D. Jones fried wieners for lunch over the open fire.[74] Clyde spotted movement and cried out, "The law's coming!"

A torrent of gunfire hummed and sizzled into the campsite as the Barrows scrambled to take cover, return fire, and get the car started. Jones ran for the Ford and tumbled to the ground from a blast of buckshot. Blanche dragged Buck behind a stump. Clyde tossed Jones into the Ford's back seat and started the engine as a sleet storm of bullets pelted the metalwork. Bonnie made it to the passenger seat and looked back at Blanche holding Buck's still-bleeding head and crying, "Don't die, Daddy! Don't die!"[75] Buck Barrow continued to fire his .45 automatic blindly, shot after shot, until a posse member kicked the gun out of his limp hand.

Clyde floored the gas, and the Ford lurched through a gauntlet of fire to break clear. A bullet chopped into Clyde's arm and he lost control, crashing the car into a stump. Taking what guns and belongings they could manage, Clyde, Bonnie, and Jones took to their heels and ran. The posse, with obvious concern for the families who would mourn their passing, did not pursue.

In May 1934, Bonnie and Clyde were still on the road, still driving yet another Ford V-8 sedan, gray with bright yellow wheel spokes. The back seat was crammed with BARs, semiautomatic rifles, pistols, and shotguns. On the floor beneath the front seat were fifteen sets of license plates.[75] They had once again drawn Henry Methvin into their sphere, but now he wanted out, and together, with his father, Ivan, hatched a plan to turn the couple over to the closely pursuing feds. Ivan Methvin was to meet the Barrows on the road between the towns of Sailes and Gibsland near the Texas–Louisiana border on May 23.

It was still dark when automobiles carrying six lawmen eased off the road into some trees and gazed down at an empty strip of hilly highway that meandered past them. The tall grass was still damp, but the location was perfect. At sunup, a truck belonging to Ivan Methvin drove up and came to rest down below on the road's shoulder. Special agent of the new FBI, L. A. Kindell, waved at Ivan, who climbed out and proceeded to remove the truck's left front wheel.

Next to Kindell stood Arcadia County Sheriff Henderson Jordan with three deputies, and next to them, stood former Texas Ranger and current member of the Texas Highway Patrol, Frank Hamer. At the request of his chief, who had lost a patrolman to the Barrows, Hamer had tracked the gang through nine

Blanche Barrow in her riding habit, captured at the abandoned amusement park campsite with a fatally wounded Buck. *Wikimedia Commons*

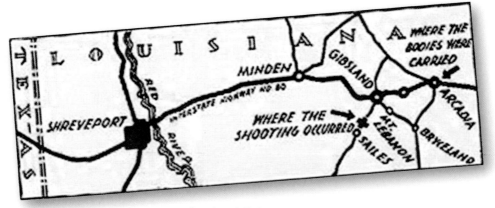

Bonnie and Clyde ambush map—where Methvin and his father arranged to have the law waiting on a hillside. *Wikimedia Commons*

The shooting posse assembled to ambush Bonnie and Clyde on a Louisiana road pose after the success of their assignment. Former Texas Ranger Frank Hamer is seated far right and Ted Hinton, the finger man, is standing at the far left. *Wikimedia Commons*

states to the expected meeting on this stretch of Louisiana highway. He was thoroughly familiar with the pair and, in his own mind, decided they would not escape this ambush alive. Taking a page from the Barrow playbook, the six men were heavily armed. Both Kindell and Deputy Sheriff Ted Hinton hefted Colt Monitor BARs firing .30-06 armor-piercing bullets; Hamer shouldered a .35-caliber semiautomatic rifle, as did Jordan; the deputies carried semiautomatic shotguns crammed with buckshot.

Flies and mosquitoes had risen with the sun and added their buzz to the morning breeze that hissed through pine trees higher up the slope. Soon, a rumble of tires on gravel turned into a gray Ford V-8 climbing over a nearby hill. The men rose on stiff legs from their dew-damp stand. The automobile, with its distinctive yellow wheel spokes, reflected the morning sunlight as it approached, slowing and passing Methvin's disabled truck. At that moment, from the opposite direction, another truck hauling a load of firewood came into view.

The outlaws and gangsters had no regard for pinching pennies when it came to dropping the hammer on anyone who got in their way or was listed for execution. They embraced the new auto-loading pistols coming from Europe and from Colt in the United States. Dillinger was an exception. He once said, "Never trust a woman or an automatic pistol," and was proved right on both counts.

John Browning was a veritable fount of new designs coming from Belgian and American factories. His Colt Model 1902 was the forerunner, in .32- and .38-caliber to the ubiquitous Model 1911 Colt .45. The Browning Highpower *Fabrique Nationale* was a powerhouse, loading thirteen rounds of the new .9mm Parabellum cartridge from a double-stack magazine in the grip. The Baretta Model 1934 from Tullio Maregoni and the Walther PPK were also popular.

The legacy of the derringer hideout pistol carried over from the Wild West to the era of the motor bandits and urban gunzels. Pocket guns became must-have sidearms for last-ditch situations.

Gun breeches closed levering cartridges from their magazines, safeties clicked off; six gun barrels tracked the Ford car as Clyde in his shirtsleeves and dark sunglasses slowed and hollered out the window, "You got a flat? Did you find Henry?" He then depressed the Ford's clutch and applied the brake with his stockinged feet. Bonnie sat up straight in her bright red dress. The wood truck came closer. Sheriff Jordan couldn't wait any longer and shouted, "Put 'em up Clyde! You're covered!"[75]

At the same time, a single rifle shot cracked and the bullet tore through Clyde's head. Bonnie screamed a piercing shriek of fear that disappeared under a thunderous fusillade of gunfire from the hillside.[76] Hot cartridge cases and smoking shotgun shells rained down into the grass as the roar of guns merged with the rattle of holed steel and shattering glass. The car rolled slowly forward and, as if tired from a long journey, slipped off onto the opposite shoulder and stalled.

The wood truck driver and his helper stared from where they'd run into the woods. Old Man Methvin crawled out from under his decoy truck as the posse quickly advanced on the virtually shredded Ford. Hamer, his pistol in hand, opened the passenger door. Bonnie, bent forward with her head between her knees, slumped into his arms. He heaved her bloody torso up onto the punctured seat and felt a thready pulse in her throat that eventually faded

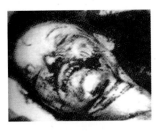

Bonnie Parker was shot to pieces by the posse on the side of the hill. One of the posse members said her scream was like a "terrified animal." *The Horror Zine*

Clyde never knew what hit him. As he turned with his sawed-off shotgun, one of the first bullets punched through his left eye and out the back of his head. *The Horror Zine*

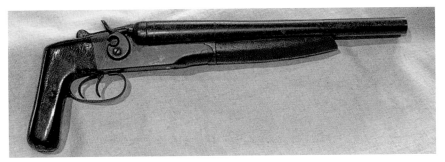

Clyde's sawed-off double-barreled shotgun was on his lap when the shooting started. *Texas Ranger Hall of Fame and Museum, Waco, Texas*

away. Her upper lip had been almost shot away giving her a blood-slick grin. He propped her sideways against Clyde who lay with his head on the closed door's window ledge, mouth open, one eye open, and one eye gone.[44] Of the 184 bullets that slammed into the Ford, Clyde had absorbed 48 hits while Bonnie had been holed with 37 wounds. A sawed-off shotgun with seven notches carved in its grip lay in his lap.[75] What became known as the Death Car has toured the country for years afterward to large crowds.[77]

The lovers were planted in different cemeteries against Bonnie's request in her postmortem published poem, "The Story of Bonnie and Clyde," to be buried side by side. The legendary Texas man hunter, Frank Hamer, had the final word: "I hate to bust a cap on a woman; especially when she's sitting down."[44]

While many gunmen believed the intimidation factor was enhanced by nickel plating the slab-sided pistols, at least one preferred a more exotic solution. Jack "Legs" Diamond, a jack of all trades in the outlaw market from rum running to body guard, hijacker, drug trafficker, or hit man for hire, lived life on the edge. After surviving four assassination attempts, he bragged about how "they haven't invented the bullet . . . that could kill me." His associates in the trade called him "clay pigeon of the underworld."[44]

Legs's signature handgun was a 1908 Model Luger pistol in 9mm caliber. To enhance its firepower, he also used a Luger Snail magazine that, in effect, put a Thompson submachine gun drum of cartridges at the end of an extended grip magazine. The Snail coughed up thirty-two rounds of semiautomatic fire and was trumped only by Hyman Lebman's Colt .38 Super twenty-two-round blitz of fully automatic fire carried by Nelson and Dillinger.

In any case, on the afternoon of December 17, 1931, there was a knock on the door of a boarding house at 67 Dove Street in Albany, New York. Apparently, someone had found that magic bullet and fired a half box of them into Legs. He died just steps away from his favorite Luger resting on the bed's nightstand.

This Deutsche Waffen und Munitions Fabrik (DWM) Model 1908 9mm Luger pistol belonged to Legs Diamond, who was a step up in murder technology. It was the state-of-the-art pistol of the 1920s, 1930s, and 1940s. *Rock Island Auction Company*

To give the Luger pistol added punch, Legs slid this thirty-two-round Snail magazine into the pistol's grip. He just had to get to it on the nightstand next to the bed before the two guys kicked in the door. *Rock Island Auction Company*

Jack "Legs" Diamond was a bootlegger and a hit man who had the unfortunate ability to make enemies. Gang boss Dutch Shultz said, "Ain't there nobody who can shoot this guy so he don't bounce back?" *Wikimedia Commons*

CHAPTER 20

SAGEBRUSH ROBIN HOOD

Charles Arthur "Pretty Boy" Floyd

IT WASN'T UNUSUAL in the 1930s for a housewife to hear a knock at the door and open it to find a man asking if she could see it in her heart to spare a simple meal. So, when the nice young gentleman, bedraggled but polite, appeared at her farmhouse in northern Ohio, Ellen Conkle didn't hesitate to offer him a seat on the porch while she went to the smokehouse for a side of meat. She always believed beggars might be angels in disguise. Later, after gulping down a plate of ribs, potatoes, and freshly baked bread, and finishing it off with a piece of pumpkin pie and coffee, the man told Ellen it was a meal "fit for a king." He reached into his pocket, pulled out a roll of bills, offering to pay her

Charles Arthur "Pretty Boy" Floyd from his mug shot. The "Pretty Boy" moniker was hung on him as a young man and stuck—but was never mentioned to his face. *Wikimedia Commons*

Most of the locals in Floyd's home town, as well as other acquaintances, referred to Charles Floyd as "Choc." The moniker refers to Choctaw beer, a local brew concocted by the Choctaw Indians and illegal to manufacture, but people made it regardless. The story goes that Charley and his brother were working at their father's still when they noticed a stud horse in a nearby field was having problems mounting a young mare.

They watched for several minutes, getting a kick out of the poor steed's struggle to perform. Then, Charley had an idea. He scooped out a handful of mash, called the mare over, and slathered the mash on the horse's behind. With the mare well-lubricated the stud did his duty in no time. The story spread rapidly and, from then on, until he died, Charley was called Choc by his friends.[78]

whatever she asked. She said no, one dollar was quite enough. His stomach full, he leaned back and watched the clouds roll by, thinking this was one fine day.

The nice young man was Charles Arthur Floyd, better known as "Pretty Boy." The FBI had him on its most wanted list. The date was October 22, 1934. And this would be his last meal.

Charles Arthur Floyd was born on February 3, 1904, in the Georgia mountains, but grew up in Sallisaw, Oklahoma, a town situated in the cotton and cattle country near the Cookson Hills. For a boy fascinated by the exploits of the Jesse James and Dalton gangs, and the war raging in Europe, this was a perfect spot to have a childhood. Summers were spent playing games in which tree branches became mighty swords and tomato stakes served as Enfield rifles. He attended school until eighth grade and from then on he learned his lessons in the saloons and brothels in the area.

At the age of sixteen, he left home, hopped a freight car and, after a series of farm labor jobs, he found work for a local scoundrel, John Callahan, who had a reputation as a fence dealing in stolen jewelry, automobiles, bank securities, and whiskey.

As he watched bank robbers and thieves exchange stolen goods for as much as twenty cents on the dollar, Floyd saw his future laid out before him. He returned home, still restless, eager for adventure, and obsessed with stories of outlaws such as Al Jennings and Henry Starr. He committed his first felony in 1922, stealing $350 in pennies from a local post office. Since this was also a federal offense, officers from Muskogee showed up to investigate. Floyd, the main suspect, was brought in for questioning. Even though Charley and his father seldom saw eye to eye, the old man provided an alibi, saying his son had been home that night.

After that scare, Floyd busied himself with farm work, gambling, and selling moonshine. He spent the rest of his spare time romancing Ruby Hardgrave, a local farm girl, and in June 1924, they married. Six months after their nuptials, Ruby presented Charles with a son, Charles Dempsey Floyd. The husband and father adored his wife and child, but the few dollars he earned from planting corn and peddling moonshine paled compared to what he might bring in taking money from banks and payrolls. The old restlessness set in once again. The following summer, he traded five gallons of liquor for a friend's pearl-handled .44 revolver, boarded a freight train, and headed east toward St. Louis. While camping among the grasses and sagebrush of Missouri, he met Fred Hildebrand, another troublemaker bent on making easy money.

In less than a month, Charley and Fred committed armed robbery of a Kroger Company payroll and made off with over eleven thousand dollars. Unfortunately, they made the same mistake as so many other criminals had in the early days of their careers. They flaunted their earnings. When they rolled into Sallislaw, Oklahoma, driving a flashy new car and wearing custom-tailored suits, the local sheriff cast a suspicious eye. Floyd had told his wife and everyone else in town that he left to find farm work in Missouri. No one, the sheriff knew, could possibly earn enough picking cotton in a month's time to buy what Floyd now sported. To make matters worse, two rolls of bills totaling two thousand dollars were found on Hildebrand. The two were hauled back to St. Louis for questioning. Hildebrand confessed and implicated Charley in the crime. A Kroger paymaster who had witnessed the robbery sealed Charley's fate. One of the men was young, the man said and "had kind of a pretty face." For the next several years, Charles Arthur "Pretty Boy" Floyd received his mail at the state penitentiary in Jefferson City, Missouri.

If prison were college, Floyd might have walked out with a degree in criminal arts. Like so many before and after him, he registered at "Outlaw U"—the modern-day equivalent of the owlhoot trail. Thanks to his fellow inmates, he learned how to avoid police searches, the best banks to rob, how to skirt around federal and state laws, the latest most sophisticated weapons, which officials could be bribed, and the names of the more experienced gangsters.

In 1929, Charles Floyd was released on parole. Now free and ready to take his place in society—more or less—he found work in an Oklahoma oil field, but was fired when the foreman learned of his prison record.

He was arrested for vagrancy three times in three different states, returned to bootlegging, and frequented several bawdy houses in Kansas City, where he met up with Beulah Baird, a local prostitute who is also credited with giving him the name Pretty Boy. Eventually, the name stuck, much to Charley's disgust.

Yet, people were drawn to Charles, partly because of his good looks, but mostly it was his charisma that made those in the criminal underworld anxious to be counted as one of his cohorts. It didn't take long for Floyd to assemble a cadre of individuals with a fair amount of well-executed heists to their credits: James Bradley, Bob Amos, Jack Atkins, and a shoplifter who currently called herself Marie Maxwell. Marie had offered to serve as cook and housekeeper for the lads.

On February 5, 1930, Floyd and his gang strode into the Farmers and Merchants Bank of Sylvania, Ohio, just outside of Toledo. They all carried pistols; some had one in each hand. Charles, brandishing his six-shot, double-action .32 Smith & Wesson revolver, ordered the cashier to open the vault. His smile faded and his demeanor switched from friendly to furious when he learned that the vault was on a timer and couldn't be opened for another five hours. Another henchman, also angered by the delay, hit the cashier, who fell to the floor.

Outsiders noticed the commotion and fetched the bank vice president in another office down the street. He turned on a fire alarm, whereupon the local exchange operator set off an ear-piercing siren and alerted the sheriff's office and the Toledo police. At the sound of the alarm, the Floyd gang grabbed a few dollars from the cash drawer, ran out, and jumped into their car. They swerved in and out of downtown traffic. At one point, Floyd's wheelman glanced up into his rearview mirror and saw it filled with the front end of a huge hook-and-ladder fire truck. Behind the wheel was the fire chief in hot pursuit and, at his side, a fireman cranked the siren for all it was worth. Sylvania traffic parted like the Red Sea for this noisy parade. But Floyd's driver mashed the gas and his big Ford flathead engine had the upper hand. Soon, the smaller car easily outran the fire chief's mammoth vehicle.

Not only did Floyd's efforts result in a meager take, but he was arrested in a hideout when law officers broke into a bedroom and found Marie Maxwell bathing the wounds Bradley had suffered in a shootout a few hours earlier. The policeman noticed heavy breathing under the bed, reached down, and grabbed Charley Floyd by the heels, dragged him out in a cloud of dust bunnies, and handcuffed him. Lawmen also seized a submachine gun, two sawed-off shotguns, a high-powered rifle, five pistols, and—gingerly—vials of nitroglycerin.

Floyd pleaded guilty to the Sylvania Bank Robbery and, after spending time in the Akron and Toledo jails, he was sentenced to twelve to fifteen years in the Ohio State Penitentiary. During the train ride to Columbus, he squeezed his frame out a bathroom window and dropped into a steep ditch, once again eluding his captors.

Smith & Wesson Lemon Squeezer .32 Short-caliber double-action revolver for down-at-the-heels hoodlums looking for their first big bank score. The revolver got its moniker from the grip safety. Also called a safety hammerless. *Wikimedia Commons*

Floyd worked his way west, hooking up with Willis Miller, a low-life better known as Billy "the Killer" Miller. While traveling through Kentucky, they got into a gunfight with two police officers; Billy and one of the cops were killed. Again, Floyd escaped. He later engaged in a gunfight with federal agents. And yet again he escaped.

Floyd's charm and elegant clothing attracted a new partner, George Birdwell. In addition to their easygoing manner, the two made a striking pair in their custom-tailored suits, carrying well-manicured submachine guns and polished revolvers. Folksy conversations with bank employees while loading cash into containers helped give an air of class to otherwise aggravating crimes. People turned a blind eye to Pretty Boy because he had learned to share. While his Robin Hood reputation earned him the respect of the common man, his cleverness in eluding the law while making off with cash from so many banks made him the hated enemy of police and bank officials.

Floyd committed his boldest heist in his own hometown of Sallisaw, Oklahoma. At noon on November 1, 1932, he, Birdwell, and a kid they had hired as a driver cruised into town in a Ford V-8 sedan, waving at people on the street. The sedan pulled up in front of the Sallisaw State Bank and Floyd got

Although numerous crimes, including armed robbery, killing a police officer, and even vagrancy filled Charley Floyd's rap sheet, years after his death, his name lives on in song, literature, and film. What set him apart from all the other armed gangsters of the 1930s? None of the other hardened criminals handed out a few bills to bank customers before they took off in the getaway car. Pretty Boy Floyd did that and more. He ripped up mortgage papers, thinking that he had freed the homeowners of debt. He sent groceries to families on the brink of starvation.

In 1939, folksinger Woody Guthrie wrote ballads honoring the downtrodden and his song "Pretty Boy Floyd," contained the following stanza:

> But a many a starvin' farmer
> The same old story told
> How the outlaw paid their mortgage
> And saved their little homes.[79]

George Birdwell became Floyd's partner and they went on a bank-robbing spree causing Oklahoma bank insurance rates to double between 1931 and 1932. Eventually, Birdwell tried a robbery on his own and was shot while in the bank's vault. *Wikimedia Commons*

out, his submachine gun hefted rakishly under his arm. He walked into the bank, took $2,530, and strolled out within several yards of the police chief who was parked nearby. The officer claimed he had no knowledge of the crime. Locals, who had lost their farms and their homes to foreclosure, silently cheered.

Not only did Floyd have their support, but when federal agents stopped at a farmhouse or home, the folks of the Cookson Hills denied any knowledge of their fellow Oklahoman's whereabouts. No, never saw him, they'd say, shaking their heads.

Later in the month of the Sallisaw robbery, Birdwell attempted a bank robbery on his own and died during a gunfight. For the next several months, whenever a police officer was killed, law enforcement officials fingered Floyd as the suspect. That same year, retired officer Erv Kelley offered his services in the attempt to capture Floyd. Kelley and other lawmen staked out a farm where Floyd had been seen. A middle-of-the-night shootout between Floyd and Kelley left Kelley dead. The wild shots from the officer's submachine gun were no match for Charley's own .45-caliber bullets. Charley stumbled away in the dark, shot in the foot, but alive.

After a discreet physician treated him, Charley became more nervous, looking twice at every gas station attendant, people in a diner, jumping whenever he heard a siren.

Floyd is said to have played a major role in the Kansas City Massacre, one of the most notorious escapades recorded in the FBI files. Others have maintained that Floyd was nowhere near the area when the event took place. Yet, according to the federal agency's account in its website, on June 16, 1933, Charley, along with a new buddy, Adam Richetti, joined in plans to free Frank "Jelly" Nash, a federal prisoner. Nash was being transported by law enforcement officers to the penitentiary at Fort Leavenworth, Kansas.

Just prior to that, Floyd and Richetti had stopped in Bolivar, Missouri, for car repairs. As they waited in the garage, they noticed the local sheriff strolling into

Adam Richetti opened Floyd's door to some higher voltage thugs, such as hired killer Verne Miller. Verne ended up beaten to death because of his big mouth. Richetti allegedly was replaced by Floyd at the last minute for Miller's attempt to spring Frank Nash from custody at the Kansas City train station. *Wikimedia Commons*

Frank "Jelly" Nash was an old-time career outlaw being transferred by the FBI from a train to the Kansas City lockup. An accidental discharge from an FBI shotgun ended his life. *Federal Bureau of Investigation*

the building. Richetti grabbed a machine gun; Floyd took out two .45-caliber automatic pistols from their car and took the sheriff hostage. They dumped him and the guns into another car and stole it. The pair drove to Deepwater, Missouri, released the sheriff, and when they arrived in Kansas City, met with Verne Miller, who let them in on the plan to free Nash. The three arrived at the Union Railway Station the following morning and waited.

This .38-caliber Colt is one of the usual pair that Floyd carried with him constantly once he had achieved true outlaw status. *J. M. Davis Arms and Historical Museum*

At this time, FBI agents could not legally carry firearms unless deputized by local police. Armed with pistols and shotguns given to them by the Kansas City police department, the agents and police officers led the handcuffed Nash to a Chevrolet sedan, and ordered him into the front seat. Three agents climbed into the back seat and, as other agents and officers paused outside the car, they spotted a suspicious-looking green Plymouth. Two men, one with a machine gun, ran out from behind the car. One of the men shouted, "Up! Up!" Shots rang out from all directions. The two officers standing outside the Chevrolet were hit and tumbled to the ground, dead. An agent was shot in the left arm and, as he tried to reach his fellow agent, that agent suffered a bullet wound to the head. Ironically, stray bullets from the outlaws' guns killed the man they had intended to free. Nash died at the scene, along with the police chief seated next to him.[80]

That was Hoover's version. A closer postmortem examination of Nash showed the back of his head carried steel ball bearings the same as loaded into the FBI agent's 1897 Winchester shotgun. This weapon had been given to him and he was seated behind the prisoner. In a panic, the agent, unfamiliar with the shotgun, might have inadvertently worked the pump action while gripping the trigger so the gun fired as he swung its muzzle past Nash, blowing off the back of the prisoner's head.

Other biographers insist Floyd was never a part of the failed attempt to free Nash, because Floyd only cared about crimes that would benefit him. Helping a fellow criminal didn't appeal to him, especially if it meant putting his life in danger. Charley himself continually denied taking part in the massacre. Nevertheless, the manhunt was on. Roadblocks throughout Oklahoma, search parties, questioning people who knew Floyd came up empty. Meanwhile, Floyd managed to elude the law once again and, along with Richetti and two lady friends, departed for points east, ending up in Buffalo.

They hid out in Buffalo for nearly a year, but life holed up in an apartment finally resulted in cabin fever for the four. Floyd and Richetti wanted to go home to Oklahoma. In mid-October 1934, Charley instructed the women to purchase a Ford Tudor sedan and they set out heading south and west toward Ohio. Luck was not on their side; as Charley tried to maneuver the car through a dense fog, he lost control and hit a telephone pole. He told the women to take the car to a mechanic. Meanwhile, he and Adam were discovered by a local resident as they rested on a hill overlooking the Ohio River. The local hunted up a telephone and notified authorities.

A patrol car soon rolled up and a police officer with two deputies got out. Richetti drew his .45 automatic and began firing; the officer got off several shots with his .32-caliber revolver. Adam's gun jammed, so he ran, but was caught and

At the Union Station in the aftermath of the Kansas City Massacre, where four officers and their prisoner, Frank "Jelly" Nash, died in a hail of outlaw bullets and one from friendly fire. *Wikimedia Commons*

arrested a few minutes later. Charley fired off a few shots with his submachine gun, wounding one of the deputies, and started running. He used his two .45s to commandeer one car, then another when that ran out of gas. Both drivers were taken hostage. Meanwhile, police had been alerted and spotted the second car. They managed to trap it on the side of a road. There were gunshots but, in all the confusion, once again, Charley Floyd slipped away.

The hunt was on. FBI agents, including Melvin Purvis, descended on the area near East Liverpool. Charley, dirty and hungry, knew how to survive the backwoods. He found a farmhouse, begged for a sandwich and a chance to wash up, got it, and left with ginger cookies and apples to continue his journey.

Later that day, October 22, 1934, Floyd reached the home of Ellen Conkle, who served him a dinner of ribs and coffee after which he offered to pay her. He asked if she could get him a ride to Youngstown, but she suggested, instead, that her brother, Stewart, and his wife, who were husking corn in her fields, could drive him when the work was done. She indicated Stewart Dykes's Model A

Ford out back. Charley got in and waited. When the Dykes returned, they told Charley they could only take him as far as Clarkson. He agreed.

Just then, two Chevrolets drove up, Melvin Purvis and his agents in one and East Liverpool officer Chester Smith and his officers in the other. When Charley spotted the cars, he ordered Dykes to drive behind the corncrib, then jumped out of the car, and started running toward the woods. Officer Smith spotted Floyd, leaped out of his car, and ordered him twice to stop. Floyd ignored the orders. Smith hoisted his .32-20 Winchester rifle, took aim and fired, hitting Floyd in the elbow and knocking the .45 out of his hand. In an interview decades later, Smith stated he only wanted to wound him. Purvis had other ideas. A volley of shots rang out from the pursuing agents. A second shot from Smith stopped Charley in his tracks, alive, but unable to go farther. When the lawmen reached him, they picked up the dropped Colt pistol and grabbed another .45 automatic from his trouser waistband.

Purvis asked if he had a part in the Kansas City Massacre. Charley said, "I ain't telling you sons of bitches anything."

Melvin Purvis began his FBI career as Hoover's go-to guy and ended it in disgrace because he was too good at garnering publicity reserved for Hoover. He was a nervous, stressed man who eventually was forced out of the FBI and committed suicide. *Wikimedia Commons*

Purvis asked him if he was Pretty Boy Floyd. Charley said, "I am Charles Arthur Floyd."

He died minutes later at 4:25 p.m.

Smith later claimed that Purvis ordered one of his men to "fire into" Floyd, so that the FBI could claim full credit for the outlaw's capture. FBI officials deny that Smith had any role in bringing down the No. 1 man on the agency's most wanted list.

The man they called Pretty Boy, the "Phantom Terror," Choc, and the "Sagebrush Robin Hood" was just thirty years old when he died, yet his story has all the drama of a Shakespearean tragedy. While souvenir collectors cut swatches of cloth from his suit, and East Liverpool police kept leftover .45 bullets and took $122 in cash from his pants, back in Washington, Hoover removed Charles Arthur Floyd's name as Public Enemy No. 1 and replaced him with Lester Gillis, better known as Baby Face Nelson.

Ma Joad, in John Steinbeck's *The Grapes of Wrath*, worries that her son Tom might follow in the outlaw's footsteps and become mean and bitter like "*Purty Boy Floyd*." She implies that Floyd, underneath it all, was a good man with strong religious upbringing until he did "a little bad thing an' they hurt 'im, caught 'im an' hurt him again and again, so he was 'mean-mad' and finally unable to be saved."[81]

CHAPTER 21

SHORT, LETHAL OUTLAW

George "Baby Face" Nelson

EVERYONE WHO HAS grown up wanting desperately to be part of the in-crowd, the club, or the gang can at once remember the bad kid. There was always a tough runt who had an angle, who hatched the schemes, who defied authority, and who all the neighbors said would come to no good. Lester Gillis was that runt on Chicago's Northwest Side. Born on December 6, 1908, he was the last child of Mary and Joseph Gillis, and from the beginning, he understood that size mattered. In his circle, he was all mouth: skinny, short, with sandy blonde hair and blue-gray eyes with flecks of color that changed with his mood. Always the gofer, never the boss, Lester adopted a dual personality to get the respect that he demanded. To his friends and family, he was light-hearted and loyal. To his enemies, he was brutal with an almost total lack of empathy.

His parents sent him to good neighborhood schools and to the discipline of boarding schools. On July 4, 1921, after some scrapes with the local law, he

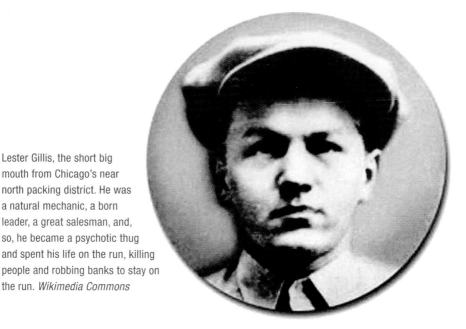

Lester Gillis, the short big mouth from Chicago's near north packing district. He was a natural mechanic, a born leader, a great salesman, and, so, he became a psychotic thug and spent his life on the run, killing people and robbing banks to stay on the run. *Wikimedia Commons*

and a friend were in a garage sitting in a car belonging to the dad of one of his other friends. Lester noticed a loaded revolver wedged into one of the door's side pockets. It was not uncommon in that tough meat-packing neighborhood to pack some heat when abroad on alien turf. These guns were forbidden fruit to Lester. His dad, Joseph, would not even permit toy guns in the house. Lester and his friend decided to take the gun to an alley and have some fun with the rest of the guys. It was Independence Day and fireworks reverberated throughout the neighborhood. When they arrived, Lester brandished the small revolver like an old-time Western cowboy and, as his friends scattered, he pulled the trigger of a gun for the first time. The gun bucked in his hand with a loud bang and its bullet struck a fence post. Another boy shrieked and fell down, digging at his face. The slug had shattered against the post and a fragment had punched into the kid's jaw.

When Lester's mom returned home, neighbors told her he had been arrested. At age twelve, his rap sheet now began with a year's stay at the Cook County School for Boys. He might have gotten off with a warning, but his reputation as a troublemaker caught up to his day in court. This first lockup imposed routine on his chaotic life and he thrived, becoming a model inmate. But young Gillis had an itch and one rainy afternoon, on the way back to the reformatory with his mother—because of exceptional behavior he had been granted brief paroles to go home on weekends—he offered to spare her a block's walk in the wet from the trolley stop and promised he would head straight back to the county home. Off he went with another boy who was on the trolley and disappeared into the rainy day. Later, the superintendent's office called Mary Gillis. Lester had disappeared.

He and the other boy had hopped on another streetcar to Cicero, where they stole a car and headed south toward Florida. Only when they were on the road did the length of the anticipated trip occur to them, so they turned around, abandoned the car, and Lester showed up at home in time for breakfast. So, by age thirteen, Lester Gillis had shot somebody, did some time, and swiped his first automobile. Life only got better after that for the outlaw-in-training.

He shifted his attention from his packing-house neighborhood called "the Patch" to a tougher environment and a mixed bag of hard cases who hung out at the Circus Club. He struck up acquaintance with an older kid named Tony Accardo and another, Vincent Gibaldi, who would become infamous as "Machine Gun Jack" McGurn, a rumored participant in a future gangland massacre on Valentine's Day. Still, Lester was the runt, the gofer who was more mascot than member of his criminal club. His string of petty thefts, car stripping, tire thefts, and joy rides in "borrowed" transport were still penny ante. He wanted respect and a bigger piece of the action. His joy rides in stolen cars to impress the girls finally got him the attention he sought. A fed-up neighbor blew the whistle on Gillis and, on October 10, 1922, he was bundled off to the Illinois State School for Boys at St. Charles.

St. Charles was originally planned as a kindly, charitable institution for deprived city youngsters, but as real money was poured into its facilities, the state's desire for payback turned help for poor boys into a lockup to keep the little crooks off the street. Once again, after a rough start, Lester showed natural skills in the machine shop and became a showpiece jewel of this latest reformatory. In the meantime, his parents opened a restaurant that eventually failed and Joseph Gillis, despite the rigor of Prohibition, became a raging alcoholic who killed himself by sucking gas from a lamp fixture.

Lester was granted parole as the institution's top student on July 20, 1925. Once again, he stayed the course, working as a mechanic for a Chrysler dealership while he sized up the financial opportunities. Prohibition had rejuvenated the Patch and brought great wealth to the older felons of the Circus Gang. Their boss, Johnnie Torrio, had been frightened into retirement by an assassination attempt, turning the whole operation over to his protégé, twenty-six-year-old Alphonse "Scarface" Capone. Al had made his bones first as muscle and later as Torrio's right-hand man, gaining the polish needed to take over such a vigorously defended turf in Chicago's booze war. Lester Gillis had learned a lot during his reformatory stays. Like Capone, he had made himself useful. Short, scrawny Gillis had cultivated friends that could watch his back. He had

Moon-faced Al Capone was given Johnnie Torio's south-side turf and organization to build on.
Wikimedia Commons

conned the administration, even conned his own mother into giving him space, granting favors and, what he most craved, respect. In Chicago's rigidly partitioned territories, he moved in the company of the "Terrible Touhy" brothers, professional thieves; "Three-fingers" Jack White, a freelance hit man; and was tolerated on the Irish turf of the O'Donnells—William, Bernard, and Miles, who controlled a chunk of profitable landscape on the near Northwest side between Chicago Avenue and Madison Street. Their combined knowledge and bloodied experience provided a perfect curriculum for Lester's postgraduate days from Outlaw University.

On June 17, 1927, Gillis hit the streets for the last time as a reformatory parolee. In six months, he would turn over his eighteenth year and become eligible for adult prison if he screwed up again. Still, he gave the straight and narrow another try as a mechanic in a car dealership and quickly won promotion to the sales floor, trading in his coveralls for a suit, shirt, and tie, and a decent paycheck. Though his knowledge of cars helped the dealership's

continued on page 240

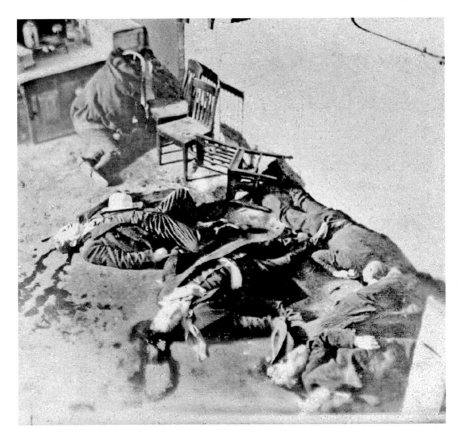

On Saint Valentine's Day 1929, at the SMC Cartage Company, a homely garage on Chicago's North Clark Street, seven of "Bugs" Moran's henchmen and wannabes waited for news of a shipment of beer. Instead, they kept most of about 150 bullets from gouging a nicely painted white brick wall and soaked the cement floor with quarts of blood. *Wikimedia Commons*

By the time the real police arrived at the SMC Cartage Company's North Clark Street garage and discovered the mess heaped at the foot of a bullet-pitted far wall, the fake police and their fake police getaway car were long gone. The smell of gunpowder still stung the air and a dog was whining piteously from where it was tied up behind a nearby truck. Six dead men lay where they had fallen after being raked with 150 rounds from two Thompson submachine guns and at least two blasts from shotguns. One body gurgled. Frank Gusenberg was still alive. Police Sgt. Tom Lofus bent over him as the gunman sucked in breaths of air.

"Do you know me?" Loftus asked.

"Yeah, you're Tom Loftus," Gusenberg exhaled, paused and then added, "I won't talk." And then his eyes cleared for a moment and he whispered, "cops did it."

Gusenberg went out the door on a stretcher as soon as an ambulance arrived — along with the press. By this time, the first law on the scene had made another discovery. Lying on the cement floor, clear of the spreading lake of blood, was a snub-nosed Colt .38 Special revolver with its hammer cocking spur ground off by Chicago's machine gun dealer to the mob, Peter von Frantzius. Professionals frequently did this to hideout guns to keep them from hanging up on clothing when needed in a hurry. Frank Gusenberg was truly a professional and the gun had apparently been discovered by the "police" when they patted him down before

Frank Gusenberg was a hit man for George "Bugs" Moran and was waiting with his brother, Peter, for Moran to show up at the garage with information about a shipment of beer. Moran was late. Fake police showed up instead and killed everybody. Gusenberg lived long enough to mumble: "Cops did it." *Wikimedia Commons*

A lone souvenir left behind by the shooters was a Colt revolver taken from Frank Gusenberg just before they put fourteen slugs into him. He lived long enough to explain, "Nobody shot me." *Rock Island Auction Company*

rearranging his internal organs with a spray of bullets.

The mistakenly fingered "Machine Gun Jack" McGurn was later chopped down in a bowling alley at 805 Milwaukee Avenue just after midnight on February 15, 1936, just minutes after the seventh anniversary of the Clark Street murder party. A comic valentine was found atop his perforated body. A bystander suggested he rolled a gutter ball. One member of the Circus Club Gang, Tony Capezio, was definitely involved and almost incinerated when he tried to burn a make-believe police car in a garage ten minutes from the crime scene garage that belonged to the club. After he came out of the hospital, he was known as "Tough Tony" Capezio. Fred "Killer" Burke was sent to prison for life.

Frank Gusenberg's Colt .38-caliber, two-inch barrel hold-out gun carried for emergencies. The hammer's cocking spur has been ground down to prevent it hanging up on clothes in an urgent situation. *Rock Island Auction Company*

continued from page 237

bottom line, the business went bust and he was out on the streets again in his new wardrobe.

For a year and a half, he drove a truck and lived at home with Mary, his mother, who still held out hope for him. He scraped together enough to buy his first car, but his love of speed and growing hatred of authority earned him tickets for scorching, squealing his tires up and down the neighborhood streets. He became a shakedown favorite of cops who visited his place of work looking for poker money, threatening to spill the beans about his reckless driving record.

To augment his income, he hired out to the booze bosses as a freelance truck driver, running whiskey and beer shipments through the usual gauntlet of hijackers. At no time did he seem to consider full-time employment for Capone, O'Donnell, O'Banion, Moran, or the other outfits who had carved out bloody slivers of income. His hatred of authority extended to whoever held the leash to an employee's collar. The cops and the reformatory clerks had pushed him around long enough. Any allegiance he made had to profit him in some way: money, schemes, techniques, anything to advance his own goal: running his own show.

By 1928, he was married. His wife, the former Helen Wawrzyniak, was a shy youngster of fifteen when they met, but his bluster had drawn her out of her shell. Now she was expecting their first child. They would be inseparable through-out his life. He was a fixture in the Chicago mob scene, but his acquaintances and employers were the ones showing up in the newspapers.

On February 14, 1929, members of the "Bugs" Moran gang and some hangers-on made a pile of

Fred "Killer" Burke arranged for the garage massacre to gun down the Gusenbergs and leave no witnesses. Burke died in jail nine years after his capture in 1931. *Wikimedia Commons*

bloody corpses in a Clark Street cartage garage. Everybody in the Patch and the Circus Gang were certain the Saint Valentine's Day Massacre was the work of "Machine Gun Jack" McGurn. A year earlier, Moran torpedoes, Peter and Frank Gusenberg, had trapped McGurn in a phone booth and machine-gunned him near to death. The "near" was his motivation.

As it turned out, a group of imports headed by Fred "Killer" Burke called The American Boys, dressed in police uniforms, did the deed with third-hand orders from Al Capone. Both Peter and Frank added their gore to the garage floor, along with the other cooling bodies on Clark Street, who were strictly collateral damage.

The year 1929 was also a watershed for Gillis. He had finally gone all in on a life of crime. His education at Outlaw U had included instruction from the best in their respective fields, and for his debut he chose big-dollar jewelry heists. Lester also chose his first *nom de outlaw*, "George Nelson." What could be more white-bread American? It would be his name on his first FBI wanted poster. The gangland moniker, Baby Face, chosen by his associates and the press—but not to George's face—reflected his preternaturally youthful appearance. Even adding a scraggly mustache to what was eventually his bullet-riddled corpse, he looked like a bloated baby pretending to be a grownup.

Between his 1929 epiphany that crime really should pay and when the cops entered his Cicero apartment in 1931, catching him steps away from his .45 Model 1911 automatic pistol lying atop a dresser, George had graduated from jewelry holdups in Chicago's Gold Coast apartments to suburban bank heists. He and his crew were rounded up—mostly due to witnesses fingering his unique youthful appearance and ice blue eyes. George was whisked off to the old Civil War hellhole prison in Joliet, Illinois. In the newspapers, an obscure criminal nobody had become Baby Face Nelson, ringleader of a dangerous robbery gang. He was finally his own boss. He was also inmate number 5437.

For the first time, incarceration was unbearable and all he wanted was to escape. He stayed in Joliet for a few months and then was transferred out to stand trial for an earlier charge. While in transit, after a farewell meeting with his friends and family, and handcuffed to a large burley officer, a .45 automatic magically appeared, nuzzling the ribs of his cop escort in the back seat of a taxi. The cop and the cabby wound up standing on the shoulder of a rural road next to a cemetery watching the cab disappear into the dark. The cop's wallet was also lighter by ten dollars.

Nelson packed up his wife and son, leaving his daughter with his wife's sister in Chicago, and headed west to San Francisco. There, he adopted yet another alias, Jimmy Williams, and fell into a variety of schemes from bootlegging to

Homer Van Meter and Baby Face Nelson became fast friends as they shared many interests such as firearms and fast cars. They were chums until Van Meter was turned into chopped meat on August 23, 1934, by four St. Paul, Minnesota, cops with machine guns when trapped in an alley. *Wikimedia Commons*

Lester's mug shot in Joliet in 1931. He became determined never to do time again. *Wikimedia Commons*

murder for hire. He also met his future faithful sidekick, John Paul Chase, who, despite Nelson's brutal mood swings, remained on call or at his side until the end. His first job was to drive back east and fetch George's mother-in-law to help Helen recover from an operation, and then the whole family drove to Minneapolis.[7] There, George met Eddie Bentz, a St. Paul hoodlum and bank robbery aficionado, who became Nelson's mentor for a planned hit on a Grand Haven, Michigan, bank.

Nelson was a sponge for Bentz's courses at the Minnesota campus of Outlaw University. Eddie was obsessive about covering all bases from casing the bank, drawing interior maps, clothing to wear, the get-away car, to the firearms required. They noted in particular that the swing bridge exit from Grand Haven could be closed, blocking that escape route. Nelson also met Homer Van Meter, a Bentz associate who was part of John Dillinger's loose crew. They became pals over long talks about guns and cars. It was during this planning that Nelson and his family, along with Bentz associate, Chuck Fisher, drove down to Texas to pick up a pair of Thompson submachine guns from the gun repair shop run by Hyman Lebman.

Jack Perkins, an old Chicago crony, showed up with his wife and kids in time to provide bulletproof vests at two hundred dollars each and later procured the getaway car, a practically brand new seven-passenger Buick sedan. Nelson insisted on three-fingered Freddie Monahan as wheelman against Bentz's request to drive the Buick.[65] Finally, on August 18, the large Buick rolled into Grand Haven, Michigan, closely packed with robbers in coveralls over bulletproof vests, except for Nelson who was decked out in a suit, tie, and straw boater hat. Freddie parked across from the bank and left the motor running.

Once in the bank, Bentz, wearing old gray coveralls, headed for the bank president's office to drag him out and open the vault. Nelson got in line in front of a cashier who waited on him almost immediately. In the back offices, Bentz waited for the president to get off the phone. Nelson grew nervous as the cashier eyed him, the basket he was carrying, and the bulky man in coveralls behind him carrying a cloth-covered bundle. Nelson fished out all the cash he had—two singles and asked for nickels. The now flinty-eyed cashier immediately produced two rolls of nickels. Chuck Fisher, peering over Nelson's shoulder, chuckled at the pathetic ploy causing Nelson to break up. The cashier was not amused. At that tense moment, Bentz came into the lobby with the bank president in tow. Nelson and Fisher produced submachine guns. The cashier had slipped his toe beneath the silent alarm that required raising from the floor. He raised it.[65]

At the sheriff's office, local police stations, and the distant state police, alarms blared. In the bank, employees and customers were face down on the floor as the bank president fiddled with the vault door, claiming he did not often have to open it himself. Everything was taking too long as the inside crew cleaned out the cash drawers. One of Bentz's cautions was "never actually shoot anyone. Make a lot of noise, but no killing—and treat women with courtesy to keep men from coming to their aid, or provoking the ladies into screaming fits."

A second clerk was dragged over to the vault and the president was shoved aside to become a hostage with a gathering gaggle of employees. The clerk also fiddled nervously, but motivated by the guns in his ribs, he finally opened the vault. Outside, aware citizens were fetching guns. A shoe clerk ran from his store with his .38-caliber pistol. The owner of the furniture store next door to the bank ran out with a Remington repeating shotgun, jacking a shell into the chamber. He saw the big Buick idling across the street and shouldered his duck gun. Freddie Monahan, behind the wheel, ducked down, clashed into first gear, and floored the gas. With tires squealing and smoking, the sedan surged down the street and disappeared into the distance.

Out of the bank came five of Nelson's crew behind eight hostages. Their two outside men fired shots in hopes of scattering the crowd. No luck; the crowd of gawkers grew, curious about the fuss. Nelson hefted his Thompson and raked the street, shooting high, stitching brickwork, shattering windows, and puncturing parked cars. The crowd took the hint and sought cover. At that moment, two events happened. Eddie Bentz began screaming, "Our car! Where's our car?" The second event was a county sheriff's patrol car braking to a stop in the middle of the street. They had thought the alarm was probably false and now were in the middle of a hot robbery.

Two deputies leaped out, brandishing shotguns. Baby Face Nelson swung his Thompson toward the sheriff's car and triggered a long burst of .45-caliber lead, turning the shiny vehicle into a ripped heap of junk. The policemen wisely

fled to cover and began firing alongside the armed storekeepers. The hostages dropped flat on the sidewalk or flung themselves under parked cars. Bentz shouted for the crew to follow him and took off down the street.

Legs pumping, carrying flour sacks bulging with cash, handfuls, and armloads of firearms, and cursing the twenty-four-pound bulletproof vests, the desperados burned up the asphalt as every gun that could fire sent a hail of bullets into their retreat. Heavyweight Earl Doyle caught a blast of birdshot across his forehead that knocked him off his feet. The crowd closed in and one citizen grabbed his gun hand. As they struggled for the pistol, it went off, blowing a hole through Doyle's other hand. He screamed and fell again, twisting his leg and breaking it with a snap. His big day was over as he raised his bloody hands.

Meanwhile, the footrace to freedom continued as the out-of-shape bandits huffed and puffed to an intersection. Bentz spotted an unwitting pair of ladies motoring into town in an old mid-size Chevrolet. Wheezing, he stepped in front of the car. Sweaty hands firmly evicted the two women and the motley mob began to crowd in with their guns and money bags.

"Wait! Don't take our babies!" screamed one of the women.

Four small children—three boys and a girl—looked up from the back seat floor. Disregarding the ferocious crowd at their backs—who were pounding down the street firing as they ran—the coughing, sweating robbers stepped out of the car and carefully handed the children to their mothers and then climbed back in. Nelson sat next to Bentz, who had taken the wheel. Baby Face twisted

Little Bohemia Lodge as it looked after the FBI raid. The askew window screen on the second floor marks where Homer Van Meter held back the FBI agents with a Thompson while everyone got out the back door and left the FBI with a "learning experience." *Wikimedia Commons*

in his seat and fired one last parting salute to the Grand Haven citizens as Bentz circled the Chevy for their getaway.

"We gotta go back for Doyle," Nelson growled.

Eddie realized he had also dropped the bag of money he had been carrying and considered Nelson's demand for a brief moment. The wheelman glanced up into the rear view mirror at the angry faces of the rapidly approaching crowd as bullets and birdshot spanged off the car's paintwork. "We ain't goin' back there," he countered and floored the gas.[65]

One bit of advance planning did pay off. The swing bridge over the river at the other end of town was swung closed by the bridgekeeper on the sheriff's orders. This move effectively trapped the state police rushing to the scene on the far side of the river as the robbers fled in the opposite direction.[65]

Springtime in Manitowish Waters, Wisconsin, with cool breezes off Little Star Lake hissing through pine and spruce trees—this is the way life was meant to be. George Baby Face Nelson, now known as Jimmy in the Little Bohemia Lodge, felt at ease in the three-room cabin with Helen, Tommy Carroll, and his wife, Jean. In the main lodge were friends: Homer Van Meter, Ray Hamilton, Patricia Cherrington, and the man himself, John Dillinger. Everyone was tired—tired of running, tired of trying to remember which name to use this time, tired of counting bullets, and tired of counting nickels and dimes until the next big job, the next big score. They could relax in the lodge, play poker, eat steaks cooked in garlic, and, since repeal of Prohibition the previous year, drink all they wanted.

The lodge owner and bartender didn't seem to mind that everyone at the poker table wore at least one .45 Colt in a shoulder holster, or the other machine guns stowed in the parked cars with the rifles and spare pistols and boxes of ammunition. The locals came and went like normal—even if Nelson was a loose tail on some of their errands into town. Even the collie dogs were friendly, enjoying bones and scraps from the dinner table. As night closed down the woods on April 22, 1934, George and Helen retired to their cabin as the night insects shrugged off the evening dew and began their mating chatter. By 8:00 p.m., the woods fell silent.

Melvin Purvis, FBI agent in charge, tugged at his uncomfortable bulletproof

Protecting the body from ravaging weapons goes back to pre-Biblical times. As weapons matured from cleaving and slashing attacks to high velocity puncturing, armor makers needed a game changer. Steel plates did the job, but mobility suffered. An unhorsed knight sheathed in steel could be killed by any tin-pot foot soldier with a long nutpick to poke in through the crevices and get at the soft bits. Bank robbers in the 1920s and 1930s faced a similar problem.

Cole Younger, back in the day, wore a steel chest plate under his shirt, which saved him from some of the firestorm of bullets during and after the famous 1876 Northfield bank raid. Later, bank robbers and hit men needed something more fashionable and flexible for ducking in and out of cars and presenting themselves at bank teller's windows.

Various armored vests were tried in the 1914–1918 Great War, but tradeoffs for protection were too extreme to be practical. Finally, manufacturers developed vests capable of stopping handgun rounds such as the .25 ACP, .32 S&W Long, .32 S&W, .380 ACP, .38 Special, and .45 ACP bullets. These were made of thickly padded cotton and dense cloth. Law enforcement countered with the .38 Super and the .357 Magnum.

A better vest was designed by Al Dunlap, publisher of the *Detective* magazine, working with metallurgist Elliot T. Wisebrod and gun dealer Peter von Frantzius.[44] This vest used hard armor encased in cloth with a leather liner more contoured to fit the body. The vest only weighed eleven pounds ("as heavy as a thick winter overcoat") compared to cheaper Duralumin vests that weighed about twenty-four pounds and were more practical than fashionable.[82]

Testing a bulletproof vest outdoors with a revolver. *Wikimedia Commons*

vest and rubbed his hands together as the night brought with it a numbing chill. All around him, shadows moved toward the Little Bohemia Lodge where the lights still blazed. Two dogs on the lodge front porch started barking. Why hadn't anyone mentioned any dogs? The front door opened and five men walked out onto the porch. Two were bartenders intent on quieting the dogs and three were customers: a gas salesman and two members of a nearby Civilian Conservation Corps camp. Purvis tensed. The gang was trying to get away. The three customers piled into a Chevrolet parked in front of the lodge. One of them pressed the ignition and the radio came on at the same time—so loud they never heard the officers shout at them to surrender. The ring of agents closed in from three sides. Machine gun bullets ripped into the vehicle, shattering glass and tearing into the metal. Two of the men tumbled out wounded and fled. The third was dead in the front seat.

Nelson grabbed his Lebman Special machine pistol, stuffed a .45 automatic into his waistband, scooped up extra magazines for the Lebman, and ran for the lodge as the lights winked out. Gunfire was ripping into the lodge and agents were firing at shadows, anything that moved. Van Meter had clambered up on the roof and was trading machine gun bursts with the feds. Nelson spotted one agent cradling a submachine gun and triggered a burst from his Lebman Special at the man. It was Purvis, who dove back into cover and returned fire. Bullets stitched the ground across Nelson's path from another agent and Baby Face scurried back to the rear of the cabin.

By this time, all the gang had made their way out of the lodge, heading down an embankment and jogging away along the lake shore. Nelson also ran down that unguarded embankment, but turned to the left instead of following Dillinger and the others. It didn't take long before he was lost, thrashing around in the woods.

By now, the agents, who had been tipped by the locals about the Dillinger gang's Wisconsin hideout, were still hammering streams of bullets into the building. Only the lodge owner and three gang women—including Helen Nelson—remained behind, cowering in the basement. Other FBI agents were tangled in an unreported barbed wire fence or wallowing in an unreported deep ditch at the side of the building.[75]

All the gang members had a good head start when the FBI men finally peeked inside and discovered they were alone in the woods. Agents ran to the autos they had commandeered at the nearby airport or driven to the scene from their offices. Their miserable capture plan and one civilian death, with no gang members in the bag, demanded the roads be scoured. The fledgling agency could not endure another total failure.

Using commandeered cars and later loping along the dark rural roads, Nelson ended up in the driveway of a local family's home where he had corralled eight hostages. He was in the process of stealing yet another car that refused to start when a sedan motored slowly toward them, rolled onto the shoulder, and stopped. Nelson saw heads wearing hats inside, slipped his .45 into its holster and drew out his Hyman Lebman Special.

Inside the vehicle, the suspicious FBI agents, armed with revolvers, shotguns, and one Thompson cradled in the arms of a large young agent named W. Carter Baum, eyed the shadowy group of people around the car in the driveway. Nelson didn't wait. He jumped toward the car and thrust his machine pistol into the side window. The driver, agent Newman, jumped out wielding his .38 revolver. Nelson tapped a burst at him, shattering his elbow. Another agent, Christensen, tried to bail out of the back seat, but caught a round in the back, at which point Baby Face Nelson found himself staring down the muzzle of Carter Baum's Thompson submachine gun.

Two agonizing seconds passed with Baum's white-knuckled hand squeezing the machine gun's grip and trigger. Nelson fired another tapped burst, catching Baum across the throat and above the edge of the agent's bulletproof vest. Christensen attempted to flee, but was caught in their car's headlights, and Nelson's final burst from the .38 Super Lebman machine pistol dumped the agent on the ground. Baum managed to crawl a few yards, but toppled over a low fence into a ditch where he gasped his last breaths. Later examination showed he had forgotten to move the Thompson's safety lever to fire.[65] Out of ammunition, Nelson slid into his latest stolen getaway car and sprayed gravel out onto the main road. Baby Face drove until the car conked out and spent the next few days living in a shack in the woods with a local Indian. He had killed his first FBI agent and now the noose would draw tighter.

The year 1934 was a bad one for outlaws. First, Bonnie and Clyde were shot to pieces, and then Pretty Boy Floyd was cut down in a farm field. John Dillinger was drilled in an alley after seeing a movie in Chicago. Toughest of all, Nelson's pal, Homer Van Meter, was machine gunned by cops who weren't looking to

A close-up of the Thompson submachine gun safety that Agent Baum forgot to switch from safe to fire before taking on Baby Face Nelson in a gunfight. *Franklin County Historic Preservation Society/Photographer: Dave Cooper*

A Hudson Terraplane sedan of the type used by the FBI agents. *www.carnut.com/ghn.html*

take him alive. Now, the dice were rolling for Baby Face Nelson. He had become the FBI's final high profile Public Enemy No. 1 and agents seemed to be behind every tree, in every car, and outside every window. Worst of all, after the Little Bohemia fiasco, he'd been labeled by the press and the FBI as a member of the John Dillinger gang rather than the top banana.

Nelson had become jumpy and his already short temper now lay just below the surface. He and Helen, together with John Chase, were holed up in Chicago after a brief flight to California. They had plans to rest up at a Lake Como lodge near the Wisconsin border in Lake Geneva. As they arrived at the reserved villa, they spotted an FBI trap when the agents mistakenly jumped a Ford just ahead of him. He turned around and headed back toward Chicago on Northwest Highway.

Along the way, an FBI team in a Hudson spotted Nelson's Ford and gave chase, but Nelson managed to turn his car around and got on the FBI's tail. Now, the pursuers were the targets. Nelson roared up behind the Hudson and, with Helen crouched on the right front floorboards, Chase fired through the Ford's tilted-up front window, hammering away with a Colt Monitor, .30-06 civilian stripped-down Browning Automatic Rifle. One .38 Super shot snapped off from the FBI punched through the Ford's radiator and shattered the fuel pump. The riddled Hudson was able to pull ahead out of danger.

Inspector Cowley — "Baby Face" Nelson — Agent Hollis — John Chase

Combo photo from the FBI telling the story of the Battle of Barrington. All the characters are assembled: Hollis, Cowley, Chase, and Nelson. The drama played out on Northwest Highway near the suburb of Barrington, Illinois. When the shootout was over, Hollis and Cowley died at the scene and Nelson died later. *Federal Bureau of Investigation*

At this time, another FBI car, heading up to Crystal Lake, spotted the limping Ford. As they passed through Barrington, the FBI car driven by agents Sam Cowley and Herman Hollis turned around to take up the chase. At the Barrington City Park, Nelson abandoned his stalled car. When the FBI Hudson approached, he sent Helen to take cover in a ditch. The Battle of Barrington commenced as soon as the agents braked to a halt.

Hollis, the FBI hero who had put the first bullet into John Dillinger at Chicago's Biograph Theater, pumped his shotgun at Nelson, then drew his revolver and took off at a run for the cover of a telephone pole, but a single shot punched into his head and he tumbled to the ground. Inspector Cowley ripped a burst from his Thompson and one bullet hit below the bottom edge of Nelson's bulletproof vest, tearing through the lower stomach into Baby Face's bowels. Nelson stumbled, but pumped with adrenalin, marched toward the agent sprawled on the ground, who discarded the empty machine gun and dragged out his service revolver before Baby Face riddled Cowley with a burst from his .35-caliber automatic rifle.

Chase, Helen, and the fatally wounded Nelson managed to transfer their luggage and guns from the Ford to the FBI Hudson and Chase drove to a safe house in Wilmette, Illinois. At around 7:30 that evening, Lester Gillis, a.k.a. Baby Face Nelson, a.k.a. Jimmy Williams, muttered, "It's getting dark, Helen— say good-bye to mother," and died shortly thereafter. They wrapped his body in a blanket and laid it in the grass next to St. Paul's Cemetery in what is now the town of Skokie.

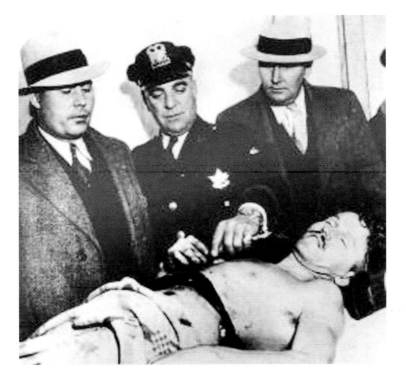

Lester Gillis, a.k.a. Jimmy Williams, a.k.a. Baby Face Nelson, lies on a morgue slab, killed by one FBI bullet that hit him below the edge of his bulletproof vest. He finally got where he was going. *Federal Bureau of Investigation*

The rifles used by Chase and Nelson were never found, but FBI forensics established the .35-caliber Winchester Model 1907 autoloader as the gun that killed Crowley. *Historical Firearms*

Being able to gather a sufficient force to raid and apprehend outlaws who have gone to ground in their hideouts allowed law enforcement to concentrate the available weapons begrudged by Depression-era civil budgets. By the mid-1920s, police had Teletype and wire photo that used telephone lines, but rapid communications between mobile police units and their dispatcher still relied on locating telephones, or street corner call boxes in the larger cities. Many small towns still used blinking lights atop the police station to alert beat cops to call in for reassignment. However, when the technology for two-way communication became available in the later 1920s and 1930s, it was local communities who led the way.

In 1923, the Detroit police received permission to operate on commercial AM radio. However, the Federal Radio Commission allotted police broadcasts on station KOP, and required the police dispatcher to provide entertainment as well as warnings of riot and rampage in the city. The Detroit police played the tune "Yankee Doodle" before each call to cops in the field. The Detroit police grumbled:

"Before much progress can be made, we must receive full cooperation from those who control the destinies of police radio . . . the Federal Radio Commission . . . The progress achieved by the Detroit Police Radio Division . . . has been obtained in spite of the federal authorities, rather than with their cooperation."

By 1928, most of the AM radio bugs had been ironed out as Detroit became the first community to use dedicated short wave radio. Some of that struggle was attributed to abuse of the system during those early years of commercial broadcast police radio. The officers were occasionally accused of using the radio to hear the results of baseball or football games. The problem was short-lived, according to authorities. In 1929, there were 22,598 broadcasts.[83]

Early two-way radio equipment was bulky and needed constant retuning and battery replacement. By 1936, however, two-way radio communications were sufficiently entrenched for Chief Rutledge, then chief at Wyandotte, Michigan, to predict:

"The time will come when every individual policeman on the beat will be equipped with a small radio receiver and be directed by radio orders. That time seems now to be arriving. Small belt radios which are carried by patrolmen began being used in the spring of 1940 by the Atlantic City (New Jersey) Police Department." To the writer's (Joseph Poli) knowledge this is the first and only department, which is today using this form of radio facility.[83]

General Electric built its last AM VHF two-way radio in time to end its production due to the outbreak of World War II in 1941. Its huge dynamotor that offered "continuous duty transmitter operation" put a huge strain on six-volt car batteries and electrical systems of that time. This load often required changing batteries at the change of each patrol's shift. According to GE, "the Leece-Neville 'flux-cutter' alternator was marketed at the end of the war as a solution to the issue, allowing high current output even at idle."[84]

G-E police radio equipment installed in rear trunk of Ford 1938 automobile. View shows, from left to right, model 4G1B1. 15-watt ultra-high-frequency transmitter. 1938.

Early radio equipment filled a police car's trunk. Because of power drain, batteries had to be changed after every shift. *Journal of Criminal Law and Criminology*

CHAPTER 22

THE LAST OF
JOHN
DILLINGER

JOHN DILLINGER LOVED to hide in plain sight. In the summer of 1934, he was back in Chicago where he enjoyed going to Wrigley Field to see the Cubs play, or to movies to watch Bogart or Clark Gable portray sharp guys who knew the score. He had even wandered into the main police headquarters at 11th and State Street with one of his girlfriends, Anna Sage, on his arm to ask after an imaginary girl prisoner. Anna shared an apartment at 2420 North Halsted near the Lincoln Avenue neighborhood with Polly Hamilton, Dillinger's latest conquest. To Polly, he was Jimmy Lawrence, who worked as a clerk in the Board of Trade downtown. He became a fixture in the shops where he bought new shirts and at the Biograph Theater, where the air conditioning beckoned on warm July afternoons.

Anna Sage ran a brothel at the Kostur Hotel and had racked up a string of arrests. The feds were waiting for her next slip, with deportation papers at the ready to return her to her native Romania. Her twenty-three-year-old son, Steve Chiolak, together with his girlfriend, often made a fun foursome along with Polly, going to the movies and eating at local restaurants where Dillinger often picked up the check. He was living like an ordinary citizen, or almost like one. He still kept aware of his environment, watched reflections in store

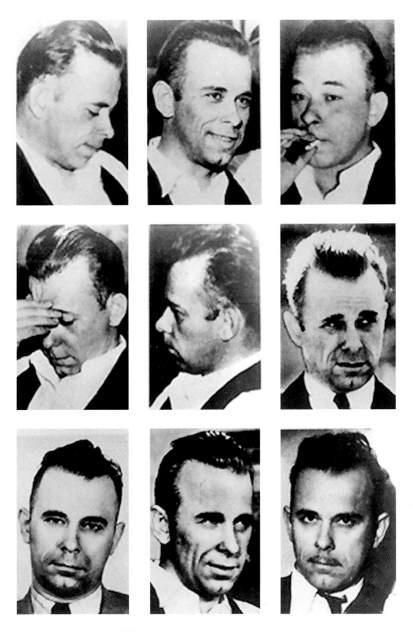

The many faces of John Dillinger kept the police on their toes as he hid mostly in plain sight during his reign as Public Enemy No. 1 on the FBI list. *Federal Bureau of Investigation*

windows for faces he had seen too many times, and kept his days random, never falling into routine. He still winced when he looked into the mirror at the botched plastic surgery job, at the ridiculous mustache and the puffy cheeks. Most of all, he remembered the pain of healing. But if people kept looking past and through him on the street, he'd live with it. Dillinger even managed to forget the suitcases in the back closet crammed with pistols, bulletproof vests, ammunition, and his favorite admission ticket to bank vaults, his Thompson submachine gun (minus its buttstock for ease of concealment under an overcoat), and the loaded thirty-round stick magazines that went with the package. Each day, he made his foray into the streets as the affable Jimmy Lawrence and left many of his fears behind with those guns in that back closet.

Dillinger gang guns confiscated in Tucson when they evacuated their hotel during a fire and were captured. by Tucson police. *Arizona Historical Society*

Anna Sage was dragged up the chain of command by her close friend in the East Chicago Police Department, Officer Martin Zarkovich. Anna was Martin's ticket to the big time, the celebrity that went with being "the man who got Dillinger." For all her savvy, she became a willing pawn of the FBI as Cowley directed Melvin Purvis to pull out all the stops and promise her anything that would keep her talking. Nervous Purvis, as he was known to many of his team, delivered. Hoover had two demands. The first: keep the Chicago Police out of the capture. He didn't

Anna Sage, a Romanian prostitute who saw a profit in hosting Dillinger's Chicago visit in her apartment near Lincoln Avenue on the north side. She's smiling because no one's told her she's being shipped back to Romania after turning in Dillinger. *Associated Press*

trust the depth of their corruption, nor did he want them to elbow the bureau aside and hog the credit. The second suggested the director was tired of having Public Enemy No. 1's yellow rats delivered up to the public on a morgue slab. He wanted a live trophy to parade through the media like a conquering general entering Rome.

The man Dillinger should have feared most, but didn't even know, was FBI Agent Sam Cowley, a former missionary of the Utah Mormon church. Sam was a relentless plodder in whatever job he was given in the bureau. After Purvis lost face at Little Bohemia, Cowley received the papal nod from the director to go after Dillinger with a special squad. Hoover wanted Dillinger's demise to be strictly an FBI show. Cowley was not a field agent, but a jumped-up desk man. However, he believed hard work would win out. What actually won out was pure blind luck and circumstance.

Anna Sage feared deportation back to Romania. Of her circle of friends, she was the only one who knew Jimmy Lawrence's true identity. She also knew the cops had a way of screwing over people like her when it came to paying big rewards. Instead, she served up Dillinger to Zarkovich on the East Chicago Police Force to begin the chain that would bring the law to her apartment and

At the end, he tried plastic surgery to rearrange some features and grew that scruffy mustache. But he still looked like John Dillinger. He even joked about the resemblance at the local Chicago tavern. *Federal Bureau of Investigation*

send John Dillinger to the electric chair—in return for her continued stay in the United States. It didn't take long for Cowley to okay a meet between Purvis and Sage in the back seat of an FBI sedan. Purvis promised her the moon: a shot at a chunk of the reward and his word that he would do what he could to allow her to stay in the States. She just had to deliver Dillinger on a plate.

Dillinger and Polly went to the Lake Michigan beach near the end of Ardmore Street on Friday, July 20, and later decided to take in a movie on Sunday, if only to cool off in the air-conditioned theater. Anna Sage called

Cowley's office with the news they were going to either the Marbro or the Biograph Theater. Now, Purvis would have to split up his field team because of the distance between the two movie palaces. Only at the last minute did Sage confirm the Biograph, about five minutes' walk from her apartment, where Dillinger was staying. The movie was *Manhattan Melodrama*, starring Clark Gable as a tough hood.

Fortunately, the obsessive habits that drove Purvis had his team in place in time to recognize Anna Sage, wearing an orange dress that looked red in the theater marquee lights, and Polly Hamilton on Dillinger's arm. As usual, John Dillinger was dapper in a light yellow straw boater, a white on white shirt, gray slacks, and gray mottled tie. His only concealing element was a pair of dark glasses. Purvis must have exhaled a sigh when he saw the most wanted gunman in the United States wore no jacket so, at best, he was lightly armed. The FBI team and the five East Chicago police carried only their service revolvers in their attempt to take Dillinger alive with minimum collateral damage among theatergoers and passersby. The Dillinger party bought tickets and went inside. Trying to take him in the theater had been ruled out, fearing a volley of gunfire and a high body count from bullets and the stampeding audience.

There was time to bring the other agents from the Marbro stakeout and reinforce the Biograph team watching every entrance and exit. The activity of strange men lounging about the street in front of the theater—all wearing suit jackets on the ninety-plus-degree day—and Purvis making three trips to the box office ticket booth, triple-checking the end time of the program—sent

Desk man Sam Cowley was jumped up by Hoover over Purvis to oversee the Dillinger trap and to get Anna Sage to drop a dime on the criminal—which she did, literally, with two phone calls. Cowley was not a field agent, but he got results. *Federal Bureau of Investigation*

John Dillinger stayed at an apartment quite near the Biograph Theater, made trips to the beach, and shopped on Lincoln Avenue. Everyone got used to seeing him. *Wikimedia Commons*

the ticket seller back to her boss in a panic. The theater had been recently held up. In a few minutes, FBI agents were shooing away a flock of Chicago police demanding ID and showing off a bevy of uniforms and shiny badges. Purvis bit off the end of his cigar and began to munch it.

Finally, as the last of the Chicago police finished peering closely at FBI identification cards under the theater's marquee lights, the program ended and patrons began filing out. Purvis was ready to light what remained of his cigar when he spotted Dillinger. He held a match poised and scanned the thin crowd making their way around the annoying Chicago cops. And then out came the slender, five-foot-eight gunman adjusting his dark glasses, tapping his straw hat onto his head, breezing past the nosy policemen, turning left toward an alley, a shortcut back to Anna's apartment.

Purvis fell in just behind Dillinger as other agents followed their boss's lead. Sweaty hands gripped gun butts as the circle closed. Dillinger seemed to sense rather than see the danger. His hand dipped into his slacks' pocket and came up with a Colt .380, Model 1908 pistol, short, flat, and deadly in the right hands. Dillinger ducked down into a half crouch and bolted for the alley. Purvis gave a strangled command to halt. No dice. Agent Herman Hollis and

For all his love of guns and his personal arsenal, the FBI claims Dillinger was caught with this Colt Model 1908 pistol holding seven rounds when the trap was sprung. He never got off a shot before three bullets brought him down. *Federal Bureau of Investigation*

two other agents aimed as Dillinger dodged, gripping the pistol. Service revolvers banged loudly, echoing off the storefront bricks and windows. One shot plowed into Dillinger's left side. A second round punctured his back and punched out through his right eye socket. He stumbled and folded face first onto the alley's cobbles. His head was pillowed on his straw hat lying on the dark glasses. An agent picked up the small automatic pistol. On the sidewalk in front of the alley, ricochets or bullet fragments had pierced the legs of two women who were weeping and in shock. The agents were breathing hard and holstering their guns. Purvis tried to worm a few words out of Dillinger who, like Pretty Boy Floyd, wasn't talking. He was too dead to talk.

By this time, Anna Sage had hot-footed it back to her Halsted Street apartment and, with her son Steve's help, lugged the suitcases full of Dillinger's weapons and ammunition down the stairs and out to Steve's car where the two of them motored down to Lake Michigan and the yacht docks at Belmont Harbor. Once there, the suitcases made big splashes as they dropped into the water from a deserted pier.

The aftermath was the predictable horrific *grand guignol* as women dipped their skirt hems in Dillinger's blood and men dabbed their handkerchiefs in what gore they could find in the death alley. The morgue was packed with morbid souls who looked upon the remains of the gunman they had only read about over their breakfast soft-boiled egg. He seemed diminished and ordinary as all persons of note appear when life has deserted the bag of skin left behind. Metal clips held his mouth shut while eyelids were cemented shut over gutta percha cups that covered the dried out grapes left behind in the sockets. The suit they put on him was too big and the casket was a cheap coroner's basket weave—good enough to load into the antique hearse driven up with Dillinger's father as a passenger, come to fetch his boy back home. There was a quiet sadness to the crowds, much like the multitude at Tom Horn's hanging, or the deep Missouri silence when people learned Jesse James had been shot. It seemed to take forever to plant Bill Doolin, because everyone in Oklahoma's Cookson Hills wanted to at least see the box he would rest in.

People didn't much cry at these gravesites as they reflected. In the twenty years since the end of the Great War to the edge of the next great conflict that hurled itself from the sky in 1941, the owlhoot trail had lured many down its muddy path. Each outlaw who hung from a stretched neck, or sprawled in manure-flaked soil leaking life, or lay face down over the fifth ace from a poker hand, or even sat propped up looking surprised from

Al Capone owned this .38 Colt revolver and carried it when he was sure no cops would be looking for a rap to hang on him. His hands were bloody from his early days, but he learned to hire wannabe outlaws to thin the herd for him when he became boss. *Bridgeman Art Library*

John Dillinger's Thompson submachine gun. It was stolen from a cop shop in Auburn, Indiana, in 1933 after his Lima, Ohio, jail break, and confiscated in Tucson when the gang was captured by local cops in 1934, and returned to Auburn in 2014. Its bullets killed some of the thirteen police officers shot down by the Dillinger gang. *Samuel Hoffman, the* Journal Gazette, *Fort Wayne, Indiana*

a hole punched through a bulletproof vest by a high-velocity rifle was, at one time, a regular guy like the curious silent faces in the crowd.

When Al Capone, the outlaw who made good stepping up into the birth of organized crime, finally died from the ravaging complications of syphilis on January 25, 1947, the last of the trade's chutzpah boiled away. All that remained were rag pickers, cannon fodder, and drug-addled psychotics. We can look at Capone's nickel-plated Colt revolver with its checkered walnut grips and appreciate the thin veneer of shine that cradled its deadly bullets. Maybe he never fired this revolver, just owned it, just kept it close. It was a symbol more than a tool. Some of the provenance guns in this book were merely owned: cleaned, loaded, put away, and taken out for special occasions in the owner's twilight years. But make no mistake, if the hand that held that gun once dropped the hammer on another human being, law breaker or lawman, the memory remains. The gun artifacts left behind will evoke that memory for generations to come, gunsmoke memories locked in steel.

ENDNOTES

1   Joyce Lee Malcolm, *To Keep and Bear Arms*. Harvard University Press, Cambridge, MA, 1996.

2   Harold L. Peterson, *Treasury of the Gun*. Golden Press, NY, 1962.

3   Mike Thomas and Scott Culclasure. Living History Programs at Guilford Courthouse National Military Park, National Park Service. www.nps.gov/media/photo/gallery.htm?id=32CF6086-1DD8-B71C-076771F96D50E588.

4   Clayton E. Cramer, *Concealed Weapon Laws of the Early Republic*. Praeger, Westport, CT, 1999.

5   "How to Make Gunpowder." wikiHow, www.wikihow.com/Make-Gunpowder.

6   Otto A. Rothert, *The Outlaws of Cave-In-Rock*. Southern Illinois University Press, Carbondale and Edwardsville, 1996.

7   Anthony Gish, *American Bandits*. Haldeman-Julius Publications, Girard, KS, 1938.

8   Gerry and Janet Souter, *The Constitution*. Thunder Bay Press, Minneapolis, MN, 2013.

9   John Boessenecker, *Bandido: The Life and Times of Tiburcio Vásquez*. University of Oklahoma Press, 2010.

10 Mark W. Geiger, *Missouri's Hidden Civil War: Financial Conspiracy And the Decline of the Planter Elite, 1861–1865*. University of Missouri—Columbia, 2006.

11 Wikipedia, s.v. "Frank James." en.wikipedia.org/wiki/Frank_James

12 kelitad.hubpages.com//hub/The-Most-Hated-Man-of-the-West-William-Quantrill

13 Cole Younger, *The Story of Cole Younger*. Minnesota Historical Society Press, 2000.

14 Mark Lee Gardner, *All Shot to Hell*. HarperCollins, New York, 2013.

15 Roger A. Bruns, *The Bandit Kings: From Jesse James to Pretty Boy Floyd*. Crown Publishers, Inc., NY, 1995.

16 www.kayempea.net/coffeyville.shtml.

17 Joseph G. Rosa, *They Called Him Wild Bill*. University Press of Oklahoma, 1979.

18 www.legendsofamerica.com/we-billcook.htm

19 Art T. Burton, *Black Gun, Silver Star*, University of Nebraska Press, Lincoln, NE, 2006.

20 "Bass Reeves." Badass of the Week, www.badassoftheweek.com/bassreeves.html.

21 mentalfloss.com/article/33537/life-and-times-deputy-us-marshal-bass-reeves.

22 BlackPast.org, n.v. "Dart, Isom (1849–1900)." www.blackpast.org/aaw/isom-dart-1849-1900#sthash.kEKPREPw.dpuf.

23 creativeone59.hubpages.com/hub/Ned-Huddleston-Alias-Isom-Dart-Alias-The-Black-fox

24 babynamesworld.parentsconnect.com/meaning_of-isom.html

25 www.vincelewis.net/blackcowboys.html

26 www.wyohistory.org/essays/tom-horn

27 www.nps.gov/history/history/online_books/blm/ut/7/chap2.htm

28 Old South Military Antiques, www.oldsouthantiques.com

29 Bill O'Neal, *Encyclopedia of Western Gunfighters*. University of Oklahoma Press, Norman, OK, 1979.

30 Sears Roebuck & Co, catalog No. 117, 1908.

31 Eugene Cunningham, *Triggernometry*. University of Oklahoma Press, 1996.

32 Billy the Kid Outlaw Gang, www.billythekidoutlawgang.com

33 Eugene Cunningham, *Triggernometry*. University of Oklahoma Press, 1996.

34 Andrew Isenberg, *Wyatt Earp: A Vigilante Life*. Farrar, Straus & Giroux, New York, 2013.

35 William B. Shillingberg, *Wyatt Earp and the "Buntline Myth"*, Kansas Collection, Kansas Historical Quarterly, 1976.

36 Al Jennings, Will Irwin, *Breaking Back*. D. Appleton and Company, 1914.

37 Mike Wright, *What They Didn't Teach You about the Wild West*. Novato, CA, Presidio Press, 2000.

38 *Encyclopedia of Oklahoma History and Culture*, s.v. "Starr, Myra Maybelle Shirley "Belle'" (1848-89)." digital.library.okstate.edu/encyclopedia/entries/s/st018.html.

39 www.history.com/this-day-in-history/pearl-hart-holds-up-an-arizona-stagecoach

40 jy3502.hubpages.com/hub/Little-Britches-and-Cattle-Annie

41 www.history.com/this-day-in-history/police-kill-famous-outlaws-bonnie-and-clyde

42 www.tshaonline.org/handbook/online/articles

43 www.biography.com/people/ma-barker-14515515?page=2

44 William Helmer and Rick Mattix, *The Complete Public Enemy Almanac*. Cumberland House Publishing, Nashville, 2007.

45 Ellen Poulsen, *Don't Call Us Molls: Women of the John Dillinger Gang*. New York, Clinton Cook Publishing Group, 2002.

46 www.nndb.com/people/367/000135959

47   The Rule of the Underworld, http://homicide.northwestern.edu/docs_fk/homicide/ICS.20.PDF

48   Bob "Red" Meinecke, "Master at Arms: William Matthew Tilghman, 1854–1924." Leverguns, www.leverguns.com/articles/tilghman.htm

49   Robert Dyment, "Whose Fault is it if Cops Can't Shoot?" *Guns*, August 1957.

50   Gerry Souter, *American Shooter*. Potomac Books, Dulles, 2012.

51   www.restaurant-ingthroughhistory.com/restaurant-prices

52   Julian S. Hatcher, *Hatcher's Notebook*. Military Service Publishing Company, 1947.

53   Seth Shulman, *Unlocking the Sky*. HarperCollins, New York, 2002.

54   Taylor Pensoneau, *Brothers Notorious: The Sheltons*. Downstate Publications, New Berlin, IL, 2002.

55   Paul M. Angle, *Bloody Williamson: A Chapter in American Lawlessness*. Alfred A. Knopf, New York, 1991.

56   www.egyptianaaa.org/SI-History3.html

57   Ralph Johnson and Jon Musgrave, *Secrets of the Herrin Gangs: An Inside Account of Bloody Williamson* IllinoisHistory.com, Marion, IL, 2010.

58   *Independent*, St. Petersburg, FL, May 27, 1922.

59   Bernie Drake, "Peoria and the Shelton Gang." *iBi*, April 2012. www.peoriamagazines.com/ibi/2012/apr/peoria-and-shelton-gang

60   Patrick Yeagle, "The deadly adventures of a southern Illinois gangster." *Illinois Times*, December 16, 2010. illinoistimes.com/article-permalink-8113.html

61   Len Wells, "Artifacts from Southern Illinois' bloody gang warfare to be on display." *Evansville Courier & Press*, August 22, 2013. www.courierpress.com/news/2013/aug/22/artifacts-southern-illinois-bloody-gang-warfare-be

62   Chief of Ordinance, Annual Reports of the War Department, Fiscal Year ended June, 1900. Government Printing Office, Washington, DC

63   Robert A. Fulton, "The Legend of the Colt .45-caliber Semi-Automatic Pistol and the Moros." www.morolandhistory.com/related%20Articles/legend%20of%20.45.html

64   "Supreme Court Justice Elena Kagan—Still a Jewish Markswoman." *Jewish Marksmanship*. jewishmarksmanship.blogspot.com/2012_10_01_archive.html

65   Steven Nickel and William J. Helmer, *Baby Face Nelson: Portrait of a Public Enemy*. Cumberland House, Nashville, 2002.

66   Scott Stroud, "Hidden History of Gangsters and Guns." *San Antonio Express News*, November 21, 2010. www.mysanantonio.com/news/local_news/article/Hidden-history-of-gangsters-and-guns-825223.php

67   Robert Loerzel interview with Chicago historian Rich Lindberg, "848" radio show. WBEZ, Chicago, July 1, 2009.

68 Allan May, "Chicago's Unione Siciliana: 1920—A Decade of Slaughter." www.allanrmay.com/Unione_Siciliana.html

69 www.myalcaponemuseum.com

70 Jonathon Eig, *Get Capone*. Simon & Schuster, New York, 2010.

71 Chris Bishop, *The Encyclopedia of Weapons of World War II*. Sterling Publishing, New York, 2002.

72 Rick Hacker, "I Have This Old Gun: Smith & Wesson 38/44 Heavy Duty." *American Rifleman*, February 2014.

73 lettersofnote.com/2009/12/what-dandy-car-you-make.html

74 Confession of W. D. Jones. State of Texas, November 18, 1933.

75 John Toland, *The Dillinger Days*. Random House, New York, 1963.

76 Jeff Guinn, *Go Down Together: The True Untold Story of Bonnie and Clyde*. Simon & Schuster, New York, 2010.

77 texashideout.tripod.com/warrencar.html

78 Michael Wallis, *The Life and Times of Charles Arthur Floyd*. W. W. Norton & Company, New York, 1992.

79 Woody Guthrie Publications, Inc.

80 www.fbi.gov/about-us/history/famous-cases/kansas-city-massacre-pretty-boy-floyd

81 faculty.chemeketa.edu/jrupert3/eng255/resources/steinbgr.htm

82 www.westernfrontassociation.com/great-war-on-land/73-weapons-equipment-uniforms/879-body-armour.html

83 Joseph A. Poli, "Development and Present Trend of Police Radio Communications." *Journal of Criminal Law and Criminology*, vol. 33, issue 2, article 9, 1942.

84 www.w5txr.net/General-Electric-Radio-History.html

INDEX